Reel Racism

Thinking Through Cinema

Thomas E. Wartenberg, Series Editor

Forthcoming

REEL RACISM

Confronting Hollywood's Construction of Afro-American Culture

Vincent F. Rocchio

Westview
PRESS

A Member of the Perseus Books Group

Thinking Through Cinema

Copyright © 2000 by Westview Press, A Member of the Perseus Books Group

Published in 2000 in the United States of America by Westview Press, 5500 Central Avenue, Boulder, Colorado 80301-2877, and in the United Kingdom by Westview Press, 12 Hid's Copse Road, Cumnor Hill, Oxford OX2 9JJ

Find us on the World Wide Web at www.westviewpress.com

Library of Congress Cataloging-in-Publication Data

Rocchio, Vincent K.
  Reel racism: confronting hollywood's construction of Afro-
American culture/Vincent K. Rocchio.
    p.cm.—(Thinking through cinema)
  Includes biblographical references and index.
  ISBN 0-8133-6710-7 (pbk.: alk. paper)
  1. Afro-Americans in motion pictures. I. title. II. Series.

PN19995.9.N4 R59 2000
791.43'6520396073—dc21   00-043984

The paper used in this publication meets the requirements of the American National Standard for Permanence of Paper for Printed Library Materials Z39.48-1984.

10   9   8   7   6   5   4   3   2   1

Dedicated to the memory of

Mary Miller-Robinson,
the heart of the class of '79
Ave Maria, Gratia Plena

Jared Tuccolo,
the soul of the class of '98
Dominus Tecum

Louise Figueroa
the head of the Rutgers Catholic mafia
Benedicta tu in mulierbus

and to my beloved RJR, who came back,
after so long away.

Contents

Acknowledgments

This book started off, simply enough, as a series of lectures for a course on racism and representation that I developed and taught in the early 1990s at St. John's University in Queens, New York. With the now infamous neighborhoods of Howard Beach, Bensonhurst, Bedford-Stuyvesant, and Crown Heights all represented in my classroom, the course was, to say the least, on the front lines in the struggle against racism. Although fraught with issues, it was nonetheless important for me as a white male scholar to participate in the struggle: To use my position from within privilege to attempt to dismantle it—to stand up and assert that racism is a social reality created, imposed, and maintained by dominant white culture, not just some complaint black people make for their own empowerment in the politics of victimization. For the teaching of students at St. John's, many of whom were working class, it was particularly important that someone who understood and shared their class status, nonetheless argued that the operations of class does not dissolve the status and function of white privilege within American society.

At that time, as I tried to teach these broader principles and concepts through the study of film and television, there was very little material that I could assign to students that dealt directly with mass media texts—at least, not in a manner and level of discourse that students could understand. Although that situation has changed somewhat, there is still a great need for students and readers in general to learn how to analyze a film for its production of meaning, and how that operation can participate in the process of racism, and often does very covertly. Hence this book. Unlike my earlier work, I did not write this text for fellow film scholars: there is enough written for them already. I wrote this book for students and for a general audience, as one small and limited attempt to get the field of film and media studies to have more of an impact on mainstream society: to make accessible specific theories that elucidate the manner in which media texts participate in the process of racism so that theory can be a tool for everyone to confront both racism and the mass media.

The process of transforming one's teaching into scholarship is as difficult as trying to turn a great book into a good movie: profound differences in the mediums complicate such undertakings. Fortunately for me, I had the assistance of some brilliant and generous individuals. The first such individual was Thomas Wartenberg, whose insistence on a book series that would combine readability with philosophical significance inspired me to launch this project. From the get-go Thomas was helpful and encouraging. I was particularly fortunate that the editor assigned to the series was Laura Parsons, the nicest, most personable, and insightful editor I ever met, let alone had the luck to work with. The fact that she is a Chicago Cubs fan also proves that she has a great sense of humor (says the pathetic Green Bay fan who waited 30 years for the Packers to win another Super Bowl). Although filling Laura's shoes would be a job I would never want, Sarah Warner certainly did so admirably, giving me support and direction during the most crucial of times. Also of enormous help was the staff at Superstar Video, who not only tracked down individual films but refrained from socking me with huge late fees when I failed to renew.

In terms of quality, this manuscript is thoroughly indebted to the two readers who dissected every argument, analysis, and description I made: Roger Simon and Joshua Bellin. As is always the case, Roger Simon brought encyclopedic knowledge of film into his readings—to the point where I think the only reason I wrote on *Le Grand Blanc de Lambarene* is that I had finally found a film that Roger Simon had NOT seen and wanted the opportunity to prove it! His ability to make connections that I did not see were of great importance. That he left the field of cinema studies to study law and then clerk for the Texas Supreme Court is of great loss to academia, but offers a glimmer of hope to our troubled society: If, as he deserves, Roger Simon ends up on the Supreme Court, the possibility for creating a more just and equitable society will have become all the more attainable—not to mention that there would be one less ideologue on the bench.

My other reader, Joshua Bellin, is likewise responsible for whatever quality exists here. A meticulous reader who pointed out every strength (both of them) and every flaw in every chapter, he was both supportive and demanding in ways that elevated the manuscript beyond my own limited horizons. I can think of no more telling an indicator of how troubled academia has become than the fact that such a brilliant scholar, superb and dedicated teacher, and outstanding human being had such a difficult time finding a place within it. If ever there were proof that the whole system (let alone the system of hiring and promotion) fundamentally is not working, it is that scores of institutions passed over Dr. Bellin before LaRoche College snapped him up like the Hope Diamond that he is.

In addition to my readers, it would be less than honest to leave out recognition for the contributions Bradford College made to this manuscript. The individuals who made up the faculty there were a constant inspiration to rise above mediocrity. As with the students at St. John's, my interactions with students at Bradford help refine and clarify my arguments of the films under discussion here. I will long appreciate those moments and their contributions. I will always be particularly grateful, however, to the Class of '98, whose collective actions gave meaning to my teaching, and allowed me to leave with dignity and recognition for my work.

Academic institutions, the problems that are overwhelming academia, and my own place within it all are very much a concern of mine as I finish this manuscript. Fortunately for me, my wife Margaret keeps me grounded in what the struggle means in people's daily lives. Where I was willing to give up on doing this project, she encouraged me to see it through, to make my contribution. Coming from a person who works daily providing health-care to the poor and disenfranchised, that was the strongest endorsement I could ever receive. To say, as I have in the past, that Margaret sacrificed much so that I could work on a book, would be far too cliché to accurately characterize the degree and scope of what she did and what she went through so that I could live and work in the world of ideas. I owe this entire book to her, without doubt–and I clearly owe so much more.

My other source of inspiration for this book is the miracle I helped bring into this world who was given the name Antonia Therese. In terms of my contribution to the world, she is beyond a doubt without compare (but only for the next 3 months!). I look forward to the time when, for the first time in her life, the household is free from Daddy having a book deadline. Antonia and her future sibling also bring me full circle back to the topic of racism. When I think about how Afro-American parents love their children as much as I love mine, but how they are nonetheless powerless to protect their children from ultimately being subjected to racism, then the tragedy of racism takes on inexplicable human dimensions. If this book could play even a small role in the struggle to rid this society of that ongoing tragedy, then I would have achieved more than a person of my abilities should hope for.

Lastly, if this manuscript began as a result of my shocking introduction to the blatant and unashamedly ugly racism I witnessed in New York, then I have my parents to thank. My parents considered racial equality and affording every individual respect and humanity as Catholic imperatives. Furthermore, they taught by example and I am convinced that whatever racial consciousness I have achieved is due to foundations they created. Somehow, Catholicism began and ended this manuscript, because it never would have been completed without the support of St. Mary's-Immaculata Concepcion Parish in Lawrence, Massachusetts. Father Bill Waters, OSA, its generous pastor, provided me with office space to work, and the rest of the parish staff gave me support and sympathetic ears. Father Jorge Reyes, OSA, kindly let me use his printer to submit this. And I would be really remiss if I did not acknowledge the wonderful ladies who cooked each month for the Bread & Roses organization, and who, when they did so, always gave me a plate of outrageously delicious Caribbean food. Significantly, what I found in the example of these dedicated women, and at St. Mary's-Immaculata Concepcion in general, is the most radical and powerful alternative to the ideology of racism and societies of inequity such as can be found in the United States and its drive for the much vaunted but vastly overrated global economy. That alternative is the body of Christ. Sadly, I could not find adequate ways to bring that alternative and all its vitality to the discussions held here. As with all the other limitations of this book, that can only be attributed to me. Fortunately for the world at large, liberationist scholars whose work I admire very much, like Michael Budde, William Cavanaugh, bell hooks, David Toole, and Cornel West have already written insightfully and eloquently on Christianity as radical paradigm and alternative (and somewhere in there is the haunting specter of Stanley Hauerwas). Their writing has inspired me and countless others, and I thank them. It would be too prideful to wish my work could live up to theirs. I do hope, however, that I can return in some measure what has been given to me by the sacrifice, example, and hard work of others.

I close by acknowledging one such example so powerful in its simplicity that it haunts me to this day. In the Fall of 1974 my family prepared to move back to Michigan from our home in Georgia. All of us children were very excited to be reunited with our friends and family up north. My always protective parents waited until moving day, however, to break the bad news to my little brother John that he would not be returning to the school he went to in Michigan because they were over-enrolled. It was crushing news to an eleven-year-old, and he cried on the front porch as the movers shuttled furniture. One of the moving men, who looked like he played defensive line for the Atlanta Falcons, threw a sofa on the truck and, upon returning, stopped to comfort my brother: he asked why John was crying, and when given the response, assured him that he would make new friends. If that does not sound like such a big deal, then the act needs to be read through the matrix of postsegregation Southern culture. The man was black, he was busy, he was hot as hell, and most importantly, he was supervised by whites who would surely chew him out for such lolly-gagging. He resisted all those pressures, however, to make a simple act of kindness across the complexity of race in order to comfort a small boy he would never know or even see again. The sofa and the truck are long gone. The act, however, endures. We do not always need theory to act in such transcendent ways, but if theory cannot ultimately lead us to do so, it is not very worthwhile theory.

Vincent F. Rocchio
Lawrence, Massachusetts

Part One

Of Racism and Representation

1
Introduction:
Revisiting Racism and Cinema

On March 4, 1991, Americans tuning into the nightly news were shocked by what appeared on their televisions: a dark and grainy home videotape recording of Los Angeles police officers beating an unarmed black motorist named Rodney King. When the case against the officers went to court, the trial was moved out of racially diverse Los Angeles and into predominantly white Simi Valley. The officers were acquitted, and rioting ensued.

A little less than four years later, in October 1995, America found itself once more glued to the TV (as it had been for almost nine months), waiting for the verdict of what many called the trial of the century: the murder trial of O. J. Simpson, famous athlete and celebrity, accused, then acquitted, of murdering his ex-wife. The torrent of media punditry and pseudo-debate that raged around the incident found its source in a wellspring of emotions about race. Those emotions were fed by witness for the prosecution Mark Fuhrman, a Los Angeles police detective who lied under oath about his use of racially derogatory remarks, specifically the word "nigger." Defense lawyers exposed his perjury by playing a tape recording of Fuhrman referring to blacks as "niggers" and bragging about his mistreatment of black suspects. The taped interviews showed that he had used the slur at least forty-one times. Fuhrman also bragged that he enjoyed lining up "niggers against the wall and shooting them."[1]

Four years after Fuhrman's chilling pronouncements, an elite street-crimes unit of the New York City Police Department nearly did just that, shooting unarmed west African immigrant Amadou Diallo as he stood outside his Bronx apartment building. The shooting was particularly notorious for the manner in which the four police officers, none of whom lived in the city, fired forty-one rounds at the defenseless twenty-two-year-old, hitting the victim nineteen times. Shortly after Diallo's death, protests and demonstrations erupted all over the city, frequently drawing over a thousand people. Like the Rodney King trial, however, the case was moved out of the large, racially diverse metropolis and into a nearby city. Unlike the Rodney King trial, however, the national media fairly ignored the trial, despite evidence of demonstrated interest. Another distinct difference from the Rodney King trial contributed to this neglect: there was no videotape to be played over and over on the nightly news, or frame by frame from the witness stand, with each side battling over the meaning contained within. Further, the trial and the trial judge went to great lengths to keep the issue of race out of the trial, a seemingly impossible, but nonetheless accomplished, task. When the officers were acquitted, despite having to prove that each individual bullet in the forty-one-round shooting was itself justified, there was no rioting, due chiefly to Afro-American leaders organizing and urging restraint, but also due to the fact that the media had stayed away. Their neglect provided an important support for race to be rendered a nonissue.

These examples, only three in what could be a very long list, demonstrate one rather obvious—though frequently denied—fact about contemporary American society, succinctly expressed by Cornel West: Race matters. These examples also demonstrate an equally obvious fact: the contemporary status of race in mainstream American culture is intimately bound to the process of representation within and through the mass media. As the King trial so clearly demonstrated, the meanings generated by images are neither inherent, nor ideologically neutral. What first popped up on American TVs seemed self-evident, but was later rendered differently, first by situating the "meaning" of the tape within a broader context—the high-speed chase that preceded the police actions—then through the imposition and application of different codes and modes of interpretation applied frame by frame.

What this book will demonstrate is that race matters precisely because racism is a social institution within American culture, and representation is the foundation upon which it stands. Indeed, racism has been an integral component of American culture since its founding upon the genocide of Native Americans, and the forced slavery of Africans and Afro-Americans. Contemporary American society is multiethnic and multiracial, but it is not color-blind—much as it would like to claim to be.[2]

Although it is morally reprehensible, racism is not just a moral problem, the result of people who are morally inferior clinging to immoral attitudes and beliefs. Neither is racism only a political problem: it cannot be made to disappear through a series of laws. Racism functions in and through specific meanings and beliefs, a domain in which the law has little power to change or effect, as the continuing public debate over abortion makes clear. For racism to be "dealt with," as such, it needs first to be conceived as a complex, multidimensional, and evolving social phenomenon that affects everyone on an individual basis. In this sense, racism is also a dialectical operation, because racism as a social dimension effects individual beliefs, attitudes, and actions, but these individual beliefs, attitudes, and actions—separately and collectively—become the support and foundation for social dimensions.

As a social dimension, racism—in its current context—is highly dependent on the conduct and the specific messages of the mass media. No other social institution engaged in the construction and distribution of public discourse has the pervasiveness and volume of consumption as the mass media, two characteristics that themselves are cause for continuing investigation. As several studies have indicated, individuals within contemporary mass society receive most of their information indirectly and through mediated texts rather than through direct experience. Individual media texts, the means by which the information is disseminated, are thus significant sites for the production and integration of meanings through which societies maintain themselves and evolve. Precisely because racism remains a pervasive component of American society, the meanings about race that are disseminated by and through the mass media demand investigation as active participants.

The study of the mass media is a complex affair, and a variety of methods and approaches are employed to understand it: history, aesthetics, economic organization, and rhetoric, to name a few. This book combines several different theories in order to analyze the messages that the mass media disseminate throughout society. It combines these theories to create methods for interpreting and analyzing individual media "texts" for how they use communication—or to use a more precise term, discourse— to reinforce the status quo of racism. Several books have already taken this approach to analyzing the content of media messages, but they are limited in their approaches and theories. Just as racism operates through several different means, and manifests itself in several different ways in society, it functions in a variety of complex and implicit ways in media texts. It is for this reason that Robert Stam and Louise Spence argue for developing new and sophisticated methods for analyzing film and television with respect to racism.

In their article, "Colonialism, Racism, and Representation," Stam and Spence demonstrate that the relationship between racism and representation is not a simple matter, as one-dimensional approaches make it seem.[3] Rather, this relationship is complex and cunning, powerful and pervasive, and—in the final analysis—unacknowledged and accepted. The work of Stam and Spence was a clarion call for the field of media studies to move beyond the "search for stereotypes," and develop the kinds of tools that would allow everyone to see these complex relationships. Their call went largely unanswered, as the work of bell hooks—one of America's leading scholars on race and culture—testifies.[4] Racism remains an entrenched problem in American society, and the media's role in the problem still goes largely unchallenged and unacknowledged by mainstream culture, which seems intent on believing the mass media's ruse that it simply reflects the culture it finds itself within.

This book attempts to make the study of racism and media accessible to everyone, not by taking overly simplistic approaches like positive-negative image analysis, conspiracy theories of media, and the search for stereotypes, but by defining terms and discussing methods that help develop more critical perspectives towards the messages of the mass media in general, and towards race specifically. An emphasis on terms is not just an intellectual exercise. Perhaps nothing is more lacking in public debates on race than common terms and definitions. The airwaves are full of debate on whether a specific incident is due to racism or certain remarks were racist, but surprisingly, there is very little discussion on what racism actually *is:* How do we define it, how is it characterized, how do we come to know it? It is as if those questions were long ago answered and agreed to, though history certainly testifies to the opposite. Not coincidentally, other words have come to be associated with issues of race, and have had their meanings distorted such that they stand in for, or are equivalent to, racism—among them, discrimination and prejudice. As Lola Young argues, "Racism is not attributable to a single factor such as capitalism, the colonial enterprise or personal prejudice."[5] Rather, as further discussion will demonstrate, racism is not the equivalent of discrimination or prejudice, and in fact, is not involved with either term so much as it is involved with the exercise of power and violence.

The distortion and confusion over terms in public discourse is not accidental, but rather serves several purposes, not least of which is helping the process of racism endure. As long as mainstream society lacks specific ideas on what racism is, then it will be susceptible to a high degree of uncertainty as to how and where it manifests itself within society. As a result, society will be less able to take remedial action. In contemporary American society, this has led to an endless stream of punditry over specific incidents and issues, like the King and Simpson trials (complete with oversimplifications, overgeneralizations, and finger-pointing), that has left the complexity of the broader social process of racism virtually undisturbed.

The King trial, for example, seemed to accomplish little towards curbing police violence, especially violence against people of color. For all its popular outcry over the issue of race and police racism, little to nothing was accomplished in terms of the structure and operation of law enforcement, within the Los Angeles police department or broader society. Indeed, the facts that came out of the Diallo trial with respect to the New York City police department showed increasing amounts of police violence, not less. Thus, as Angela Ards reports:

From July 1993 to June 1997, complaints against the police rose 45 percent and monetary settlements by the city increased 38 percent. In 1996 Amnesty International investigated more than ninety allegations of NYPD misconduct dating from the late eighties to early 1996. Its report found that the root of the problem was not 'rogue' cops but the police culture—with its aggressive tactics that disproportionately target racial minorities, its unaccountability and its code of silence.[6]

In addition to the police silence that Ards references, another kind of silence pervades the problem of increasing police violence and its disproportionate effect on people of color: the near silence of the mass media, which is far more oriented to achieving profits by hyping individual racial incidents and tragedies than it is towards analyzing racism as a broader, complex social institution.

This book starts, therefore, by defining its terms, though in a manner very much distinct from the way in which mainstream culture has come to define social phenomena. In contemporary society, the function of defining social phenomena is to limit and contain them: to put things in their place, lest they disturb the balance of a society of inequity. In this book, the function of defining terms and concepts is to expand our understanding of them: to raise questions rather than to provide succinct answers. As Cornel West has demonstrated, succinct answers about race and racism are becoming an increasing part of the problem. West argues, "most of us remain trapped in the narrow framework of the dominant liberal and conservative views of race in America, which with its worn-out vocabulary leaves us intellectually debilitated, morally disempowered, and personally depressed."[7] West thus concludes that "Our truncated public discussions of race suppress the best of who and what we are as a people because they fail to confront the complexity of the issue in a candid and critical manner."[8] West's conclusion provides important criteria for establishing a definition of racism: it must be broad in scope, confront the complexity of the issue, and be able to do so in a critical manner that will not shirk its investigation or conclusions.

Fulfilling such criteria and remaining accessible is not a particularly easy task, however. In his insightful work on race and ideology, for example, Arthur K. Spears defines racism as "behaviors which indirectly or directly support the inequality of racial hierarchy."[9] In attempting to construct a definition that is broad enough, however, Spears does not provide for the kind of precision that can analyze racism as a complex process. In this respect, Stam and Spence's work is important for their attempt to advance a more precise definition of racism that engenders a critical approach. In their work, Stam and Spence put forward Albert Memmi's multidimensional definition of racism. For Memmi, racism is not just feelings, attitudes, or actions based on race. Instead, racism is "the generalized and final assigning of values to real or imaginary differences, to the accuser's benefit, and at his victim's expense, in order to justify the former's own privilege or aggression."[10]

What is particularly important about the multiple components that comprise Memmi's definition is that together they define racism as a complex process, not a thing. Further, what Memmi's definition demonstrates is that representation is at the heart of racism. Precisely what Memmi means by "the generalized and final assigning of values" is the process of symbolism and signification; that we assign meaning (which is laden with value judgments) to the phenomena that surround us. Indeed, it is difficult, if not impossible, to refrain from assigning meaning to what we see and hear—even if that process is conducted in an unacknowledged way. Psychoanalyst Jacques Lacan has argued that we are constantly engaged in this symbolic—

naming—process, not only as children learning language, but as functioning adults negotiating their position and situation within a complex, dynamic, and evolving social reality. As a few media scholars have indicated, this "naming" process is at the heart of the talk-show formats, from *Oprah* to the more fabricated *Jerry Springer*. Indeed, the outrageous topics and situations on the talk shows demonstrate Lacan's point that when specific phenomena resist symbolization, they are conceived of as threatening and as a source of anxiety. Thus it is that a primary function for the talk show is to frame topics, no matter how outrageous, into some evaluative (and implicitly moral) term: to symbolize it so as to render it nonthreatening.

The anxieties attending phenomena resistant to a culture's symbolization are evident in the earliest, indeed foundational, instance of American racism: the destruction of Native American peoples. It is not difficult to see why early white settlers in North America conceived of the Native Americans as "savages" and closely aligned with the "devil." As members of a pre-Enlightenment society, white settlers lived and thought within what is frequently described as a "sacral society": where religion—and in this case a tightly constricted religion—is the center and dominant source of meaning for the social-symbolic system. The existence of Native Americans was fairly beyond the scope of that meaning system. Standing, as they were, outside the boundaries of the meaning system, Native Americans could logically be placed as outside the sacred, and thus belong to the profane—the devil. Furthermore, the Native American way of life constituted a threat to the white settlers' social system: Native American culture was communal in its social organization (which meant it was egalitarian and lacking in private ownership) and sacral in its ideology (the world was a sacred place and had to be treated as such). Native American culture constituted a threat to European social organization precisely because it engendered the significant aspects of Christianity that European societies had worked so hard to eradicate: communalism (which threatened the nation-state mode of social organization), egalitarianism (which threatened hierarchical modes of social organization), and sacral affinity with the natural world (which threatened certain productive modes of organization). White European settlers—though not consciously—had to assign meaning to this significant discrepancy, and they did: the Native Americans were "savages," beings without civilization (the concept of civilization neatly explaining why the radical egalitarianism and sacral ideology of Christianity cannot be applied to a social system). Further, what this example shows—as semiotics (the study of signs) will explain more fully in a later discussion—is that the meanings assigned by a culture are in no way ideologically neutral. Rather, they are replete with value judgments and a whole set of ideas about the world lie behind them.

Memmi's definition of racism challenges us to look at our own society and see the same process conducting itself today, even though the players may have changed. Thus, in the first part of his definition, Memmi identifies what earlier approaches to racism have emphasized—the act of stereotyping. The meaning that is assigned attempts to remove individuality and assign traits (or meaning) to everyone based on some identifiable difference—in this case, race. Hence, in the example of the European white settlers, all Indians were "savages." As later discussions will demonstrate, however, this generalizing process manifests itself in another way with respect to the process of representation. Within representation, the symbol can be used to stand in for a broad range of meanings—sa process that the concept of stereotyping tried to address. This is what Donald Bogle discusses in his work on racism and film: that the black women who portrayed characters in films stand in for *all* black women, and that, further, the meanings that are assigned to them are meant to marginalize black women.[11]

Precisely what Memmi's definition shows, however, is that, though the process of racism involves stereotyping (or generalizing), it goes beyond that function to include several other operations. To begin with, Memmi's definition draws attention to a frequently overlooked characteristic of signs: their contingency. Rather than being determined by reality, signs are arbitrary constructions that are dependent on outside factors to lend them their ability to make meaning, which is what the term "connotation" is meant to express. As a result of their contingencies, signs frequently change meaning over time, a point that will be elaborated further in a discussion of semiotics. One of the most vivid examples of the meaning of a sign changing over time is the swastika, which was a good-luck sign in ancient time, then symbolized the ideology of racial purity for the Nazis, and now comes to symbolize quite a number of different things today—among them the atrocities committed by the Nazis. Memmi's definition emphasizes that with the process of racism, meanings are assigned to difference in a way that is both generalized *and* final. We are not meant to question the validity of the meaning and values assigned to race. Rather, we are encouraged to accept those meanings as real, as the "truth" about race, rather than meanings that are constructed by the signs and symbols that we impose onto race.

The Semiotics of Race and Racism

Memmi's definition of racism is thus firmly grounded in theories of semiotics, the study of signs. To sustain its conclusion, it is necessary to briefly go into the main concepts of semiotics and examine their implications.

The study of signs and sign systems can be traced to ancient times, but it was not until the late-nineteenth and early-twentieth centuries that more widespread philosophical attention was paid to a fundamental aspect of signs: that there is no inherent relationship between a sign and that which it represents. In the communication act, it seems self-evident that a sign points to, and stands in for, some thing, or some object that exists in reality. In other words, because things exist in reality, like trees, birds, water, and rocks, we develop signs to name them. Viewed in this manner, communications can "accurately" or "objectively" (to use the parlance of journalism) "represent" reality—precisely what allows us to know things and determine the "truth."

Several philosophers have long since concluded that this is an inaccurate perception of the relationship between communication and reality. Most significant in codifying how sign systems function, however, was the work of Ferdinand de Saussure, one of the founding theorists of semiotics. Signs do not refer to reality, argues Saussure, but ultimately to other signs. For Saussure, the meaning of the sign does not come from the way reality is structured and ordered. Rather, the meaning of the sign depends on a system of difference and similarity between signs themselves. Christopher Norris sums up the implications of this theory: "our knowledge of things is insensibly structured by the systems of code and convention which alone enable us to classify and organize the chaotic flow of experience. There is simply no access to knowledge except by way of language and other, related orders of representation."[12] Thus, rather than language and symbolic systems coming out of reality, taking their scope and form from the way reality is structured, languages (and other sign systems) organize, shape, and structure our perception of reality.[13]

This fundamental, but often ignored aspect of language, has very radical implications for the concepts of "meaning" and "truth." In essence, things only mean what social orders want them to mean, because language and representation are only human constructs, as are the codes that govern them. The result is that truth is now relativized, if not eradicated. It is a function only of agreements and pacts, and not guaranteed by something in reality. Indeed, truth, such as it is, needs to be reconceptualized as that which is beyond representation—as that which remains beyond and behind symbolization. In other words, the truth is out there, but always and ever more inaccessible to us. This has profound implications for how we come to think of race and racism, for not only does it mean that there is no truth about race, it means that race itself is not reality, but rather, is a symbolic distinction that we make based on how we have come to perceive reality.

As a result, one component of Memmi's definition needs modification. For purposes of clarity, Memmi makes the distinction between "real" and "imaginary" difference in terms of where the generalized and final assigning of meaning gets applied. In making such a distinction, Memmi's definition attempts to emphasize that the process of assigning meaning does not depend on "real" difference. Semiotics makes clear, however, that difference is already at the level of the symbol—that real difference is not accessible to our knowledge without symbolization. Thus, what we come to think of as real difference is only our perceptions as they are shaped by a specific social-symbolic system.

What Saussure's work demonstrates is that the social-symbolic system, while not centralized (it has no one point of organization—no one group or person controls it) or localized (it is not located in any one place—like the government or Wall Street) is nonetheless a site of enormous power and influence. Clearly, to be able to name and define social groups and social processes, complete with the value judgments that are inherent in that process, is to be in a position of power. This is what led several theorists, among them Mikhail Bakhtin and Antonio Gramsci, to examine the manner in which groups and individuals compete to control the social-symbolic system, and to postulate how that competition is an inherently political process—since ultimately that process is about the distribution of power.

This leads back to the other components of Memmi's definition of racism. What Memmi argues for in his definition is that this generalized and final assigning of meaning (and the values inscribed within them) is part of a process of maintaining power. The process, according to Memmi, works to the accuser's benefit, and at the victim's expense. Precisely what Memmi emphasizes here is that a network of power stands behind the generalized and final assigning of meaning within the social-symbolic system. Further, the meanings assigned will benefit the empowered at the expense of others. This process can be clearly demonstrated with respect to Afro-Americans. Of all the values assigned to the Afro-

American race by dominant white culture, one of the most enduring is "inferior intelligence." Even as recently as 1994, two American social scientists received wide attention for producing a seriously flawed study that attempted to prove that Afro-Americans were of lower intelligence than whites.[14] What Memmi's definition makes clear is that this study was not produced by some sort of scientific neutrality. Theories of Afro-American intellectual inferiority are consistently produced by dominant white culture. Furthermore, their conclusions function as an accusation. Once meaning has been assigned and finalized (as a result of these "scientific conclusions") individual Afro-Americans and Afro-American cultures must continually prove their intelligence, since they are already pronounced guilty of inferior intellect. By incorporating the terms "accuser" and "victim," Memmi's definition emphasizes the power relations that are established in this process.

In addition, the use of these terms makes clear that existing power relations benefit from this process at the expense of the disempowered. Minorities are accused of having countless undesirable traits by the majority culture, a self-fulfilling process whose purpose is to maintain the racialized barriers upon which white privilege is established. In her discussion of the media's representation of gangsta rap, bell hooks delineates not only the manner in which the accusation process is self-fulfilling, but also, the manner in which it covers over and obscures the legacy of social operations whose function is oppression based on race. Thus, she argues, "a central motivation for highlighting gangsta rap continues to be the sensationalist drama of demonizing black youth culture in general and the contributions of young black men in particular."[15] At stake in this highlighting process is the evidence of an earlier accusation: that blacks are violent.

What hooks demonstrates, however, is that this highly selective focus on black male misogyny functions to repress the relationship between the expressions in this musical genre and the values of dominant society. She thus argues, "gangsta rap does not appear in a cultural vacuum. . . . It is not a product created in isolation within a segregated black world but is rather expressive of the . . . engagement of black youth culture with the values, attitudes, and concerns of the white majority."[16] hooks thus concludes that the media spectacle built around gangsta rap has a very specific ideological function, arguing that: "young black males are forced to take the heat for encouraging via their music the hatred of and violence against women that is a central core of patriarchy."[17] Far from defending the misogyny and male violence against women that is found in gangsta rap, hooks focuses instead on the manner in which black males, via a process of accusation, are singled out "without placing accountability on larger structures of domination."[18]

The process of assigning meaning—of making accusations about race—is thus an important component to power relations in a society. As hooks's example demonstrates, the process of accusation is very much a part of reinforcing existing power relations. Assigning meaning benefits the accuser because it functions to justify the privileges that are received from an unequal distribution of power (and resources). According to Memmi, the process of assigning meaning justifies both privilege and aggression (or violence). Here, the process of assigning meaning comes back full circle to the place where it started: the accuser (or assigner). Majority culture assigns traits and values to race in order to justify the privileges it receives at the expense of others.

Privilege is an abstract social phenomenon that has a very real impact on individuals. While it is not always readily visible, it is continually in operation. Several different social practices provide vivid examples of how privilege operates in American society. The practice of racial profiling by police departments operates such that when white people drive their cars, they have the privilege of not being a suspect of some kind by virtue of driving expensive automobiles or driving in certain areas or neighborhoods. Because they are not accused of having an inferior intelligence due to their race, white people do not have to initially prove their intelligence, or prove that they are not angry or lazy. Because they belong to majority culture, white people are treated as individuals first, and only on occasion as a member of their race. Afro-Americans and other nonwhites, however, do not possess that privilege: Majority culture is not color-blind, and minorities are seen as members of their race first—with all the accompanying racial baggage that has been assigned to them.

The operation of privilege thus has very real consequences of enormous scope. It exercises a role in medical care, education, employment, housing—in short, in every major social arena. What Memmi's definition starts to clarify is the manner in which privilege maintains itself through a process of justification. Further, this process of justification is itself conducted through social discourse—through the generalized and final assigning of meaning based on difference. Meanings are structured such that, when inequity must be acknowledged, its existence or continuation can be justified.

Moreover, by using the term "justification," Memmi's definition provides the means by which social discourses are seen to have specific and strategic rhetorical functions. Within a broader process of justifying racism, for example, social discourses can employ strategies of legitimization and naturalization. In the case of the former, discourses structure meanings around concepts of social mandates. The latter term goes one step further and structures meaning as having been dictated by reality. Further, when it comes to the process of justification, social discourses frequently employ several of these strategic modes.

The last component of Memmi's definition indicates that maintaining privilege is not dependent on discourse alone, but also includes and incorporates violence. This is clearly visible in the history of the civil rights movement, when the state itself resorted to violence in an attempt to maintain segregation and the privilege it engendered. What is not always so clear is how discourses are used to justify aggression (it was unavoidable, necessary, etc.), legitimize aggression (usually involving the actions of the state), or naturalize aggression (rendering it in a manner that makes it part of human nature, etc.).

The use of discourse to justify aggression is not limited to history; it is still a part of contemporary American society, as the ill-fated war on drugs can testify. Despite the fact that by nearly every measurement the war on drugs has been a dismal failure, its operations continue. Several social statistics—not the least of which is the disproportionate arrests of Afro-Americans for drug offenses—demonstrate that discourses about "getting tough on crime" largely function to justify aggression on the part of the state that is directed largely at nonwhites.[19]

Memmi's definition thus allows us to see that the violence and aggression so consistently linked to racism are not necessarily ends in themselves, but participate in a broader process of maintaining and justifying privilege. Racism is therefore not just a set of attitudes, or even a process of discrimination. Rather, what Memmi's definition demonstrates is that racism needs to be understood as a complex process if society is ever to dismantle the abstract and oftentimes invisible structures of privilege and the discourses and symbols that justify them. Racism should thus be understood as the generalized and final assigning of meaning (and the values that are engendered in them) to create difference, for the accuser's benefit, and at the victim's expense, to justify, legitimize, or naturalize the former's privilege or aggression.

In addition to providing a more comprehensive analytical tool, this definition puts both the communication act and the maintenance of the structure of privilege under the spotlight where they belong. Maintaining both the structures of privilege and the social-symbolic system that legitimizes these structures, as discussed earlier, centers around the distribution of power within a specific social system. This modified version of Memmi's definition therefore directly concerns itself with power and power relations as they function with respect to race. The communication process, however, is not only about power, but is also engaged with individuals and individual identity. The intersection between a social-symbolic system that shapes individual perceptions of reality and individual identity itself is also crucial for understanding the process of racism. As discussed previously, the relationship between the two is a dialectical one: Individuals are a product of, and are shaped by the social-symbolic system, but they in turn shape and affect the social-symbolic system they live within. Furthermore, individuals and individual identity are not defined entirely by the social-symbolic system: people are not just the automatons of their culture.

Psychoanalysis, Identity, and Racism

Here the theories of Jacques Lacan can provide an insightful analytical tool. By combining theories of semiotics with psychoanalysis, Lacan examines the relationship between the social symbolic system and individual identity. Lacan's work is particularly helpful in two respects. To begin with, Lacan does not treat the communication act and the symbols that comprise it as some kind of neutral tool that humans use to make their lives easier and more productive. Rather, Lacan explores the intricate relationships and effects that communication and symbols have on individuals, individual behavior, and individual identity. Furthermore, Lacan's work distinguishes between image-based symbols and language in terms of their relationship to the individual—a distinction that is of great importance for studying mass media texts.

One of Lacan's most radical contributions is particularly relevant to the study of race: the fictive nature of identity. Lacan argues that individual conscious identity does not stem from some "essence" within the person, but rather is constructed from images and signs with which the individual has identified. He bases this position on the incompleteness of being that is evidenced at birth: individuals are not born with self-knowledge or self-sufficiency, only with a few limited instinctual impulses. Individuals grow into their identity, and this progression is a process of endowing themselves with intellect to govern more instinctual processes. Standing behind conscious identity, and always in relation to it, is the instinctual unconscious (which also takes its shape from images and signs). Consciousness itself thus results from a relationship between identification with and the taking in—or introjection—of signs (like a name), terms, and concepts, that shape and model behaviors and identity. Signs and symbols are thus the hallmark of consciousness more than some essence of personhood. As Lacan argues: "That a name, however confused it may be, designates a specific person, is exactly what makes up the transition to the human state. If one has to define the moment in which man becomes human, we can say that it is the moment when, however little it be, he enters into the symbolic relation."[20]

As semiotics has demonstrated, however, the meanings of signs are not real, but rather come from their relationships to other signs and the codes that organize them. As a result, conscious identity, although giving us a sense of who we are, is fictive: it comes, for the most part, from the outside and is not based on what is real. This has very important consequences for the functioning of identity. To begin with, it means that racial and gender identity are not based on biology as much as on a social-symbolic system. Thus it is that Lola Young argues that:

> Although the division of people into racial categories is often based on the valorization of the primacy of . . . the visual signifiers of difference . . . it is generally accepted that biological definitions of 'race' which date back to at least the 18th century are spurious. 'Race' is not, then, an objective, culture-free designation of difference, and neither is the labeling of skin color.[21]

Young further elaborates the dominant role that culture exercises in the designation of race and racial categories when she references Sander L. Gilman's argument that "the very concept of color is a quality of Otherness, not of reality," noting, for example, that Jewish and Irish people have, at various times, been designated as black.[22] Arthur K. Spears thus concludes that: "The concept of race is not scientific. A mountain of scientific research firmly establishes it as a pseudoscience. . . . It is a sociocultural concept, created and sustained in the minds of humans living in or aware of racialized societies.[23]

The significance of such social construction in the categories of race is the dissolution of "essential" or "natural" identities that are determined by biology. Rather, as Lacan's work demonstrates, identity is the result of a complex and dialectical relationship between the real conditions of the individual body and environment, the social-symbolic system that it is situated within, and the individual's own dynamic history at the juncture of the two. The social-symbolic system thus exercises an enormous role in the construction and maintenance of identity, and this has significant implications for the operation of race.

Because identity is constructed around and upon symbols and the norms and values they engender, individuals have enormous psychic and emotional investment in signs, symbols, and images and in the meanings they convey. Indeed, what Lacan's work shows is that truth, on an individual level, is very much determined by its ability to confirm the identity of the individual.

The implications of this for the study of race are twofold. First, it explains why the issue of race is not just a rational social problem about the distribution of power in a society. Rather, race and racism are very much a part of each individual's identity, and their psychical attachments to the meaning of race and racism are not readily disengaged. Further, those psychical attachments are in need of continual reinforcement, and this need drives people to social discourse—whether in the form of conversation or the consumption of mass media texts. In this respect, Lacan's work offers another kind of criticism against the neutrality of symbols, language, and images. Lacan demonstrates that not only are their meanings value-laden, but people's identities are tied into them and caught up in the process of their exchange. The individual need for identity confirmation in discourse creates the economic demand for the messages of the mass media.

This dynamic can be seen, for example, in the success of a film like *Driving Miss Daisy*, which will be discussed more fully later in this book. What white audiences can see in a film like *Driving Miss Daisy* is confirmation that race does not matter, which for many individual white spectators is a truth of their identity: Growing up in American society, their whiteness did not seem to matter because the operations of privilege are frequently made to be invisible. Thus it is that Richard Dyer argues that the invisibility of whiteness "secures white power by making it hard, especially for white people and their media, to 'see' whiteness."[24] Precisely what Lacan's work demonstrates is that this invisibility of whiteness is what individual spectators need to see confirmed and reinforced through rhetorical and signifying strategies. Further, Lacan demonstrates that the necessity of this confirmation is very much rooted in the fictive nature of such social constructs.

The critical concept to analyze this process is the psychoanalytic theory of identification, and here too psychoanalysis makes an invaluable contribution to the study of media texts. Precisely what the concept of identification provides is a theoretical framework that delineates the relationship between signifying practice and the individual that it addresses. Specifically, theories of identification illuminate the individual's psychical investment in the signifying or symbolic process, and where and how they receive pleasure in it. In both Freud and Lacan, identification is the means by which identity is formed, and later, confirmed.

Identification is a much-used word, in both mainstream culture and film studies—to the point of being an overly generalized concept. In the early stages of contemporary film studies, theorists jumped on Lacan's metaphor of the mirror to describe the audience's relationship to the screen. This was due in part to the failure of earlier theories and their attempt to compare film to dreams. Lacan's use of the mirror metaphor, however, was used to describe the process of identification, which is above all a dialectical process. In the metaphor of the mirror, Lacan used the image of the "endless play" between person and reflection: the person knows he or she is standing in one place, but sees him- or herself in another, and he or she is in the other place (the mirror) only because of standing in front of that place. Another way to describe this play between reflection and being is that the person stands before the reflection, and sees him- or herself, only it is not actually them, because it is a reflection—but it really is him or her, because it is *his* or *her* reflection.

The operation of identification works analogously to this process. In the operation of identification, the individual psychically places him- or herself in the place of the other, or the object of identification. At the same time, however, the individual takes in the other (or object) in a desire to become that. Identification is therefore a dynamic process: a taking on as well as a projecting out.[25] Lacan's work on identification is significant because he distinguished between three important modes, two of which will be discussed here for their significant operations within the process of film spectatorship. The first of these is Imaginary identification, which describes a process where the individual identifies with images and forms that come into the perceptual field. The second, and less discussed mode of identification, is Symbolic identification, where the individual identifies with abstract concepts, values, and discourses.

The distinction between these two modes is important in understanding the process of how individuals engage the film or TV text. In a manner similar to the semiotic model, Symbolic identification with discourses, values, or judgments shapes or "translates" the individual's Imaginary identification with images. While it is true that any individual is free to identify with "the bad guy" in a film, the text itself organizes its discourses and symbols such that individuals are encouraged to identify with the hero. Precisely what is at stake in this specific organization of discourses and symbols is the construction of a set of values that audiences recognize as their own. At the same time, those values confer positive judgments and traits on some characters, and negative ones on others. As Daniel Bernardi points out, this process is particularly operative in the construction of the signifiers of race within media texts. He thus argues: "Representations of blackness, redness, yellowness, and browness are intermediate clues to the constructedness and particularity of whiteness . . . if only because this discourse dominates both the production and reception of these racial categories."[26] Further, Bernardi and others, such as Young, have demonstrated that the values that get assigned within the construction of these signifiers are such that whiteness is confirmed as normal, or worse, superior, while blackness is constructed to mean "dirty," "inferior," and "uncivilized."[27] Within this ongoing process, spectators are encouraged to identify Symbolically with the set of values (and the ideologies they come out of) that has been constructed, and to identify through Imaginary identification with the image and form of the character that the text designates.

The ability to analyze the manner in which the text organizes its discourses and symbols into a particular set of values and ideological orientations is an important addition to the study of racism and representation that was missing in earlier studies. These studies identified the use of stereotypes and motifs, but were not as well prepared to determine whether a film's incorporation of a stereotype was for the purpose of perpetuation or criticism. Given the potential complexity of the film or TV text, such a purpose is not always readily apparent. This led some earlier approaches into an implied and overly simplistic model, whereby:

Presentation = Affirmation

In this model, what is shown in a film, like the stereotype of the overly libidinous black man, is shown with the film's implicit approval or sanction. As later discussions of Spike Lee's work will demonstrate, this model cannot accurately interpret more complex forms of critique.

The concept of identification not only provides the means to analyze how texts organize signs and symbols around particular sets of values and ideologies, but relates that process to the audiences that such signification is directed towards, and how they engage it. What the concept of identification delineates is a process whereby spectators engage the film text as a means of obtaining pleasure by having their identities (continually in need of reinforcement because of their dependence on the signifier) confirmed. Further, because Lacan's theories of identification are based in theories of signification, it also provides a framework for rhetorical analysis: the means by which films persuade their audiences about race. Lacan's theories of identity clarify this point.

In establishing his radical critique on the essential self, Lacan, using theories of semiotics, demonstrated how identity was fictive, and how ideas of truth were relative to being able to confirm the identity of the individual. Lacan was not the first theorist to demonstrate that truth was relative (a philosophical point that can be traced back at least as far as ancient Greece). He was, however, more insistent on the role the concept of "truth in discourse" plays in individual identity. Here, Friedrich Nietzsche's assault on truth is particularly significant for introducing what Lacan would later elaborate on. Truth, Nietzsche argues, "is a mobile marching army of metaphors, metonymies, and anthropomorphisms. . . . Truths are illusions of which one has forgotten that they are illusions."[28]

Nietzsche's pointed inclusion of metaphor and metonymy in his critique of truth is not coincidental. Metaphor and metonymy are both structures of language whose function is to convey meaning by substituting one term for another. With metaphor, words or symbols take on their meaning based on analogy and similarity. Although this study seeks to move beyond the analysis of stereotypes, an examination of one stereotype can illustrate how metaphor can function with respect to race. The stereotype of the black "buck," for example, functions metaphorically to equate Afro-American men with overly developed sex drives and sexual prowess. The stereotype is based on an analogy between the physical demands of sexual prowess and the physical prowess demanded by forced labor that Afro-American men had to endure.

What this particular stereotype also demonstrates is that meaning can be a combination or compilation of linguistic structures. Ultimately, the term "buck" was used to convey the meaning of sexual drive and prowess.

The use of this term functions through the process of metonymy. With metonymy, signs or symbols take their meaning by substituting one term for another based on association, by the proximity or contiguity of one thing to another. In using the term "buck" to designate black or Native American men, a substitution is made between the male species of certain animals (like the deer) and the males of specific races. This substitution is based on a proximity. Both the African tribal cultures and the Native American cultures lived with a much closer connection—spiritually and otherwise—with the natural world. To the mind of postfeudal culture, this was the equivalent of living close to or as animals. The term "buck" then functions metaphorically and metonymically to degrade (and thus help oppress) black and Native American men by stereotyping them sexually. They are degraded or dehumanized by equating them with animals.

The substitutions discussed here are not the only factors that contribute to this stereotype, but they demonstrate the operations that are at work in linguistics, and how they function rhetorically. In each substitution, there is a preexisting truth that facilitates and anchors the substitution. Thus, in the metaphor, black men, living lives of forced labor, really possessed physical prowess. In the metonym, tribal cultures (which of course had been stripped from black men through slavery) really did live in a closer proximity to nature than white postfeudal culture. Within metaphor and metonymy, the anchor term lends its truth value to the other term in the substitution, either because of similarity (as in metaphor) or proximity (as in metonymy).

What psychoanalysis demonstrates is that this mode of persuasion is very much connected to identity. The operations of identity—the truths that make up the individual—function as the anchor upon which other terms can be associated, either through similarity or proximity, or through their opposites. What Lacan's work demonstrates, however, is that the "truth" of identity is only an effect: the reinforcement, or recognition, of the specific identifications that the individual has made to construct identity. In terms of social discourse, truth is therefore a highly self-referential process—when social discourses reinforce individual identities, they are accepted, while if they contradict or fail to reinforce identity, they are rejected.

The operations of metaphor and metonymy are important to this process of identity reinforcement for the manner in which they provide the ability to confer truth on social discourses by engaging the functioning of identity. For example, the truth for several individuals in terms of their identity is that they are white, which perception, informed by the science of biology, confirms as true. As these individuals develop their identities they introject and identify with certain traits and values but (usually) without being consciously aware of how the structure of privilege is operating within their lives. Because privilege is not consciously attached to many of the traits individuals will use to define their identity, like professional competency, financial stability, and stable family life, the truth of these traits becomes anchored elsewhere, via the process of metonymy. There is a proximity, achieved through a concept of cause and effect, between these traits and the hard work such individuals expend that would confirm the role that individual effort and merit exercise in their individual and collective identity.

Large numbers of white individuals therefore do not accept the concept of privilege as a social structure because it does not relate to their identity as it was constructed through identification and the operations of metonymy and metaphor. The semantic operations at stake there repress the fact that *most* people—regardless of race—work diligently just to maintain themselves in this increasingly complex and demanding culture. As a result, when nonwhite individuals, or groups of nonwhites, do not achieve or acquire as much, the truth for individuals within white culture appears very clearly to be lack of hard work or merit, despite evidence to the contrary.

Precisely what is significant for the study of racism and film is the manner in which the ability to maintain such beliefs is rooted in the dynamics of identity and identification: Without discourses to confirm and validate such semantic constructions the individual's ability to maintain them is severely undermined. This study results from the mass media being all too willing to offer up such discourses as a means for realizing profit. Thus it is that Ian Angus and Sut Jhally argue: "In contemporary culture the media have become central to the constitution of social identity. It is not just that media messages have become important forms of influence on individuals. We also identify and construct ourselves as social beings through the mediation of images."[29]

In his work on racism and television, Herman Gray demonstrates the degree to which media representations are structured around white audiences being able to identify with preconceived ideas about black success and failure resulting from individual circumstance. Gray delineates the manner in which these representations are constructed primarily around themes of individual effort at the expense of collective possibilities, and an emphasis on individual values, morality, and initiative. As

Gray argues: "media discourses shift our understanding of racial in-equality from structured social processes to matters of individual choice."[30]

Gray's focus on the rhetoric of television—how media discourses attempt to persuade audiences of specific ideological beliefs—demonstrates another very important principle for the study of race and representation: communication is not the expressive social operation it appears to be. Indeed, what semiotics, Lacan, and several other theoretical approaches demonstrate is that communication is at once a matter of expression (what is said) and a matter of repression (what is hidden as a result of the act of expression). Such a dialectical model of communication is crucial for analyzing the process of racism—since modes of repression are extremely important to its functioning.

Furthermore, Gray's attention to rhetoric is an important reminder that the text is the primary conduit through which the relationship between audience and the mass media is conducted. What this discussion attempts to demonstrate is that no single path or theoretical framework can analyze this relationship in all its complexity and operations. For this reason, the rhetorical analysis of film texts conducted here employs the three models previously discussed: semiotics, psychoanalysis, and marxist critical theory. The first provides a rigorous framework for analyzing the signifying operations of the media text and its construction of meaning—though in a manner that fundamentally maintains, as a result of the arbitrary nature of the sign, that there is no fixed or essential meaning to the text. The second demonstrates how the construction of specific meanings engages the individual spectator through the functioning and operations of identity, and the last demonstrates how both of these processes are involved in the struggle for power over determining meaning (itself a struggle to achieve or maintain prominence, dominance, or influence within the social system).

Conclusion

Mass media is an enormous institution within contemporary American society. At the very least, it is the primary source of information for most individuals within the society. To analyze the messages of the mass media as they relate to race is therefore to excavate an important site for determining the "meaning" of race and the process of racism. In addition, however, the earlier discussion of Memmi's definition of racism demonstrates that racism is a process conducted through representation—that the process of signification is one of the foundations upon which racism is conducted. Examining methods and applying them to media texts not only provides insight into how racism is conducted in and through the mass media, but also provides models for how the process of racism functions outside of the media and within broader culture and cultural signifying practices.

In some respects, Stam and Spence's call for more work on racism and representation is being answered. There are now several books that examine the cinema (and sometimes television) with respect to the representation of Chicanos and Latinos, Asians, Jews, and Native Americans, in addition to Afro-Americans. The scope of racism directed at non-white cultures is so broad that no study can devote itself to all of it and hope to achieve any depth. For this reason, this particular book limits its study to the process of racism as it is directed against Afro-America. The implications of the semiotic model insists that there is no one "true" reason that such an approach is a better thing to do, but there should be a theoretically justified reason for doing so. For this study the rationale is the enormous scope of Hollywood's attempt to define and oppress Afro-American culture. Almost from its beginning, the American cinema was engaged in the process of racism against Afro-American culture, and the engagement has never ceased, moving into television and other mediums as a result of, at the very least, very successful persuasive discourses about race.

The purpose of this book, as suggested earlier, is not to condemn this process. Moral pronouncements, though necessary, are not as effective as they can be when the problem is multidimensional in terms of its role within the social system, and further, largely surreptitious or hidden. Rather, the purpose of this book is to provide the reader with the analytical tools to confront the messages of the mass media as they are engaged in the process of racism. The repetition of unacknowledged associations about "truths" concerning race through an enormous volume of media texts has been highly effective in maintaining the institution of racism. This book attempts to provide the reader with the means to bring that process into the light of day, where the reader can confront the constructed meanings about race, and the goals of continued domination and oppression within those meanings, in order to disengage from it. If semiotics and psychoanalysis prove anything, it is that we have the ability to agree on a better way, a better society.

Semiotics and psychoanalysis also demonstrate, however, that meanings are incomplete and unstable. Whatever meanings are assigned to race for the purpose of maintaining privilege and domination are not only incomplete, but unable to contain more egalitarian discourses about race. The purpose of analysis, therefore, is not simply to expose the process of racism as it conducts itself through representation, but to uncover the images and discourses that resist or escape that process—images and discourses that allow us to glimpse, however briefly, more egalitarian societies and collective transformations of social structures. The necessity of such a dual approach lies in the goal of transforming a society of inequity. Until we can expose and confront the operations of inequality, they will persist unabated, and until we can imagine a more just and egalitarian society, we cannot build one. As bell hooks argues, "Opposition is not enough. In that vacant space after one has resisted there is still the necessity to become—to make oneself anew."[31] The purpose of studying racism and representation, then, is no less than playing a part in a process of liberation, a process that the mass media has been very effective in containing. It is time to confront their effectiveness.

Notes

1. Robert Garcia publishes this quote on the NAACP website in a time line that he created on Civil Rights and Police Reform in Los Angeles. See http://www.ldfla.org/time_line.html.

2. See, for example William F. Buckley's claim that "it simply is not correct . . . that race prejudice is increasing in America. How does one know this? Simple, by the ratings of Bill Cosby's television show and the sales of his books. A nation simply does not idolize members of a race which that nation despises." Quoted in Herman Gray, "Television, Black Americans, and the American Dream," in Robert K. Avery and David Eason, eds., *Critical Perspectives on Media and Society* (New York: Guilford Press, 1991). Buckley's near obsession with the word "simple" belies his purpose: to deny a complex social process by oversimplifying its dimensions and operations. Indeed, Buckley's remarks can serve as a valuable object lesson in the operations of ideology: One can usually tell that the ideological fix is in when a commentator insists that complex and dynamic social phenomena are a "simple" matter of one sort or another.

3. Robert Stam and Louise Spence, "Colonialism, Racism, and Representation," in Bill Nichols, ed., *Movies and Methods*, vol. 2 (Berkeley: University of California Press, 1985).

4. See, for example, bell hooks's discussion on developing a critical eye and moving beyond image analysis in Chapters 1, 6, and 8 in *Yearning: Race, Gender, and Cultural Politics* (Boston: South End Press, 1990).

5. Lola Young, *Fear of the Dark: "Race," Gender, and Sexuality in the Cinema* (London and New York: Routledge, 1996), 40.

6. Angela Ards, "When Cops are Killers," *The Nation,* March 8, 1999.

7. Cornel West, *Race Matters* (Boston: Beacon Press, 1993), 2.

8. Ibid.

9. Arthur K. Spears, *Race and Ideology: Language, Symbolism, and Popular Culture* (Detroit: Wayne State University Press, 1999), 21.

10. Quoted in Stam and Spence, "Racism and Representation," 635.

11. Donald Bogle, *Toms, Coons, Mammies, Mulattoes and Bucks: An Interpretive History of Blacks in American Films* (New York: Bantam Books, 1973).

12. Christopher Norris, *Deconstruction: Theory & Practice* (London and New York: Methuen & Co., 1982), 5.

13. This does not mean that language can fundamentally alter reality: when individuals walk off a cliff, they fall immediately (unlike Warner Brothers cartoon characters, who fall only after they notice they are off the cliff). By creating systems of meaning, however, human communities (and the individuals within them) no longer have to be *completely* subject to reality. Distinguishing between inside and outside, for example, allows humans to walk into the cave when it is raining, and not have to be subject to it (unlike the antelope, which will stand and get rained on). Systems of meaning therefore allow us to order, organize, and stabilize the reality that confronts us.

14. I refer here to the notorious tome authored by Richard J. Hernstein and Charles Murray, *The Bell Curve: Intelligence and Class Structure in American Life* (New York: Simon and Schuster, 1995). For extensive discussion of this discredited research, see Claude S. Fischer Voss, Ann Swidler, Martin Sanchez Jankowski, Samuel R. Lucas, and Michael Hout, *Inequality by Design: Cracking the Bell Curve Myth* (Princeton: Princeton University Press, 1996). Eric Alterman offers a critique and analysis of the reactionary politics that drives this discredited research in "The 'Right' Books and Big Ideas," *The Nation,* November 22, 1999.

15. bell hooks, *Outlaw Culture: Resisting Representations* (New York and London: Routledge, 1994), 115.

16. Ibid.

17. Ibid.

18. Ibid., 117.

19. Common Sense for Drug Policy, reports on its website (http://www.csdp.org) the results of a survey from the Substance Abuse and Mental Health Services Administration, that shows "most current illicit drug users are white. There were an estimated 9.9 million whites (72 percent of all users), 2.0 million blacks (15 percent), and 1.4 million Hispanics (10 percent)

who were current illicit drug users in 1998." The organization further reports, however, that "blacks constitute 36.8% of those arrested for drug violations, over 42% of those in federal prisons for drug violations. African-Americans comprise almost 60% of those in state prisons for drug felonies; Hispanics account for 22.5%." Other sources that demonstrate how the war on drugs is directed against minorities include David Cole's, *No Equal Justice: Race and Class in the American Criminal Justice System* (New York: The New Press, 1999); Human Rights Watch, "Racial Disparities in the War on Drugs" (Washington, D.C.: Human Rights Watch, 2000), which can be found on their website http://www.hrw.org/campaigns/drugs/war/key-facts.htm, and from the website for the Drug Policy Foundation, at http://www.dpf.org. The signature example of this state-sponsored aggression against minorities under the war on drugs occurred in 1997, when Esequiel Hernandez, a sixteen-year-old resident of Redford, Texas, was shot and killed by improperly trained U.S. Marines performing drug interdiction duties. When U.S. Representative Lamar Smith conducted an investigation into the tragedy, he found that the Marines had been informed that 70 to 75 percent of the citizens of Redford (population 100) were involved in drug trafficking.

20. Jacques Lacan, *The Seminars of Jacques Lacan,* Book I, *Freud's Papers on Technique,* ed. Jacques Alain Miller, trans. John Forrester (New York: W. W. Norton & Company, 1991), 155.

21. Young, *Fear of the Dark,* 39.

22. Ibid.

23. Spears, *Race and Ideology,* 17.

24. Richard Dyer, quoted in Daniel Bernardi, *The Birth of Whiteness: Race and the Emergence of U.S. Cinema* (New Brunswick, N.J.: Rutgers University Press, 1996), 106.

25. Despite the use of the term, identification is not to be understood as the equivalent of either introjection or projection, or the reverse of either. Identification is a continual maintenance of two positions.

26. Daniel Bernardi, "The Voice of Whiteness," in *The Birth of Whiteness: Race and the Emergence of U.S. Cinema,* ed. Daniel Bernardi (New Brunswick, N.J. : Rutgers University Press, 1996), 107.

27. See Bernardi, "The Voice of Whiteness," and Young, *Fear of the Dark,* Chapter 2.

28. Quoted in Norris, *Deconstruction: Theory & Practice,* 58.

29. Ian Angus and Sut Jhally, *Cultural Politics in Contemporary America,* quoted in hooks, *Yearning,* 5.

30. Herman Gray, "Television, Black Americans, and the American Dream," in *Critical Perspectives on Media and Society,* eds. Robert K. Avery and David Eason (New York: Guilford Press, 1991), 295.

31. hooks, *Yearning,* 15.

2
The Birth of a (Racist) Nation(al) Cinema

For many film scholars, the watershed moment of the modern cinema was the release of David Wark Griffith's epic film, *The Birth of a Nation* (1915). Although motion pictures had been around for over twenty years, and had already proved they were not a passing fad (as Edison had thought), it was Griffith's film that demonstrated the scope of what the Hollywood cinema could be: lavish productions, blockbuster ticket sales, and enormous amounts of publicity and media attention. As a result, the film has cemented a place within film history—indeed, it did so with its first sell-out crowd. The only thing that has changed over the years is the degree to which racism and representation are occluded from discussions of the film.

As Chapter 1 made clear, this book is concerned with analyzing films for their participation in racism as a process. In doing so, however, this book neither intends to be a history of racism and cinema, nor a comprehensive accounting of racism and cinema. This book begins with *The Birth of a Nation* not for historical reasons but in order to confront the contemporary issues that the film raises. One such issue is the relationship between the aesthetics or artistic value of a film, and its dissemination of ideology—in this case the ideology of racism. *The Birth of a Nation* is all too often given its status within film history despite its participation in the processes of racism. There is a pervasive attitude that Griffith's film is great art, and that the lamentable and even objectionable racist material can be separated from that.

In his discussion of the film, for example, Clyde Taylor argues that, "Mainstream cinema scholars and aestheticians . . . have kept the race

issue at arm's length from their exploration of the film's technique, refusing to synthesize these two discussions."[1] Taylor elaborates by arguing, "It is as though the film's many celebrated rhetorical achievements
and its substantial defamation of Blacks were isolated issues, discussible
as if they belonged to two separate films."[2] Further, Taylor demonstrates
that this separation between the film's art and its racism serves an ideological function. As Taylor argues, "the aesthetic [approach] not only
conceals its alliance with ideological motivations, as it always must, but
. . . in the specific instance of Griffith's movie it works to suppress important social meanings." By subordinating the aesthetics of the film to
its rhetoric, this chapter will demonstrate that the film's participation in
racism as a signifying process cannot be made distinct from the film,
and that indeed, without its racism, the film would not have the status it
has today.

In addition, the blatant racism of the film raises several issues that are
still significant to current debate—not the least of which is the issue of intention. *The Birth of a Nation* did not have to wait ten to twenty years for
film scholars to discover the "hidden" racism of the film—its pointed and
reactionary views were a cause of immediate outrage among some viewers,
especially Afro-Americans: the NAACP (National Association for the
Advancement of Colored People) denounced the film at once. As several
film scholars have noted, however, Griffith could not understand what the
fuss was all about, and claimed it was a film about war and reconstruction,
not about race. In other words, Griffith did not intend the film to be
racist, and went to his grave believing it was not. What this chapter will
demonstrate is that meaning and signification are not the result solely of
intention, however conscious the intent may be. Rather, as discussed before, meaning is the result of a relationship between signifiers as they are
constructed through specific codes. Intention is only one mediating element to the construction of meaning, and is highly vulnerable to being
supplanted by more powerful elements like connotation: previously established patterns of association that individuals can bring to the symbol or
sign.

Furthermore, the issue of codes and their relationship to social structures is significant to racism as signifying process and here too *The Birth of
a Nation* can be most instructive. The meanings constructed around the
signifiers of race in Griffith's film seem especially blatant and obvious to
today's viewer. What this chapter will demonstrate, however, is that this is
not because audiences are more sophisticated than spectators of the past,

but because the "truths" that grounded the processes of racism in the past—Afro-Americans are uncivilized and animalistic, Afro-Americans are biologically less intelligent than whites—have been by and large discredited by all but the most fanatic (though, incredibly, as discussed previously, these "truths" keep trying to make a comeback in certain academic and political circles).[3] The codes that governed certain meanings within *The Birth of a Nation* have thus been abandoned, making it easy for current viewers to see the artificiality of what was once taken for truth. In this respect, the film can function as an object lesson precisely because, although the abandoned codes of the past may seem obvious and artificial today, their reemergence into other forms, or their transformation into other codes are far less visible and meet with far less resistance, as this and further chapters will demonstrate.

The issue of codes and their construction of meaning makes *The Birth of a Nation* such a valuable object lesson precisely because the lesson cuts both ways. Current viewers do not have access to, or need of, some of the cinematic codes that governed the film, and as a result certain transitions or sequences can seem unclear and a little confusing. Because these moments occur within the context of trying to understand a specific narrative, they have a tendency to highlight the issue of accessibility to codes. At other points, the lack of cultural codes makes certain meanings seem overblown and artificial, heavily redundant or overworked. The point becomes not to reject *The Birth of a Nation* specifically as untrue (its "history" is ludicrous), but to use the film as an important example: To be able to see the codes that structure the meaning of race, and thus to determine more readily where and how these codes function in more current contexts and signifying practices.

The production of meaning in *The Birth of a Nation*, specifically with respect to race, is the main focus of this chapter. Here too, this particular discussion does not claim to be comprehensive; the scope of the film makes that goal prohibitive. Rather, this chapter will demonstrate that, Griffith's claims to the contrary, the primary signifier that organizes the narrative is not war and reconstruction, but race. Indeed, the opening of the film demonstrates this point by structuring itself around race. The film begins with an intertitle that states: "The bringing of the African to America planted the first seed of disunion." The intertitle is then followed by an image of the slave trade. It is only one intertitle and one image, but placed as they are in the beginning of the narrative, the two elements function to make race the primary signifier that organizes the meaning system of the film. In a narrative that presents itself as an epic story about war and reconstruction, the plot assigns race as a primary causal agent. This primacy will be upheld throughout the rest of the narrative as determinative of the signifying relations and the meanings the film constructs. This is the case for such narrative events as the raid-on-Piedmont scene, the death-of-the-little-sister scene, and the film's climactic scene of the rescue at the little cabin (which the raid-on-Piedmont scene functions to foreshadow), but is also the case in less dramatically visible sites like the construction of characters, and the film's "historical" discourses. Indeed, it is difficult, if not impossible, to locate a scene in the film where race as signifier is not operative.

The film's opening is thus significant for the manner in which it establishes the primacy of race within the signifying operations of the film. At least part of that primacy stems from the manner in which the narrative begins, not with the introduction of main characters, or their specific setting, but rather, with an historical thesis: the argument that the African being brought to America is determinative of the events that unfold through the narrative trajectory. In addition to presenting itself as historical truth, the intertitle is significant for the manner in which it leaves no doubt that Africans are the root of a particular problem. The film is not so clear, however, as to who is to blame for that. The image that follows the intertitle functions to imply that Africans themselves are to be blamed for their own forced abduction, bondage, and slavery.

The shot, at first, presents itself as a tableaux: it is framed by an iris matte, and characters are arranged statically throughout the frame—action is minimal. The function of the matte is to draw attention to, or emphasize (through a process of exclusion) the middle part of the frame. What becomes emphasized here is a line of African slaves, bare to the waist and flanked on each side by slave traders, some of whom hold whips at the ready. In the foreground and to the left of center is a parson (or minister) intoning a blessing. The first slave stands bowed passively before him, the second gazes intently but in wonder at the parson, and the third glances around furtively.

Several different elements work to establish difference within the shot. The first of these is costume. The whites in the shot are fully dressed in the clothing of colonial times, the clothes of civilization: the parson and a soldier have topcoats and shirts with ruffles, they wear shoes or boots and have pressed hats. Even the barefoot slave trader wears a vest rather than be topless like the Africans, who are bare to the waist (though some wear

The opening image of the film introduces race as central to the narrative.
Courtesy of the Academy of Motion Picture Arts and Sciences.

cloth caps). Figure movement and expression also work to establish difference. Despite the tableaux's minimization of action, the actions of the white characters are conducted with confidence and certitude: they know what they are doing and why they are there. The Africans, on the other hand, are bewildered and passive.

All these elements, in relationship to the intertitle, serve to suggest that blacks themselves are to be blamed for slavery.[4] As the intertitle states, blacks were brought to America, not forcibly abducted. The language suggests a willingness to the action—similar to bringing a date to the prom. The image then reinforces these semantics. It does not show slaves being abducted by force; rather, it shows them waiting passively in line as if to get in. Further, the bewilderment and passivity function to suggest that this "bringing" would not have happened if blacks were not so inferior as to put themselves in the position of being slaves to begin with.

From the beginning, then, the film brings to bear several different elements to convey meanings about race that are clearly to the accuser's benefit and at the victim's expense: Africans themselves are to blame not only for slavery, but for the problems that slavery caused white people—problems that will be shown as the film continues. The beginning thus establishes a pattern by which it will attempt to persuade its spectators of the "truth" about race: presenting itself as history and then incorporating codes of realism in its imagery to enhance the claims of objective history.

Such a rhetorical strategy is operative in the raid-on-Piedmont scene, where the film attempts to persuade its audience of the inherent destructiveness of blacks. The film demonstrates at several points what kind of destructive potential blacks have as a result of their being so unruly and uncivilized, but the most prominent example is the scene in which the city of Piedmont, the Camerons' hometown, is ravaged by guerilla forces during the war. Not only does the scene provide one of the most vivid examples of black destructiveness, it also foreshadows—and in the process reinforces the meanings constructed by—the film's climax and ending. In this respect, the scene not only images black destructiveness, but insists on their inferior intelligence by showing their dependence on white leadership. In the raid on Piedmont, this dependence is conveyed through the figure of the "white scalawag" captain who leads the irregular soldiers to do his bidding—looting and pillaging.

The raid-on-Piedmont scene is introduced with the intertitle:

> Piedmont scarred by
> the war.
> An irregular force of
> guerillas raids the town.
> The first negro regiments
> of the war were raised in
> South Carolina.

Here, the intertitle functions through the pattern established in the beginning: the voice of history precedes narrative events. Thus, after the intertitle the quaint and quiet town of Piedmont is shown in its tranquility, then disrupted by marauding black soldiers who shoot down the citizens, begin looting houses, and kill those who get in their way (though for narrative convenience, they only wound the elder Cameron when he attempts to protect the house). The scene is characterized by the lack of order and the destructive chaos inflicted upon the heretofore quiet town by lawless former slaves. Indeed, one shot demonstrates how readily blacks lose control by showing a slave woman in a dress laughing and kicking at one of the victims of the rampage. She clearly is not one of the soldiers, but at the first sight of unruly and destructive behavior, she joins in.

Although the raid scene does not last very long, and its necessity for understanding the overall story is minimal, it carries a high degree of narrative significance. The scene serves as the nightmare image of the film, as a vivid presentation of the destructive potential of blacks in out-of-control rampage that threatens life, property, and person. Furthermore, through the figure of the white scalawag captain, it raises the specter of how willing opportunistic and immoral whites are to take advantage of blacks' destructive potential and their inherent dependence on white leadership. This problem, and its moral reprehensibility, are emphasized through a comparison. There is a noticeable difference, for example, between the pandemonium caused by the scalawag captain influencing the black irregulars to do his bidding, and the scene of "The Great Conqueror," General Sherman, laying waste to Atlanta. Sherman's scene is constructed as the horror of war that played a role in ending the conflict, while the raid on Piedmont is an assault on civilization itself. There is a significant lack of military objective or strategic goal to the raid on Piedmont. It is thus characterized not as war but as complete civil breakdown and gratuitous destruction, demonstrated by the pillaging, the setting fire to the Cameron estate (and other houses of Piedmont) and the threat to the personal safety of the Camerons.

The scene thus functions to construct the meanings of "destructive" and "inferior intelligence" around the signifier of the black race. The former is conveyed through the violent actions of the soldiers, the latter through the inherent dependence the blacks have on white leadership. Further, through its opening and conclusion, the scene creates an opposition where blacks are uncivilized whereas whites, conversely, are civilized. This opposition is emphasized by the manner in which the complete devastation of Piedmont is prevented by the townspeople's ability to enlist the aid of a nearby regiment of Confederate Army soldiers. Once the soldiers receive word of what is happening in Piedmont, they charge into the town. When the black irregulars—and the white captain—hear the charge, they panic almost immediately and begin a hasty retreat. The Confederate soldiers arrive and, with minimal engagement, effectively restore order to the town.

The ability of the Confederates to restore order and tranquility to the town associates the white soldiers with reestablishing civilization. Conversely, the chaos that ensues from the pillaging and destructiveness associated with blacks insists on their being uncivilized.[5] The generalizing process that the film assigns to these representations is then finalized through, among other things, the appropriation and articulation of history. This process of general and finalized meanings constructed around the signifier of race is not limited to narrative events, as mentioned previously. Rather, it also functions through the construction of characters within the plot.

Early on, for example, the film introduces the Camerons, one of two families around whom the story will revolve. During this introduction, the film cuts to a close-up of two puppies playing at the feet of the Cameron father. As the puppies frolic, the family patriarch picks up a kitten, and places it on one of the puppies. After he does so, discord and fighting ensues among the animals. The image clearly calls to mind a folk expression: fighting like cats and dogs. Placed within the function of introducing the Cameron family, the image—isolated as it is through close framing—functions metaphorically by creating a parallel or analogy to the wider story world. Conveying, as it does, a "natural law" about mixing species, the analogy is extended to the mixing of races via its association with the patrician, slave-owning Camerons, who understand the natural superiority of whites and the unnaturalness of mixing the races.

The introduction of the eldest Cameron son also functions through the signifier of race. The introductory shot of the eldest Cameron sibling is fleeting: the camera is barely able to show his image before the plot cuts to the front of the house, revealing a wagon full of slaves rolling by. As the wagon passes, two slave children fall off the back of the wagon, conveying a sense of clumsiness and unintelligence—each a result of a lack of affinity for an object of civilization, in this case a wagon. Their natural buffoonery is then the cause to be set upon by a black elder brandishing a stick, who punishes them for being so foolish. As the man whacks the children, the film cuts back to the original shot of the eldest Cameron son, who looks on approvingly.

This very simple scene nonetheless articulates the problem-solution structure that will be repeated on even larger scales throughout the film. The problem, in this scene, is the black inability to interact competently with modern Western culture. The wagon is so alien to the poor dumb slave children that they do not know to hold on as the wagon continues moving. The solution the film proposes is violence: the children are beaten as a way of making them learn and become more competent. Furthermore, what the scene presents is an ideal solution, for whites do not even have to get involved—and hence, mix—with the race, but only have to look on from a position of authority. As the pattern is repeated throughout the film, violence as a means of controlling the unruly and un-civilized blacks becomes a consistent narrative solution.

The process of constructing characters and character relationships through the signifier of race is also operative with the Cameron mother and the little "pet" sister. As the characters are introduced they are shown sitting on the porch of their mansion, a large column occupying a portion of the frame. Suddenly, a wide-eyed black girl pokes her head out from behind the column, then runs out of frame. In a shot dominated by stasis, the action is very noticeable. Consistent with the film's signifying struc-tures, there are dramatic differences between the main white characters and the black girl, who is used as setting more than character. The first of these is appearance. While the Camerons are dressed in upper-class fash-ion, the girl is in much more simple clothing. Where the Cameron women have hair that has been combed and tied up or back, the black girl has hair standing straight up in pigtails.

What is significant here is the context in which the comparison takes place. Codes of setting, lighting, and costume all emphasize the realism of the scene. The function of this realism is not to persuade the audience that the Camerons are real, but rather, to convince its viewers that what the Camerons stand in for is real: a "quaintly" way of life "that is to be no more," as the intertitles describe it. Through codes of realism and histori-cal voice, the film attempts to persuade its audience of the truthfulness of the plot's depictions of a certain time, and in the process attach the mean-ings it constructs about race to those depictions.

One of the clearest examples of this process is the scene where the Camerons take their northern guests on a tour of the plantation, includ-ing the cotton fields and slave quarters. Before the group arrives in the fields, the film shows black slaves picking the cotton. As the group of main characters enters the frame, they are strategically placed in the fore-ground—the black slaves remain in the background picking cotton. Their "place" is to provide backdrop for the main characters.

In a certain respect, it is too easy to excuse this shot as conforming to the codes of cinema. Placing the main characters in the foreground pro-vides for readability of the frame, and since much narrative exposition is delivered here—especially the love interest between Ben and Elsie—this explanation is certainly accurate. The sequence of shots immediately following, however, demonstrates that such racially neutral discussions—however accurate they may be in one arena—are not comprehensive: they are insufficient for ruling out that the process of racism is active within the scene.

The close correspondence between the sequence in the cotton fields and the sequence in the slave quarters demonstrates this point. The latter sequence is introduced with the intertitle:

In the slave quarters.
The two-hour interval given for
dinner, out of their working day
from six till six.

The next shot shows Ben Cameron leading his group to where the slaves have gathered. In the foreground, he shakes the hands of a male slave, who bows to him and offers Ben a seat. Ben declines, but nonetheless gestures to the man to participate in the actions of the other slaves in the right of the frame: they have begun to dance and to clap. What is clear from this shot is that the slaves have begun to dance and clap for the entertainment of the white masters and their guests. They are happy, if not grateful, for the opportunity to entertain the white people.

This is where the process that has been described as the construction of meaning can be so readily seen. The intertitle suggests that the film is going to look at life in the slave quarters, but it does so only in relationship to the white masters. Rather than emphasizing the injustice, destitution, and misery of slavery, the film chooses to show how happy slaves are to entertain their masters. It has clearly chosen to privilege one interpretation of slavery over another, and done so in a manner that makes black subordination to whites seem natural. As a result, it creates a repetition of the meaning that the scene in the cotton fields worked to convey. The narrative subordinates the black characters to the white characters, and the framing accomplishes the same process. The narrative value of these black characters is limited to their ability to provide a setting through which the white characters move—but in such a way as to invest the white characters with authority, or superiority. Clearly, the scene would not be the same if the characters went through cotton fields that were empty of laborers. Thus, although the cinematic code of "readability of the frame" is operative here, the narrative subordination that results, and the subordination by framing that reinforces it, are not themselves independent of constructing meaning with respect to race. They work to naturalize the idea of whites building and maintaining "a quaintly way of life" that depends on black subordination.

A final example of how this meaning gets constructed centers on the character of Lydia Brown, Congressman Stoneman's mulatto housekeeper. The scene that introduces Lydia shows her fantasizing about higher stations in life. The fantasy is interrupted, however, by the arrival of a white Senator, who slights her. Lydia subsequently becomes enraged and ends up throwing a hysterical, orgiastic fit. She tears at her clothes, writhes on the floor, fondles her breasts, becomes wild-eyed, and licks her own hand. The performance strongly suggests a kind of animalistic sexuality that erupts literally at the drop of a hat: the Senator intentionally dropping his as a means of demanding her servitude. In a later scene, where Silas Lynch is positioned to achieve power, she again displays the wild, orgiastic behavior that is analogous to animalistic sexuality. Her vicarious celebration emphasizes the link between the two mulatto characters that is significant for the meanings the film constructs around race.

Lydia's behavior is especially pronounced through her comparison with the other white characters, who display no such traits and behavior. Indeed, by comparison, Elsie Stoneman's sexuality is not only contained, but when it finally erupts, after a courtship with Ben Cameron, it is portrayed as adolescent and innocent. Lydia's behavior is replicated, however, by the other mulatto in the story, Silas Lynch—who will also be unable to control his sexuality when he lusts after Elsie Stoneman. Through these comparative structures, the film makes clear that the source of this animalistic sexuality is the characters' blackness. The film thus equates the meaning of blackness as being naturally uncivilized because untamed impulses seethe beneath whatever veneer of white sophistication black people may try to assume.[6]

In addition to defining its characters through the signifier of race, the film's rhetorical operations are grounded through the appropriation of the voice of history. As discussed previously, the discourse of the film—the manner in which it "speaks"—is authoritative and unequivocal, giving it the appearance of history. That appearance is further constructed by the film's use of mise-en-scène.

In addition to the use of realist mise-en-scène such as setting and costume, the film mixes its fictional narrative with historical accounts quoted from sources and depicted in tableaux. These tableaux shots are introduced with intertitles that further work to convey their historical accuracy. The first of these intertitles quotes Nicolay and Hay's *Lincoln: A History,* and depicts Lincoln signing an order calling for 75,000 volunteers. As the film progresses, several more such moments in history are "faithfully" depicted: the surrender at Appomattox and the assassination of Lincoln at the Ford theater among them. Furthermore, the second half of the film begins with long quotations from historian-turned-politician Woodrow Wilson. This repetition of historical discourses functions to lend the authority of history to the film's generalizations about race, and thus to achieve finality for the meanings constructed.

As the film progresses, the fictional narrative will draw from this authority to lend credence to itself and its allegorical history: that is, to make the story of the Stonemans and the Camerons stand in for actual history. This allegorical history exercises a dominant role in the construction of meaning about race and how those meanings will be justified or naturalized. Here too *The Birth of a Nation* provides a contemporary lesson by forming a relationship between privilege and aggression. The film goes to great lengths to justify and naturalize privilege. It then constructs aggression as a necessary function for protecting the social order embodied in privilege, providing a vivid example of what Memmi describes as the construction of meanings to the accuser's benefit and at the victim's expense.

The Birth of a Nation divides its plot into two parts: the war and Reconstruction. Perhaps not coincidentally, these two different parts roughly divide the film's textual strategies of naturalization and justification. The first half of the film abounds with meanings about race that construct Afro-Americans as uncivilized—along with the connotations that can be drawn from such a meaning, some of which have already been discussed. What is important to note here is the manner in which the film uses the codes of realism (as well as the authority of history) to make that construction seem natural. With the second half of the film, however, textual strategies shift from a process of naturalizing the meanings the film constructs, to justifying and legitimizing ideas and discourses about race—specifically (and not surprisingly) privilege and aggression. This shift from one to the other is not an exclusive process, as the scene of Silas Lynch organizing in Piedmont demonstrates.

The function of the organizing scene is to begin establishing a string of atrocities once black Southerners gain political power. It is thus organized around the strategy of justifying privilege and aggression. Even within this strategy, however, the film makes use of the naturalizing mode. As the plot shows Silas arriving in town and beginning his work, it underscores its point by demonstrating how naturally inferior blacks are. Outside where the black vote is being gathered, blacks are shown playing music, dancing, and drinking. Characters gather around these festivities; a few are shown to be eating watermelon as they look on. As the scene plays out, two blacks who are at work in the fields are persuaded to come and join the party.

Aside from the blatant watermelon-eating stereotype, the scene uses the codes of realism to make it seem natural that blacks are like children: they would much rather play than work. Within the second half of the film, however, these naturalizing discourses are pointedly enlisted for a process of justifying the ensuing discourses about race. The organizing scene, for example, demonstrates that organizing the black vote is not about equality, but abuse of the system: It takes "the charity of a generous North" and misuses it "to delude the ignorant."

As the second half of the film progresses, these abuses accumulate. Immediately after the organizing scene, Ben Cameron and his sister are confronted by black soldiers marching on the sidewalk outside their house. Silas Lynch, who has witnessed the event, insults Cameron even further by reminding him that the sidewalk is as much for blacks as it is for whites. For Cameron, who has suffered and lost much from the war, Lynch's intervention is an outrageous affront. In terms of the film's overall strategies of justification and legitimization, it is only a sign of what is to come.

As the plot progresses, the "discourse of history" shows blacks cheating at the ballot box, while whites are illegally denied their vote. Then, as related by Ben Cameron, other atrocities occur. A verdict is rendered against white people by a black jury and a black magistrate. A white family is shown being evicted from their property by black Union soldiers. The plot then shows that even as Cameron speaks, his own faithful black servants are punished by black Union soldiers for not voting with the Union League and the carpetbaggers. One servant is shot dead while trying to rescue another from a whipping.

Following these atrocities, the film then shows "the riot in the Master's Hall." In another of its historical facsimiles, the film shows the "negro party in control in the State House of Representatives—101 blacks against 23 whites" in the 1871 session of the South Carolina legislature. The intertitle informs the audience that the facsimile is taken from photographs of "The Columbia State House." The facsimile then shows the ludicrousness of the "riot," assuring the audience that these are "historic incidents from the first legislative session under Reconstruction." The first such incident is a black legislator drinking whiskey at his desk. This image is followed by an image of another legislator standing at his desk eating fried chicken (reminiscent of the earlier scene of watermelon eating). In the foreground of this shot are the feet of another legislator on top of his desk as he reclines. The legislator removes his shoes, which causes an outburst, and a ruling from the speaker that "all members must wear shoes." The shoes are placed back on the bare feet as the other legislator continues to eat his fried chicken leg. This mockery of a legislature then passes a series of outrageous laws: first, a law decreeing that all whites must salute Negro officers on the streets; next, one providing for the intermarriage of blacks and whites. The passage of the latter is occasion for riotous celebration in the house chambers both by the legislators and the black characters in the gallery.

As later plot events will demonstrate, the purpose of these scenes is to establish the grounds for legitimizing actions (especially violence) and discourses that protect privilege. The film first delegitimizes the institution of government by showing how all three branches—judiciary, legislature, and executive—have been co-opted by blacks who are led by immoral whites like Stoneman, who only seek to increase their power and wealth. In turn, the government's illegitimacy endows collective revolts with the qualities of necessity and credibility.

Before the film concludes its strategy of legitimization, however, it shifts to strategies of justification and naturalization in the attempt to build its narrative impact. The strategy of naturalization is directed at the meanings constructed around the signifier of blackness, specifically the natural ignorance or intellectual inferiority of blacks, and the uncontrollable sexuality of blacks. The first of these is articulated through the scene where Ben Cameron drifts off to "ponder the plight of his people," and comes across two white children playing. The white children cover themselves in a white sheet, and spook the black children who are chasing after them. To Cameron, and to the rhetoric of the film, the event is an "inspiration" and gives rise to the Ku Klux Klan. The inspiration, however, is grounded in the strategy of naturalization. By modeling behaviors on children, the film returns to the theme of black people's "natural" ignorance: what Cameron sees is not the ability to wage terrorism through anonymity, but the natural tendency of black people to be spooked. Rather than seeing how children behave, he sees how all black people will react—a realization guided by the perception that black people are naturally ignorant like children.

Building on this naturalization, the film then constructs its justification for the Klan. To begin with, the film introduces the Klan through an intertitle that describes them as "the organization that saved the South from the anarchy of black rule." What is significant in terms of the film's rhetoric is that this intertitle functions as an introduction when it is more of a conclusion. The film has been establishing the anarchy of black rule for quite some time, and indeed, as a situation of injustice that needs resolution. The introduction of the Klan provides just such a resolution.

The film continues its strategy of justification through one of its more blatant acts of collapsing "history" with narrative. Throughout the film, there has been sophisticated mixing of historical facsimiles, history, and narrative fictional events. With the introduction of the Klan, the boundaries that separate those discourses are blurred beyond recognition. An intertitle states that the Klan's first visit is to terrorize a Negro disturber and barn burner. The film then shows the character walking out and finding the Klan waiting for him. The Klan issue him dire warnings, and the character runs back into his house.

Then, according to the history of the film, "Lynch's supporters score first blood against" the Klan. As the Klan rides down a road, a group of black Union soldiers hides behind trees with Silas Lynch. The Negro disturber runs up to them and informs them of what happened, and the group ambushes the Klan as they ride by. These scenes are significant to the film's rhetoric of justification. Although the Klan had been armed, they were not engaged in violence. Violence began with the Negroes' attacking the Klan in an ambush (hence, without provocation). Within this context, the violence that the Klan may conduct is responsive and justified. Further, this conclusion is constructed under the ruse of history—the line between the fictional account of Ben Cameron and the history of the Klan is blurred beyond recognition. This was supposed to be a fictional narrative event—it did, after all, depict what Ben Cameron was doing. Just as the film cloaks Ben Cameron in a Klan costume, however, it cloaks the narrative event as history—relating the event more through the discourse and mode of history than through fiction.

In addition to providing truth value to the film's construction of meaning, rendering the narrative through the discourse of history exercises a fundamental role in the process of obtaining spectator identification. As the rhetorical operations of the film organize signifying elements to encourage identification with the Camerons, and subsequently, the Klan, at the expense of black characters, the discourse of history becomes the site that authorizes such an identification. The voice of history that pervades the narrative functions as a guarantor of truth whose purpose is to validate spectator identification with the associations the film constructs around character. As Manthia Diawara demonstrates, this alignment of spectator identification is clearly evident in the Gus chase sequence, where the black soldier lustfully pursues the little sister Cameron, and narrative elements "all combine to compel the spectator to regard Gus as the representation of danger and chaos; he is the alien, that which does not resemble oneself, that from which one needs protection."[7] What Diawara's analysis does not discuss, however, is the manner in which the alignment of spectator identification with the little sister and against Gus is first established through the film's construction of meaning through the voice of history.

The Gus chase sequence, itself embedded in the "history" of reconstruction abuses that comprise the second half of the film, follows the more historical account of the raid-on-Piedmont scene in the first half of the film. Each of the scenes functions to build on the film's construction of the threat of uncontrolled sexuality around the signifier of blackness established in the raid-on-Piedmont scene, where the virtue and virginity of the Cameron women is threatened by the onslaught of black soldiers. Here the film introduces one of the dangers that the uncivilized Negro represents to civilized society: black men unable to control their lust for white women. The Cameron girls hide in the cellar as the pillaging rages on, waiting with fear and apprehension, hoping that they will somehow be spared.

The significance of the scene is not only its previously discussed function of foreshadowing the film's climactic scene, but also the manner in which it demonstrates the impossibility of separating the film's aesthetics from its meaning. The raid on Piedmont builds its drama by crosscutting between the ravaging blacks, the virtuous girls, and their rescuers, the Confederate Army. The drama, so constructed, revolves around the protection of white women's virginity from the threat of black sexuality. Abstracting these elements out of an analysis of the crosscutting technique, as if they did not contribute to the drama that is at stake there, is reductionism to absurdity. Furthermore, such an abstraction ignores the dynamics of identification that the plot is structuring. The Cameron women are characters that have been established by the narrative, they have specific traits and a place within the ongoing narrative through which spectators can invest their identification. The black soldiers, on the other hand, are an undifferentiated mob, upon whom only negative signifiers are attached: violence, wantonness, destruction, and incivility. It is precisely the voice of history, however, that authorizes such an identification: validating such a depersonalizing construction of black identity and the oppositional structuring to the dynamics of identification.

The threat of black sexuality to the virginity of white women is thus a significant site for the film's rhetorical operations and their ability to procure identification. While the raid-on-Piedmont scene establishes both the threat and the dynamics of identification that get structured around it, the death-of-the-little-sister scene articulates the tragic proportions of that threat, a task it accomplishes through the character of Gus the "renegade" Negro soldier. Gus comes upon the little "pet" sister playing with Elsie Stoneman and follows her to the Cameron house. There he is rebuffed by Ben Cameron and told to stay away from the house, an order that infuriates Silas Lynch and creates an uneasy standoff between the men. The scene concludes uneasily with the reintroduction of the threat to the virtue of white women that the uncontrollable lust of black men constitutes. Although temporarily suspended by plot, the narrative nonetheless makes manifest the tragic potential of this threat, when the little sister disregards her brother's warning and goes off into the woods by herself. There she is followed by Gus, who proposes marriage to her, then lustfully pursues her when she rejects him and runs off.

Here too the film makes recourse to Griffith's signature crosscutting technique, but in a twist that will emphasize how calamitous the threat of black sexuality is, the rescue is unsuccessful: the Little Colonel does not arrive in time to save the little sister, and she leaps from a cliff to her death rather than give in to the uncontrollable lust of the black soldier. The sacred status afforded to the little sister's death not only makes manifest the danger that unregulated black sexuality constitutes, but becomes a site through which the rhetorical operation of justification can function. Whereas other narrative events work to justify the creation of the Klan, the little sister's death provides justification for the actions of the Klan: the lynching of Gus.

That the rhetorical function of this narrative event is justification of violence is evidenced by the manner in which an array of textual elements is brought to bear before the film shows the Klan lynching the black soldier. To begin with, the character who is lynched is Gus, a man responsible for the deaths of two characters, one by outright murder. In addition, Gus is executed only after there has been a trial with evidence presented. And lastly, the Klan deposits Gus on the steps of Silas Lynch's house as a means of restating that all these events have occurred under the context of political illegitimacy: the black anarchy that is growing across the land.

The justification of white aggression against the "natural" threat of black sexuality is thus firmly established by the film when Elsie Stoneman is abducted by the lustful mulatto Silas Lynch. Elsie's abduction, and the threat of rape that comes with it, is thus part of a rhetorical strategy that will combine naturalization, justification, and legitimization to the film's climactic scene, and in the process, align spectator identification with white privilege and violence. Moreover, Elsie's entrapment by Lynch serves such a rhetorical function precisely because of the manner in which the threat of black sexuality, introduced with the raid on Piedmont, and manifested in the death of the little sister, is fundamental to the film's discourse. Lynch's uncontrolled desire for Elsie, defined by the previously discussed comparative structures of plot as emanating from his blackness, is thus a culminating site for a principle narrative element. As Taylor argues, the scene functions "to communalize the threat that by Gus's action alone might be taken as individual aberration."[8] The film thus seeks to procure identification with the justification of violence through a process of repetition and reaffirmation of the threat of black sexuality.

The entrapment of Elsie by the carpetbagging mulatto Lynch, and its subsequent threat to her virginity, functions as a significant site where the film culminates the threat of black sexuality through its ability to resolve its own historical contradictions. As was discussed previously, the rhetorical operations of the film historicize the cause and creation of the Klan as a democratic response to the illegitimacy of the politics of reconstruction. Within the dynamics of plot, however, the abstract machinations of power are not enough to justify the violence necessary in maintaining privilege. Through Lynch's abduction of Elsie, the plot can combine the threat of black sexuality with the threat of black anarchy—itself the logical result of the narrative's insistence that blacks are uncivilized. The plot makes clear that Lynch's ability to force himself on Elsie is dependent on his manipulation of the laws of an illegitimate, and quickly disintegrating society. Drawing on previously established structures of identification, the scene attempts to align spectator identification with the violence that will save Elsie.

The plot's alignment of identification with the justification of violence is thus an important part of the film's rhetorical operations. In addition, however, it constitutes a significant metatextual operation that undermines the claims about the nonracism of the author's intent. As Manthia Diawara has pointed out, the strategies of identification employed by the film are directed towards white privilege at the expense of black characters. Thus it is that, as Diawara argues, "the dominant reading compels the Black spectator to identify with the racist inscription of the Black character."[9] In constructing an epic that is intended to center around the war and Reconstruction, Griffith created a film where identification is reserved for whites and excludes blacks. The structure of the film's narrative and its strategies of identification thus deny the very existence of the black spectator.

This kind of effacement or denial of the existence of the black spectator is reproduced in another metatextual operation of the film: casting. Cheryl Chisolm and Clyde Taylor both point out how all the major characters of the film are cast with white actors, even if the role is that of a black character. The most prominent example within the film is the character of Gus, a white actor in blackface—most probably burnt cork. The construction of the film thus denies the existence of both the black spectator and the black actor. Taylor documents Griffith's outrageous assertion "that he could not find any qualified Negro actors in the Los Angeles area," a claim that was further buttressed by the argument that "he wanted to cast from his own company."[10] This kind of aesthetic justification for the politics of exclusion that denies jobs to blacks would serve as a template not only for Hollywood film production, but for broader culture as well. In addition, however, the claim betrays the contradictions at stake in the maintenance of privilege. Ultimately, it was Griffith himself that could not find Negro actors, not because they did not exist, but because he could not see them. The term "qualified" is the linchpin in the signifying system of the politics of exclusion. It presents itself as some kind of objective measure, but instead, rests in the eye of the beholder, shifting and sliding in order to please the viewer. Griffith's inability to find qualified black actors functioned to confirm his own view of blacks as childlike and intellectually inferior. In this respect, the metatextual practice of casting reproduces meanings articulated, repeated, and reaffirmed through the film's narrative.

The climax and conclusion to that narrative is thus an important site for reasserting the primacy of race in the signifying operations of the text, and for finalizing the meanings constructed through those operations. As mentioned previously, the film's climax builds upon the threat of black sexuality with the abduction of Elsie Stoneman by Silas Lynch. In addition, however, the film significantly expands the dramatic tension by extending the threat of danger to other principal characters of privilege: the Camerons, who become victims of black anarchy and have to seek refuge in a remote cabin. Within the construction of this narrative dynamic, the film structures a finalized validation of the necessity of violence for the maintenance of privilege.

In the process of articulating that finalizing validation, the plot makes recourse to a rhetorical device that is still often used in contemporary discourses and texts, but frequently ignored in discussions of the film: the use of crossover characters. The film consolidates its finalization of meaning around the signifier of blackness through the construction of the "faithful souls" characters, two former Cameron slaves who have remained loyal to their former owners. Rhetorically, the faithful souls characters further establish the innate goodness of the Cameron family, but just as significantly, their characters allow the plot to avoid absolute racial division in the film. Through these characters, the film avoids an all-out attack on the black race by showing instead an image of the solution to blacks being uncivilized: obedience and loyalty to upstanding white people. The faithful souls function as a corrective against "bad" Negro characters, and allow the film to escape from being absolute in its condemnation of the race. Not coincidentally, then, they will also become a key site of contradiction for the film's rhetoric, as future discussion will demonstrate.

Further, however, the faithful souls exercise an important function within the film's finalization of the meanings assigned to blackness by having black characters themselves validate those meanings. The faithful souls provide evidence to the "truth" about black excess and anarchy, by rejecting the mean-spiritedness of the revolutionary blacks and siding with the white characters who stand for civilization and goodness. The power of the discourse that is built around their characters is further demonstrated by the manner in which their actions initiate the rescue of the Cameron patriarch that puts the film's climax into motion—no small contribution given the narrative and dramatic complexity of the climax.

Indeed, while the climax of any narrative is normally a crucial point for narrative analysis, it is particularly so for *The Birth of a Nation*. The film's climactic scenes are a primary reason for its status within film history. Even today, spectators who find the pace of the film outdated and boring, and take objection to the film's racism, can find themselves drawn into the drama that unfolds at the cabin. What this analysis will demonstrate, however, is that despite an increased narrative pace, and the weaving together of several plot elements—the abduction of Elsie, the flight of the Camerons to a remote cabin to escape rampaging blacks, the organization of the Klan by the Little Colonel—the film's climax is a repetition, reaffirmation, and culmination of the primary meaning it first assigns to the signifier of blackness: uncivilized. As previously mentioned, two predominant themes articulate this meaning: the threat of black sexuality and the danger of black anarchy. The film's climax, like the raid-on-Piedmont scene, gives image to the destructive potential of black anarchy—its violence and excessiveness—both at the site of the cabin, where the Camerons desperately try to defend themselves against an army of vengeful blacks, and in the city of Piedmont, where Elsie tries to preserve her virginity in the midst of a complete social breakdown at the hands of black citizens.

The film's climax thus serves the narrative function of restabilizing the narrative by eliminating these threats from the main characters and their ability to function as sites of spectator identification. Restabilization is thus a significant site for the plot's finalization of meaning. In *The Birth of a Nation,* this finalization is accomplished through two structures of plot. The first is the restoration and affirmation of privilege through the elimination of its antagonists. The ride of the Klan restores order to Piedmont, which had been taken over by black anarchy; saves Elsie from a fate worse than death—as the film so clearly articulates through the character of the little Cameron sister; and rescues the rest of the Cameron family and friends in the cabin. Just as significantly, though, the ride of the Klan successfully disarms the blacks, and sends the rabble-rousers packing.

The narrative stability that is achieved is then conferred upon privilege itself as the site of stable social relations—and its necessity for maintaining them. In this manner, the climactic scenes become the culmination of the strategies of legitimization that have been conducted throughout the film, with the Ku Klux Klan as the legitimate response to the "overthrow" of existing civilization. In addition to narrative stability, the resolution of the climax works to finalize meaning through the process of denouement: where the plot no longer seeks to advance the narrative so much as it does confirm the equilibrium that resolution has established. *The Birth of a Nation* structures such a denouement through its incorporation of the melodramatic practice of public recognition of the signifier. The parade of the Klan through Piedmont provides a point where the crowd in the film can function as surrogates for the audience, publicly acknowledging the order and civilization that the Klan represents. The crowd thus provides a finalizing validation of the meanings the film constructs. Chief among those meanings is the threat of black sexuality. Not coincidentally, the virtuous women ride at the head of the Klan parade—signifiers of the necessity of white-on-black violence as a means of preserving the virginity of white women. The narrative logic and aesthetic sensibility of the placement of the female characters at the head of the parade evidences the fundamental role that the threat of black sexuality exercises within the signifying operations of the film.

Despite being several hours long, and engaged in several textual strategies to enhance its drama, *The Birth of a Nation* is organized around constructing a very basic meaning that it presents as truth: that blacks are uncivilized. As demonstrated through this discussion, the film employs a variety of codes to persuade its audience of this theme, and constructs other meanings to support it: the threat of black sexuality and the inferior intelligence of blacks being two important examples. In the end, the film is far more a narrative about the necessity of white privilege and aggression than it is a history of the Civil War and Reconstruction.

If *The Birth of a Nation* is a good object lesson in how codes operate to construct meanings about race, it is also a good object lesson in how this process is never complete. Despite the film's enormous efforts to persuade its viewers of the necessity of white privilege and aggression, several aspects of the film escape or resist this rhetoric, and point to the potential for either a more egalitarian society, or for the collective transformation of a status quo of privilege. Indeed, the film consistently points to the power of the collective and its potential for transformation, an important aspect of the film too frequently overlooked.

Starting with Eisenstein, Griffith has been routinely characterized as hopelessly bourgeois and Victorian in his worldview. Despite this, *The Birth of a Nation* shows distinct differences from the contemporary Hollywood cinema, specifically with respect to an emphasis on the individual and individual actions. In contemporary film, the trend is on *the* hero, and how that hero shapes the narrative world around him through his actions and desires. Through the continued repetition of this structure, the status of the individual is given almost sacred status, at the near exclusion of the collective. In a society dependent on widespread alienation and individual powerlessness, such a strategy is clearly symptomatic.

Griffith's film, however, was produced and viewed in another era, one that was not yet the fully realized mass society. Not surprisingly, then, it is not so dependent on an individual hero, and indeed, resists giving that status to any individual character—insisting instead on the power of the collective. Thus it is, for example, that although the plot credits Ben Cameron for the idea of the Klan, as soon as he has conceived it, the film emphasizes the collective nature of the Klan *over* Cameron's role in it. The Klan is not merely a backdrop through which the character of Ben Cameron can be raised to the status of hero. Rather, the film emphasizes how powerful the Klan is because of its collective cohesion: Lauding, for example, how Southern women kept the secret of the Klan without fail, though certainly the plot's purpose in constructing the Klan as it does is to legitimate and justify its violence, as discussed previously. That function, however, cannot repress either the value or the power of the collective.

Furthermore, the Klan is not the only site of collective power within *The Birth of a Nation*; the film also extends the power of collective transformation to black culture. Admittedly, it does so negatively—as proof that society is no longer legitimate because blacks have power—but it nonetheless shows how readily social situations can be changed if groups can organize and act collectively. Even though the film attempts to qualify and contain the potential for black collective organization and action (it always shows whites as leaders), it still begrudgingly grants blacks that potential and demonstrates its power.

In addition to articulating the power and potential of the collective, the film also gives image to the elements and dynamics that sustain the collective. It provides object lessons for the basis of collective organization: how it comes into being and is maintained and sustained. Further, and counter to much of the film's rhetoric, it invests these elements most visibly in two black characters, the faithful souls. As their designation suggests, and their actions will confirm, faith is one of the elements that brings a collective into being and maintains it. The faithful souls characters, for example, maintain faith and subsequent loyalty to the Camerons. As previously discussed, many of the strategies behind the construction of the faithful souls are negative and thus they contribute to the film's overall rhetoric. Despite these strategies, however, the "faithful souls" anchor several meanings that resist the overall construction of meaning. Indeed, as a result of their characters, the film ends up creating—in the cabin-under-siege scene—the very image it argues against: the multicultural, multiethnic collective that struggles together for the good of all.

The faithful souls create the models for individual behavior that make the cabin community so cohesive. To begin with, they remain faithful to those with whom they have built personal relationships. This includes not just the Camerons, whom they served as slaves, but others in the community—it is how the male faithful soul is lured out to be punished. In addition, the faithful souls look past race and/or current social realities, in order to maintain bonds and serve the needs of others. The faithful souls can be read as Uncle Toms, but that would be a one-sided and incomplete reading—especially in terms of resistance and liberation. There is also a sense in which they do not participate in the growing political organization of blacks in Piedmont because the aim of such organizing is defined strictly as empowerment. The faithful souls, however, are constructed in such a manner that they reject power in favor of service. Here too, although such a construction operates within the film's racist agenda, it nonetheless provides an oppositional ideology to the logic of the individual, and places great value on its transformative potential. By consistently putting others before themselves, the faithful souls engender the logic that provides for the maintenance and preservation of the collective—a logic that others within the collective of the cabin will come to adopt.

The repetition of this theme occurs at the site of the cabin belonging to the characters of the retired Union soldiers. Where the soldiers could have seen the former "enemy" in the group formed around the Camerons, they see instead people in need, and assist them to the point of sacrificing their own lives. This point is emphasized by Dr. Cameron offering himself up to save the group—again, actions taken for the good of the collective, not the individual. The members of the cabin, led by the soldiers, reject this individual sacrifice, even though it may result in the sacrifice of their own individual lives. What the film fails to contain is that these individual sacrifices are all structured around the preservation of the multicultural, multiracial, egalitarian community—however brief its existence may be (privilege will certainly restore itself when the siege is over). Furthermore, by associating the multicultural, multiracial, egalitarian collective with survival itself, the film bestows on the small community a primacy not shared by even "the quaintly way of life that is to be no more."

These sites of resistance within the film's rhetoric do not deny, erase, or render acceptable the manner in which the film participates in a process of racism described here. Rather, what this discussion attempts to demonstrate is that film analysis can provide us with two different but interrelated ends. The first of these is what the bulk of this discussion has accomplished: analyzing the film text for the manner in which it covers over its participation in the process of racism. The second of these is to see at what points the discourses and meanings films construct fail, and to see instead the manner in which images and discourses provide examples of creating and maintaining the egalitarian community.

Notes

1. Clyde Taylor, "The Re-Birth of the Aesthetic in Cinema," in Daniel Bernardi, ed., *The Birth of Whiteness: Race and the Emergence of U.S. Cinema* (New Brunswick, N.J.: Rutgers University Press, 1996), 16.

2. Ibid., 17.

3. I refer readers again to the discredited work of Richard J. Hernstein and Charles Murray *The Bell Curve: Intelligence and Class Structure in American Life* (New York: Simon and Schuster, 1995) as an example of this reemergence of the enduring quest to prove white superiority. As before, I also refer readers to the extensive discussion of this work in Claude S. Fischer, Michael Hout, Martin Sanchez Jankowski, Ann Swidler, and Samuel R. Lucas, *Inequality by Design: Cracking the Bell Curve Myth* (Princeton: Princeton University Press, 1996). Eric Alterman offers a critique and analysis of the reactionary politics that drives this discredited research in "The 'Right' Books and Big Ideas," *The Nation*, November 22, 1999.

4. The issue of what noun to use as a signifier for people of African descent is a complex one that I gave much consideration to. As the title of this book demonstrates, I chose the noun "Afro-American," persuaded in part by the work of Cornel West, and the concerns of many that the term "black" was beginning to have connotations of hierarchical status based on pigmentation (an issue that the film *School Daze* will raise). The term does not quite seem appropriate to a discussion of *The Birth of a Nation* precisely because of the history that the film sets itself in. The term would be a misnomer when applied to African slaves (as in the slave-trade scene) precisely because it reproduces the imposition of American culture and society where no such affiliation was sought, desired, or chosen. Given the history of the slave trade, it is then not quite possible to accurately distinguish all characters as being either Afro-American slave by birth or having originated from Africa. Furthermore, as the discussion of this chapter will demonstrate, the rhetorical operations of this film are structured around constructing meanings through the signifier of race, which the film distinguishes as white, black, and mulatto—the latter functioning as signifier for the mixing of

the two races. For these reasons, it seems to me that the noun "black" would more accurately characterize the significations at stake in the film.

5. The few blacks who escape this characterization in the film are portrayed instead as being dependent on their white masters and unable to command the English language—thus rendering them childlike.

6. Further, because Lydia is a mulatto, it suggests that the power of these animalistic behaviors is not tempered even by the mixing of the races.

7. Manthia Diawara, "Black Spectatorship: Problems of Identification and Resistance," in Manthia Diawara, ed. *Black Cinema* (New York: Routledge, 1993), 213.

8. Taylor, "The Re-Birth of the Aesthetic," 22.

9. Diawara, "Black Spectatorship," 213.

10. Taylor, "The Re-Birth of the Aesthetic," 26.

Part Two

Cinema and the Maintenance of Privilege

3
The Gods Must Be Crazy
(Privileged, but Crazy)

Chapter 2 demonstrates how films incorporate and create different codes to persuade their audience that the meanings they construct about race are true (despite their delivery in the form of fiction). *The Birth of a Nation* was analyzed not so much to begin a history of racism and representation, but rather to demonstrate how several of the film's strategies are still used by current films and media texts. Indeed, this chapter will jump from 1915 to 1986 to demonstrate that point with *The Gods Must Be Crazy*. An analysis of this film will show not only that some of the same strategies are still used, but that the basic meaning that *The Birth of a Nation* constructed—that blacks are uncivilized—is operative within *The Gods Must Be Crazy*.

What this chapter will demonstrate is that *The Gods Must Be Crazy* persuades its audience of that truth by eliminating some (but certainly not all) of the negativity and malevolence that *The Birth of a Nation* attached to the meaning of uncivilized. Indeed, much of the film portrays the concept of "uncivilized" in positive terms. Nonetheless, this analysis will show that the positive attributes lavished on the "uncivilized" serve as a ruse to disguise the manner in which the film assigns a generalized and final meaning based on difference to naturalize, justify, and legitimize the accuser's privilege and aggression at the expense of the victim.

Like *The Birth of a Nation*, *The Gods Must Be Crazy* will build its persuasive rhetoric for privilege and aggression on a strategy of naturalization. It begins this process, not surprisingly, within the film's opening. The film starts with an image of Africa as seen from space. The image shows the surrounding oceans, and conveys a sense of the globe as round. Over

that image is the film's title: *The Gods Must Be Crazy*. There is a relationship between the framing of the image—with respect to distance—and
the language of the title, as the subsequent images will confirm. The view
of Africa that the spectator is seeing is the gods'-eye view. The images
that follow are introduced through quick zooming and dissolves whose
function is to bring the position from which the spectator looks from the
previously established place of the gods into the specific space of the story,
the Kalahari Desert.

As in *The Birth of a Nation*, framing functions as an element within *The
Gods Must Be Crazy* that constructs meaning about race. The spectator begins from the space of the gods, looking down upon the story world.
What the film's narrative will consistently reinforce is that the spectator—
because he or she belongs to the civilized world—is a god. The story will
qualify that position by demonstrating that civilization is crazy and therefore, as the title states, so are the gods, but nonetheless the civilized world
is the place of power. As suggested earlier, the film replaces the malevolence found in *The Birth of a Nation* with respect to the concept of being
"uncivilized." It replaces the malevolence with condescension: tribal culture may actually be a better way of life, but civilized people are in the
place of the gods because they "know more."

The Gods Must Be Crazy attempts to persuade its viewers about the
truth of this discourse by adopting a variety of strategies. The first of these
is incorporating the voice-over narration of the documentary film. *The
Gods Must Be Crazy* begins by looking and sounding more like a Public
Broadcasting Service documentary about the African continent than a
contemporary narrative. This includes the style of the voice as well. The
voice-over that describes the Kalahari Desert is not the old-fashioned
basso "voice-of-God" narration characteristic of earlier documentary
style, and of films like *The Ten Commandments*, but the clear-pitched,
soft-spoken voice reminiscent of the evenhanded and objective scientist
employed by nature documentaries in the contemporary era.

The use of this voice-over is key to the film's rhetorical strategy. To begin with, it aligns the film with an established code for conveying the
truth: the nature documentary. This code then allows the specific discourse of the voice-over to take on truth value. Because later on in the plot
The Gods Must Be Crazy will suspend cinematic codes of realism to advance its comedic operations—a signifying practice *not* used in *The Birth
of a Nation*, or most dramatic films: This voice-over strategy is integral to
the film's rhetorical strategy. It will function as one of the few places that

will be unaffected by the comedy and complications of plot, and thus will consistently contribute an authoritative view and interpretation about the story world.

The film thus seeks to establish early that it conveys the truth about what it is representing. The function of its representation and description of the "little people" of the Kalahari Desert is thus to create a frame by which spectators will evaluate fictional narrative events as allegorical of the truth of contemporary Africa. The film will then create a dichotomy separating the "little people" of the Kalahari from white civilization, attempting to persuade its audience of the naturalness and necessity of privilege (and aggression) because *all* blacks (not just the Bushmen) are uncivilized.

The film structures this dichotomy right after the introductory scene that describes the Kalahari Bushmen and their society. The Bushmen are "pretty, dainty, small, and graceful," and their society has "no crime, no punishment, no violence, no laws, no police, no judges, rulers, or bosses." The voice-over further concludes that "the one characteristic which really makes the Bushmen different from all the other races on earth is the fact that they have no sense of ownership at all. Where they live, there's really nothing you can own. . . . They live in a gentle world." After examining the cultural life of the Bushmen in these thoroughly positive terms, the film then looks at modern (white) civilization only 600 miles away. With tongue-in-cheek assessment, the voice-over makes a comparison with "civilized man" evaluating him over images of modern civilization and with decided consternation. The voice-over thus points out that:

> The more he [civilized man] improved his surroundings to make his life easier, the more complicated he made it. So now his children are sentenced to ten to fifteen years of school just to learn to survive in this complex and hazardous habitat they were born into. And civilized man, who refused to adapt himself to his natural surroundings, now finds that he has to adapt and readapt himself every day and every hour of the day to his self-created environment.

The rhetorical point that the comparison makes is that civilization is crazy, and that the cultural life of the Bushmen is far more pleasant and acceptable. As alluded to before, this early comparative structure is actually a very clever ruse. To begin with, it acts as a further truth-building device; the film's veracity is emphasized by its apparent willingness to criticize the very culture from which it comes. Furthermore, with the discourse of the film so clearly siding with tribal culture over modern civilization, it is difficult to imagine that the film could participate in the process of racism.

What an analysis of the film's narrative will show, however, is that the comparative sequence in the beginning of the film is an important rhetorical device for naturalizing and justifying privilege. As the story unfolds, it makes clear that while tribal culture may be preferable, modern civilization is not only here to stay, but is too complicated, crazy, and dangerous for black Africans to be entrusted with. The Bushmen, for example, are "little people" who are "dainty," and "very gentle"; in addition, they have never even seen something as hard as a rock. These descriptions of a society, which has "no sense of ownership at all" function to make Bushmen culture look far preferable to modern civilization, but also define the means by which modern society can be seen as regrettably superior, having more scope of knowledge about reality (rocks, steel, technology in general) and being populated by people who are neither little nor dainty, nor gentle—as narrative events will evidence.

Indeed, the regrettable but necessary superiority of modern (white) civilization will come to be a principal structure around which the narrative trajectory will begin. This is introduced first with the film's initial contact point between tribal culture and civilization: a careless slob of a bush pilot throws a Coke bottle out of the window of his plane. This event will cause another event, the discovery of the bottle by the Bushmen, who first marvel at it, then find that it improves their quality of life in many ways: for curing snake skins, harvesting roots and tubers, and ornamenting clothing—with the implication that more uses are discovered almost daily. Soon after, however, the bottle starts to impact the community negatively: it introduces ownership, covetousness, jealousy, anger, and violence. Since there is only *one* bottle, and it provides for so many useful functions, people within the tribe are introduced to object-desire. They all want the bottle and want it at the same time. The members of the tribe are not prepared for these new desires and emotions, and the sequence shows them unable to handle them, ending with one member striking another with the bottle. So traumatic are the ill effects that the tribe concludes that the bottle is an evil thing and attempt to give it back to the gods. When the first few attempts to do so fail, !Ky, one of the men within the tribe, makes the decision to journey to the end of the earth to give it back.

This scene in the film is important for several reasons. To begin with, it inaugurates narrative, whereas before the film was organized and struc-

Discovering one of the products of modern civilization inaugurates a narrative trajectory that affirms the "natural" superiority of Whites.

tured much more along the lines of a documentary. It therefore begins to organize its signifying elements in a structure that imposes drive towards resolution and restabilization on the meanings it will build, meanings that are then applied to the interaction between cultures. Furthermore, the scene introduces the first evidence of the film's rhetoric of naturalization, demonstrating that black Africans cannot handle civilization. Here, the film goes to great lengths to make civilization seem like the problem: the bottle, after all, intruded on the tribe's Edenic life. The intrusion of civilization into the culture of the Bushmen comes as a threat to the stability of tribal society, a threat that must be resolved through the trajectory of narrative. The imposition of narrative is significant for the manner in which the shift is itself "caused" by tribal culture not being able to handle the effects of civilization: Their timeless, cyclical way of life is broken by the trajectory of narrative precisely because they cannot successfully integrate the object-driven, linear mode of organizing reality that is civilization.

The next scene then confirms that the film is decidedly given over to narrative. Immediately after !Ky begins his journey, the narrative introduces a new plotline: a group of terrorists attempt to assassinate the president and cabinet of an African country to the north of the Kalahari. Unlike *The Birth of a Nation*, which made the threat of black violence a cornerstone of its rhetoric, *The Gods Must Be Crazy* only indirectly uses such a meaning in its strategy of naturalization. Indeed, in the assassination scene, the film goes to great lengths to contain the spectacle of violence. What is more crucial to the film's overall rhetoric is not the blacks' supposed propensity for violence, but rather, the argument that blacks are not able to control civilization.

This argument gets buttressed very early on in the assassination scene. Just as the Bushmen were not able to control the impact that the bottle had on their lives, so too the film makes clear that the terrorist assassins are not adept at handling the mechanical objects of modern civilization. This is first demonstrated when they burst through the doors of the cabinet meeting, only to have the doors swing back closed, temporarily trapping their machine guns. As the scene continues, several elements combine to downplay (or contain) the violence of the scene—replacing it with comedy. The rate of projection is speeded up at some points to give the assassins the Keystone Kops effect, slow motion is used to avoid showing bullets ripping through flesh, and one assassin is fended off by an office secretary throwing trash at his head.

As the scene continues, the humor is maintained by a consistent recourse to physical comedy, most often a variation of black ineptitude with the products of modern culture. Thus, the government soldiers pursue the guerrillas, but the car they commandeer runs out of gas. The guerillas try to shoot down a helicopter, but hit a bunch of bananas instead and give away their position. Further, as the scene plays out, the guerrillas continually attempt to reshoot, but the missile keeps falling out of the launcher. Another sight gag occurs when one guerrilla has to correct his compatriot because the latter's machine-gun shells are discharged into his face.

The comedy of the scene is mediated by two elements of plot. To begin with, the scene introduces the leader of the guerillas, Sam Boca, who, unlike his followers, is not a black African. Through the signifier of race, his character stands with, but separate from, the black buffoonery that goes on around him: the site where competence with the white civilized world comes into contact with and organizes black violence. That potential is then realized, briefly suspending the comedy, when (more by luck than skill) the missile remains in the launcher, and the guerrillas blow up the government helicopter leading the attack. Even here, the film attempts to contain the gruesomeness of such an attack somewhat by having the guerrillas laugh and cheer, and showing the two who worked the missile launcher casually return to a game of cards.

The progression of the scene, however, makes clear that the film's rhetoric does not attempt to contain completely the violent spectacle of the helicopter blowing up. After the short celebration, Sam Boca, the leader of the guerillas, hears the armored vehicles approaching. The guerrillas flee in the jeeps amidst a sea of artillery fire and explosions from the armored vehicle. The tone of the scene decidedly shifts from comic-action to action. The spectacle of the helicopter blowing up thus serves as an important transitional device for the shift in the film's rhetoric, and begins to indicate what the function of the scene is. Prior to the helicopter's explosion, the scene is organized as comic action. Through the repetition of physical comedy, the film makes its argument that blacks are naturally not competent to control the products of modern civilization. This point is humorously driven home when the one guerrilla attempts to keep the missile in the launcher by stuffing a banana leaf in the back of the launcher. The physical bit of humor goes to the heart of the ideology the film is constructing: What blacks "know" is the jungle (despite bananas not growing naturally in groves the African jungle), not modern technology.

The film's primary strategy at this point is thus naturalization, and the comedy functions towards that end. Because the film's rhetoric will not rest solely on naturalization, however, the helicopter explosion serves as a brief introduction to the strategy of justification. As the narrative develops, the plot will try to persuade its audience that blacks are naturally not competent to control modern civilization, and that this can have violent and tragic consequences. The armored car attack on the enclave underscores this point by creating the shift from comic action to action. That shift is of fundamental importance to the film's rhetoric because it underscores how inept blacks are with civilization, while demonstrating how potentially dangerous that incompetence can be. As the government-guerrilla conflict trajectory advances, the film will frequently return to physical comedy built around black ineptness with modern civilization, but always in relation to the tragic potential that the mix between black incompetence and the penchant for black violence creates.

This delicate balance is of crucial importance for the plot's rhetorical operations. As Peter Davis argues, "It has long been a tranquilizer to white unease, in fact essential to [their] sense of superiority, that even if black guerillas exist, they are incompetent."[1] Crucial to maintaining a balance between black incompetence and the potential for black violence is a plot technique as old as *The Birth of a Nation*, the mixed-race character. The guerilla leader, Sam Boca, is not black, but neither is he all white. He looks far more like a Latino insurgent than an African, and this racial incongruity is significant. Because he is not black, his knowledge/control of modern technology and leadership skills can be attributed to his whiteness: this gives him command and authority over his black followers, who are learning (ever incompetently) to interact with the technology of modern warfare through his knowledge/leadership. Sam Boca's propensity for violence and trouble, however, can then be attributed to his darkness—or, more accurately, his nonwhiteness—which is further emphasized by his dark hair and beard. In this manner, the film maintains both the threat of black violence and a belief in white superiority.

The film further articulates the ideology of white superiority through several other elements of plot. Chief among these, however, is the manner in which the character of !Ky is used to demonstrate how the complexities of civilization are beyond *all* black Africans, not just the Bushmen. This rhetorical operation is structured by the plot in the events surrounding !Ky's hunting of a goat. Not knowing the concept of private property, !Ky hunts a herder's goat. He is then shot by a policeman, taken to court, and sentenced to jail. The events are crucial to the rhetorical operations of the narrative because the scenes eliminate whites entirely from this part of the plot. As a result, it demonstrates black on black justice, and renders it incompetent. The court has no sensitivity to the linguistic and cultural complexities in which it is engaged, and consequently blunders its way into an unfair verdict. It is thus shown to be incapable of a fundamental responsibility of civilization: administering justice. It thus serves as a kind of ironic confirmation to the voice-over's opening description of Bushmen culture: there are no judges.

Furthermore, the scene implicates a potentially refractory character, Mbuti, in the inability to render justice, and thus exercises a measure of containment to his character. Prior to this scene, Mbuti was introduced as the faithful assistant to Andrew Steyn, and, significantly, his mechanic. In this respect, he is a black character who is adept at engaging modern technology—the by-product of modern civilization. Mbuti's inability to translate the profound and complex differences between the two cultures and languages, however, implies that he is not so masterfully in control of the nuances and complexities of modern civilization. He is powerless to prevent the kangaroo court from rendering an unjust verdict.

In addition to these operations, the construction of the white characters within the story contributes, not surprisingly, to the ideology of white superiority. This is strikingly articulated with the arrival of the journalist-turned-schoolteacher, Kate Thompson, in a small village in Botswana. Upon Kate's arrival and introduction to the village through the Missionary Reverend, the village suspends its activities and sings a song of welcome to the figure who will bring education to their rural and remote existence. Peter Davis notes that the scene is structured around the cliché of black gratitude to whites for help being given—a cliché that is reinforced earlier with the black journalist informing Kate that "they're desperate" for teachers. More than the appropriation of a cliché, however, character placement, and the exchange of looks, also functions to articulate white superiority. At the signal of a bell, the villagers stop their routines and sing their welcome to Kate. As they do, however, Kate is placed high on top of a rise, the villagers all stand below. Even those villagers closest to the new arrival are segmented from the space where she stands, and greet her from below. Camera placement and editing then reinforces this spatial arrangement by showing Kate's eye view as looking down on the scene, while the villagers look up at her. All these elements function together to transform what is perhaps the film's most extensive exhibition of African culture, from greeting the new teacher into adoration for the position she occupies through her status of giver of knowledge.

In a telling moment for the scene, Kate turns to the Reverend and Jack Hind to ask what her response should be. The spatial segmentation is extended such that the white men are above Kate. The trajectory of the narrative will confirm that this arrangement of space is symptomatic of the film's ideology of white male superiority. As the film progresses, it maintains either comedic or comedic-action modes, but as further analysis will demonstrate, the function of this comedy is to render acceptable, through a process of disguise, the ideology of white male superiority. The principle means of that disguise is the character of Andrew Steyn. Steyn is introduced, and will be continually presented, as a caretaker to the wildlife of Africa. He is a soft-spoken, gentle man, but the film places him firmly within the sphere of modern civilization because he is a scientist: the plot makes clear that he is working on a doctoral thesis, situating him within the world of white elitist education.

What the film will emphasize about his character, however, is that he continually shuns privilege: he dresses simply, lives in a tent, and drives a jeep so dilapidated and troublesome it is nicknamed the Antichrist. In addition, he accepts modernity only insofar as it assists in caring for the wild. He possesses a computer, a scanner, and a high-powered telescope, but only because these objects assist his work. The film also introduces another aspect of his character in this scene: he is awkward around women. As he puts it, his brain switches off when he is in the presence of a woman. This will serve as a source of much comedy within the film, but it will also serve an important rhetorical function.

As the plot progresses, and Steyn tries incompetently to deliver the new teacher to the missionary school, the film introduces a character who is the opposite of Steyn, Jack Hind. Unlike Steyn, Hind is not a caretaker of the wilderness but an exploiter of it, making money from running hunting expeditions (safaris) for tourists. Also unlike Steyn, he is not awkward around women, but self-admittedly suave. In addition, the film will later show him to be self-absorbed, cowardly and less than honest.

The comparison between the two characters is enormously important for the rhetoric of the film. By setting up such a comparison the plot creates a love triangle between the new schoolteacher, Kate Thompson, and the two men. The narration is then able to bring together all the different plot lines into one: !Ky joins up with Steyn and Mbuti, the guerrillas kidnap Thompson and the schoolchildren, and Jack Hind joins with the government police in their capture/rescue efforts. What had once been different strands weaving through the narrative are now bound together with urgency—an urgency that underscores the drive to resolution and restabilization.

From this situation, it is the gentle, bumbling Steyn who emerges as the competent man of action, the man capable of gaining control. What is significant for the film's discourse is the manner in which the narrative shifts between Steyn's previous bumbling and his newly found competence. As soon as he is aware of Kate's dire circumstances, Steyn swings into control. He devises a plan, improvises when it goes wrong, and effects a rescue. His ability to improvise is a key to the film's rhetoric. Finding himself in a shoot-out with two remaining guerrillas, Steyn not only competently holds his own with a submachine gun—as if it were part of every biologist's training—but just as importantly, calls nature itself to his aid. In order to outmaneuver his armed adversaries, Steyn makes use of a large tree snake lying in the branches to capture one guerilla, and the acidic sap from another tree to immobilize the other. Tellingly, he makes use of nature with a knowledge and familiarity that the black African guerillas do not possess. In this manner, Steyn shows himself to be more African than the guerrillas (a pun the film has been working since the banana grove).

Just as importantly, however, Steyn and modern technology come to the fore within this scene, displacing the effectiveness of tribal herbal technology. The narrative long ago established the efficacy of the Bushmen's herbal tranquilizing hunting techniques in its opening descriptions of Bushmen culture, elaborating on how Bushmen hunters sedate their prey with tiny darts dipped in an herbal compound. Rather than using that to effect the rescue, however, the film has recourse to the tranquilizing chemicals that Steyn uses in his work. !Ky still does the hunting of the men with guns, but he uses the product of modern science, not of tribal culture. The urgency of the situation is used to confer a primacy to the former that it denies the latter.

The narrative trajectory thus uses the drive for resolution and restabilization to both naturalize and justify privilege through the ideology of white superiority. Throughout the scene white characters are "naturally" seen to take control of a complex situation. The naturalness with which that control is appropriated is evidenced through Jack Hind's character. Throughout the film, Hind is constructed negatively: pompous, self-absorbed, and cowardly. Despite these constructions, however, Hind actually leads the black military in their pursuit of the guerrillas. The naturalness with which trained military personnel defer to his leadership—he actually appropriates a gun from them—is another means for the plot to articulate the natural relationships between the races: Hind can take control because he is naturally superior.

Through the comedic actions of the plot, and the comparative structure of the two male characters, the film attempts to disguise its discourse of white male superiority. In Steyn's rescue of Thompson and the schoolchildren, for example, the film is quick to reestablish his bumbling characteristics. As soon as the guerrillas have been immobilized, Steyn starts to lose control of the situation, as his out-of-control jeep disrupts the newly attained narrative stasis, providing more physical humor that emphasizes Steyn's tendency for mishap. As further analysis will show, this reestablishing of Steyn's earlier traits is important for the film's rhetorical operations. It prevents Steyn from evolving into the virile man of action—a development that would have important political implications.

Rather than develop into such a character, Steyn remains as capable, gentle, awkward, and scientific—rearticulated through the conclusion, where Kate Thompson and he finally become a couple despite all the obstacles. The function of this rearticulation and the narrative conclusion lies in the film's rhetoric of justification. Andrew Steyn, who first suggested taking care of !Ky, is the figure of white paternalism—a figure that replaces that distasteful image of white colonialism that has scarred Africa. Jack Hind serves as a reminder—but a thoroughly depoliticized one—of the ugly reality for which Steyn is a corrective: exploitation of the virtue of Africa. Steyn is not the techno-scientific-bureaucrat looking for oil, diamonds, gold, or agricultural possibilities, but rather, a naturalist who looks to care for the "natural" state of affairs in Africa. Thus it is that in the complex state of affairs that is now Africa—which includes civilizations that are crazy, and cultures that are not even aware of the existence of those civilizations and need to be protected—the nonmenacing, paternal Steyn is the figure who can best control such difficult and incompatible interrelationships.

The protracted scene of Steyn attempting to pick up Kate from the bus stop and deliver her to the mission is thus critical for the manner in which the film justifies this white paternalism. Throughout the scene, Steyn's awkwardness around women and general bumbling complicate what should have been a relatively simple task. Kate, coming as she does from the city, is completely unclear about what is going on. Her first suspicion, somewhat confirmed by Andrew's awkwardness, is that Steyn is making sexual advances towards her. She continually thinks she should fend him off, and narrative events are seen from her point of view as confirming such suspicions. Indeed, the narrative brings several elements into the plot to create a situation of mock sexual tension that it can disperse: Both characters are reduced to their underwear, Andrew has to embrace Kate in that state of undress to extricate her from stinging plants, and when she does try to separate from Steyn, she is frightened into rejoining him.

The latter development is particularly significant in terms of the film's ideology. After seeking to be alone from Andrew, Kate is shocked by the unseen arrival of two black men. She immediately elicits Steyn's help/presence, despite his former sexual advances. The scene thus cleverly uses the motif of "strangers" to motivate Kate's inherent fear of the black men. Given her state of undress, she is naturally afraid for her vulnerability. She quickly concludes however, that she is safer with the sexual advances of Steyn than with strange black men.

The function of these discourses is to construct Steyn's character in a manner that replaces the colonialist who raped and pillaged Africa with the paternalist who is there to care for it. It is for this reason that the film clearly links his awkwardness to sexuality: in his own words, his brain turns off in the presence of a woman. To underscore this point, the film has Mbuti comment that he will have to tell Steyn about "the facts of life." This construction of the bungling asexual paternalist is precisely the corrective to the virile man of action that colonialism created within its iconography and discourse of justification.

That Steyn can function as a corrective to past images of white excess is achieved through the manner in which the plot consigns the abuses of white colonialism to the past. It accomplishes this task through the character of Mbuti. In the scene where Steyn and Mbuti discuss !Ky's situation in the hands of the legal system, Mbuti discloses how, as a younger man, he fled into the Kalahari after striking a British police officer, an event that took place back in the days when Britain ruled Botswana. Mbuti survived because the Bushmen found him dehydrated and saved him.

The significance of this scene is that Mbuti, in recounting a tale from the past, locates white European colonialism in that period—the past. Coming as it does after scenes in which government officials are all shown to be black, the tale functions to convey the impression that white privilege—or even white rule—is gone from Africa. The film's production and distribution, however, occurred during the 1980s—a period of white rule, and Apartheid, in South Africa. The scene is thus an attempt to cover over, or deny, not just the white rule of South Africa, but the continued economic and political colonization of Africa by Cold War superpowers and multinational corporations. It substitutes in South Africa's place the mythical country of Botswana, where natives still ride buses carrying live chickens, and ride past villages made of straw huts. As Peter Davis notes, this is a mythical Botswana, and not the actual country of the same name because the geographical-political dimensions of the film's setting exist only in the imagination of the film and its makers. Davis thus argues, "features of the landscape, dress and custom are not to be found in the real Botswana," and the film "could not have been set in South Africa itself" since "the free movement of people across a landscape, with . . . which *Gods* is filled, is simply not possible in South Africa."[2] The film's setting is thus a complex rhetorical strategy of denying the political existence of privilege.

With the manufactured disappearance of white rule and the demonstrated incapacity of blacks to control modern civilization and its technology, the place of white male paternalism becomes necessary to the stability of Africa, as the film's resolution confirms. The plot thus attempts to assure its audience that white privilege—in the form of paternalism—is necessary to maintain the virtue of Africa. The story confirms this point when, unlike previous historical encounters with white Western culture, the contact between !Ky and Andrew does not end in tragedy—like the historical encounters did, and like it could have if Steyn had not intervened and !Ky had remained in jail. Rather, the film concludes with !Ky successfully throwing the bottle off "the edge of the world" and returning to his home, his virtue and the virtue of the Bushmen community intact thanks to his contact with the benevolent Steyn. The film makes clear that only white paternalism is in a position to maintain such a state of affairs in Africa, precisely because Africans, in the form of their incompetently run Western-style governmental bureaucracies, are not able to maintain such a delicate balance—as is confirmed by the mishandling of !Ky's case.

The rhetorical operations of the plot thus offer its spectators the opportunity to identify with the superiority of the white race, as confirmed by the narrative trajectory. In the process it draws on several deep-seated beliefs, not least of which is that Africa is an uninhabited and unspoiled wilderness. Thus, while the film may assert that civilization is "crazy," it also assures its audience that its effects are highly contained: that Africa as natural wilderness is not being despoiled by modernization, as the film's closure so strongly suggests. Audience identification towards the naturalness of white superiority is thus structured upon the antinomy between the spectator's own sense of the alienating effects of mass culture and the natural existence and contentedness of the Bushmen. Indeed, part of the reason the film's comparative structure works so successfully as a ruse is that audiences bring their sense of alienation from material technological culture to the process of viewing the film. What they see in the comparison is an incredibly astute analysis of the form and structure of their alienation: it is very much rooted in becoming further and further detached from the natural physical environment. The narrative places that identification into a trajectory that justifies white privilege as a means of protecting and maintaining the natural world.

Several elements within the film, however, escape this process of the justification of privilege built on naturalization. To begin with, the criticism the film levels at material technological culture is contained, but it is not erased. The film confirms the myths of resilience and permanence—the belief that material-technological society is too massive and strong to merely fade away—yet the necessity it bestows on that society does not resolve its problems. Though necessary, material technological society is too detached from the natural world to ever be healthy, its neurosis located, indeed, in its very detachment.

Furthermore, the film goes beyond the criticism itself to offer images of alternatives to material-technological society. The first of these is the society of the Bushmen. Here, too, strategies of containment are exercised. The film makes clear that no one can survive in the Kalahari *but* the Bushmen. In the figure of Mbuti, however, the film creates a strategy of containment that works very ambivalently. Mbuti's tale of political flight into the Kalahari at once confirms and denies that only the Bushmen can survive there: he would have died if the Bushmen had not buried him in the sand to stop the dehydrating effects of the sun, then forced water and food into his body. According to the tale, the Bushmen intervene and save Mbuti, but he then lives with them for three years.

Precisely what the tale teaches Steyn and the audience on a literal level is that people other than the Bushmen *can* survive in the Kalahari if they learn from the Bushmen. On a more figurative level, the tale teaches that people can learn to survive from the Bushmen—that the lessons can be taken and applied beyond the Kalahari. What the Bushmen teach is precisely the opposite of material-technological society: how to survive by being attuned to the physical environment and adapting to it. The Bushmen prove more than almost anyone else can—since they live in one of the most unforgiving places in the world—that the earth will provide if one lets it.

In this respect, the Bushmen constitute the most basic form of resistance to material-technological culture: complete isolation. What the film demonstrates, however, is that there is another degree of resistance: limited engagement. Within the images of the villages of Botswana, the film demonstrates that isolation is not the only way to exist outside of material-technological culture. The straw-hut villages that Kate will pass on the bus, and eventually enter in order to teach, are still organized around the land, and are nonindustrial in terms of their use of technology. They are shown to not have running water or cookstoves, and are decidedly more peaceful than the noisy city where Kate first picks up the bus.

The scene of Kate taking the bus makes clear, however, that there is some—albeit very limited—interaction between material-technological culture and village life. The bus, for example, goes to (or at least by) the villages, making it possible to travel to and from the villages for whatever reason. In this manner, the villages can remain remote and detached from material-technological culture, without being completely isolated from it. As a result, village life can benefit from material-technological culture without being bound to it. The latter is clearly an idealized image, but it nonetheless constructs a point of resistance to material-technological culture through that ideal.

Furthermore, what the film makes clear is that race is not relevant within this ideal. The white minority in the film, although privileged for the purpose of the film's rhetoric on race, nonetheless acts seamlessly within the black world. The character of Kate emphasizes this point. Coming to the village from city life, Kate has to learn to become more comfortable with the ways and customs of the black Africans she is there to help. As the film goes on, she accomplishes just such a transition. The signification that resists the film's discourse on race is that societies organized around sustaining themselves through the physical environment will do so communally and will consequently not have need for the signifier of race.

The film's discourse on race can exceed this signification, and justify a structure of privilege precisely because none of the white characters actually participates in the work of sustaining the community, in laboring directly with the earth's production. Rather, all of these characters, even Steyn, are once removed from such a relationship with the land, either taking care of the community (Kate and the Reverend) or taking care of the environment itself (Andrew). Indeed, the only white character who comes close to laboring on the land is portrayed negatively, Jack Hind. The film makes Jack out to be an exploiter of the environment, not a worker of it. This point is underscored by a play on his name: "hind" is another word for rear end, as is the word "ass." Jack Hind is thus a coded way for the film to call his character a jackass—which is by and large how the character behaves. At least part of the negative construction of his character is the manner in which he remains as European exploiter of the land: He is detached both from the indigenous culture that populates the land, and from the environment itself, which he uses to make profit.

For all the rhetoric that attempts to persuade the audience that white privilege is necessary to maintain the delicate balance between communal culture rooted in the physical environment, and material-technological culture, the film's discourse cannot cover over one inescapable conclusion of its own images: That the ability and power to create and maintain communities that are superior to material-technological culture lies within black culture, not white. In many respects, such a conclusion is itself firmly rooted in the film's paternalistic view of Africa and its indigenous peoples. As "primitives" blacks have a natural affinity for the land, which whites—having fallen from grace via their intellectual prowess and affinity for creating technology—no longer possess. In addition, however, this idealized and condescending view of both the African continent and its indigenous peoples, articulates an anxiety and insecurity about technological-materialist culture that the film's opening attempts to contain with humor: That whites are no longer in control of their societies, but controlled by them. The gods, while superior, are ultimately crazy.

Notes

1. Peter Davis, review of *The Gods Must Be Crazy*, *Cineaste* 14(1) (1985), 52.
2. Ibid., 51.

4

Driving Miss Daisy (Because She's White and I'm Not!)

Chapter 3 on *The Gods Must Be Crazy* demonstrates that the naturalization of privilege and aggression can be a very effective rhetorical tool. Appeals to nature or the natural state of things can function rhetorically as a means of persuading people not to act; to maintain something (like privilege) by accepting it as inherent, rather than to act upon it. Naturalization is therefore a popular mode of rhetoric for maintaining the status quo of inequity and its modes of categorized oppression—race, class, and gender. This chapter analyzes the film *Driving Miss Daisy* to examine more closely a different rhetorical mode: the discourse of justification. This is not to say that the discourse of naturalization is absent from *Driving Miss Daisy*—it is certainly present—but the dominant mode that organizes the film is justification.

Thus, whereas both *The Birth of a Nation* and *The Gods Must Be Crazy* began with the discourse of naturalization as related to biology and used that as a foundation for discourses of justification and/or legitimization, *Driving Miss Daisy* takes a different approach. The film begins with naturalization, but a different kind of naturalization, before it shifts to justification as a more predominant means of organizing its discourse on race and privilege. With *Driving Miss Daisy*, naturalization gets a new look. In both *The Birth of a Nation* and, to a lesser degree, *The Gods Must Be Crazy*, the discourse of naturalization was associated with biology; Afro-Americans or Africans were "naturally" uncivilized in both. In *Driving Miss Daisy*, naturalization shifts to another arena. It is thus not so much associated with the biology of race as it is with the form and structure of social reality, with "the way things are."

The narrative consistently asserts that the upper-class Daisy shares minority status with her driver Hoke.

Using codes of realism and the appropriation of history, *Driving Miss Daisy* renders the segregated south as a natural occurrence—the unintended result of a specific history, rather than a particular and contingent social formation maintained through a variety of social forces and interactions. Rather than examine those social forces and analyze segregation as a social institution, *Driving Miss Daisy* presents the social reality of the segregated south as an imposed and inevitable reality that individuals cannot change, but can ultimately rise above in their own interpersonal relationships.

The conclusion to the opening sequence evidences this naturalized look at the society of segregation. As the credit sequence to the film ends, Daisy enters her car, and subsequently backs it into a ditch. The event becomes a spectacle for the entire neighborhood, who look on as the car is towed out of the ditch. This is first conveyed by a shot of two children sitting atop a large stone fence, pointing to the action of the car being towed. An elderly gentleman in a hat stands next to them and observes. The sequence then cuts to a variety of shots, each showing people involved in the process of towing or observing: two other men stand by the tow truck, watching and talking, while two well-dressed ladies stand and sit (respectively) in front of a house watching the action while an Afro-American maid brings them iced tea. After the two women reach for their glasses, the maid looks into the camera as if gazing at the car, her facial expression acknowledging the gravity of the situation. The film then cuts to another Afro-American maid who stands behind a hedge looking at the situation along with an Afro-American male gardener. He is also pointing to the ongoing action and they are clearly discussing it. As they do, an elderly white woman approaches and requests that they go back to work. The gardener gives a "yes ma'am" and the two begin to exit. The plot returns to the area of the car itself with a tighter shot of the men in suits who stand by the tow truck.

The significance of this scene is the manner in which the plot sequence makes privilege appear so natural. The event is clearly out of the ordinary, and therefore a spectacle for the entire neighborhood. Everyone is naturally looking at it and discussing it—much to Daisy's horror. Within that discourse of naturalization, however, is the fact that the Negro help should not be standing around staring at the event, but should be working. Every other constituency has the right to look at the event: the children, because they have no responsibilities, the elderly man because he is more than likely retired, and thus has no work to do, the women because as female members of the upper class in this time period they also have no job to do, and the two men in suits because—as the film will clarify later—they are involved with the car (one as son of the driver, the other as an insurance man). The one Afro-American domestic is serving two neighbor women, so she is already working, and thus allowed to look, but the other two Afro-American workers are standing by themselves, and are therefore not working. Their employer's request that they get back to work is thus rendered as a reasonable and natural request. Indeed, the film quickly returns to the men in suits as a means of asserting plot actions over examination of social structures. The film does not stay with the Afro-American employees as a means of registering the effects of such segregated rights to look. Their returning to their duties is not meant as a critique of privilege and segregation, but rather, as a means of presenting it naturally.

This naturalized view of the social reality of privilege—an operation that will be maintained through the film—allows the film to ignore the social dimensions of race and focus on individuals of privilege within the social context. It thus structures a story around Daisy that presents racism as an individual moral conflict at the expense of the social factors involved in racism and the maintenance of segregation. This individual-izing of a social process provides the means for justifying both privilege and aggression.

The character of Daisy and the narrative operations organized around her are thus a fundamental site for this process. Both privilege and aggres-sion are central components to Daisy's character, to the degree that an enormous number of textual operations is needed to contain them. The first of these strategies of containment can be located in the opening it-self. In many ways Daisy's character is not sympathetic: she is a finicky, cranky, overly proud, and too upright (if not up-tight) person. The film's opening, however, withholds these aspects of her character. Instead, the film establishes audience sympathy with Daisy's situation as the primary introduction to her character. The car accident functions to elicit empathy for her by making her a victim of old age, a proudly independent person who is going to have to face dependency.

In this manner, Daisy's conflict, the tragedy of growing old, is estab-lished as the primary aspect of the main character, and thus of the plot it-self, a means by which the plot is able to elide the social dimension of race. Daisy's tragic situation then functions to justify some of the hostility she displays to other characters. Without such motivation to her charac-ter, spectator empathy would be hard to maintain for such a cold, hostile, overly prim, and unemotional character. Indeed, even with the tragedy of her primary situation, such empathy is hard to maintain. For this reason, the winter-storm scene and Daisy's visit to Mobile, Alabama, for Uncle Walter's birthday are both significant for their ability to render Daisy in positive terms.

Both scenes modify her character by displaying a positive side to her. These modifications are part of a delicate balance that the film maintains for the purpose of justifying aggression. Daisy's hostility is rendered as a personality trait, the result of who she is as a person. Furthermore, the film structures her aggression as belonging to the issue of her unwanted dependency—a point that the winter-storm scene emphasizes when Daisy enigmatically comments that "Idela was lucky." In this respect, the film justifies her aggression against Hoke because he is the manifestation of her dependency: she must depend on him to get where she needs to go. The film thus attempts to deracialize her aggression towards Hoke by subordinating it to the issue of her dependency. It also deracializes this aggression by creating other targets and tying them to the issue of dependency, such as Boolie, her son, who forces this issue upon her, and Florine, her daughter-in-law, because of her association with Boolie.

Dependency, however, is not the only factor justifying Daisy's aggression. One of the earlier traits established of Daisy's character—that she is Jewish—also provides justification for her aggression and works to justify her privilege as well. By structuring Daisy's character as Jewish—especially a Jewish person living in the South—the film defines Daisy as a member of a minority, creating the means by which her aggression can be justified through a process of comparison and contrast. Three key sites articulate this justification of Daisy's aggression by setting it against more malevolent (and violent) forms of racism: the trip to Mobile, Christmas at Boolie and Florine's, and the bombing of the temple. These scenes are particularly significant because through them the film presents itself as antiracist, each scene offering a pointed critique of racism. As further analysis will show, however, being against the malevolent forms of racism does not necessarily prevent a particular signifying act from participating in the process of racism—specifically the process of justifying aggression and privilege. Each of these scenes demonstrates this point.

The trip-to-Mobile scene engages in this process during the sequence with the state police. Here, a tranquil scene of Daisy and Hoke parked on the side of the road is ominously disrupted by a voice from out of frame that shouts, "Hey boy!" As Hoke reacts, the film cuts to a shot of two police officers, one of whom immediately asks, "What do you think you're doing with this car?" This introduction, with its antagonistically racist overtones, sets the context of the scene as a potential point for the manifestation of malevolent—if not violent—racism. Drawing as it does on the history of Southern police racism, the scene is laden with tension as to whether Hoke and/or Daisy will be mistreated. The scene ends with

Hoke and Daisy driving away as the voice of the cop comments over the image: "An old nigger and an old Jew woman taking off down the road together. . . . That is one sorry sight." The racial vulgarity of the cop's comment, along with the tension that the scene generated, renders the overt and malevolent racism both threatening and obscene.

Within the trajectory of the narrative goal—Daisy reaching the point where she can see Hoke for who he is and recognize their friendship—the scene serves as a reminder of the obstacles Daisy and Hoke face: they live in a terribly, and often times violently, racist society. Within the discourse of justification, however, the scene serves another function; it makes Daisy's aggression seem exceedingly small by comparison, allowing it to be read—and justified—as merely cranky individual behavior. Indeed, in contrast to violence, Daisy's aggression is always limited to the verbal; to cutting, acerbic remarks, to treating individuals contemptuously or brusquely, or clearly conveying that someone does not measure up to her standards or sensibilities. Indeed, the cold and acrid nature of her treatment of people is so effectively dominating that Daisy does not have to have recourse to personally degrading someone.

The Christmas scene with Florine and Katie Bell brings out this point. Here, Florine derides her maid, Katie Bell, for not writing down instructions and, later, for forgetting to buy coconut at the store, an ingredient needed to prepare a dessert for Florine's extravagant Christmas dinner. The scene is pointedly critical of both Florine's privilege and her aggression. Florine's comment, "More I cannot do," is clearly structured to be read ironically. The spectator knows that there is more Florine can do; she can go shopping herself like most people. Further, the degree to which Florine is upset over one dessert for what will be an enormous Christmas party is exaggerated, as Boolie's apology to Katie Bell will confirm. All these elements contribute to make Florine's condescension and derision appear extremely inappropriate.

The effect of this scene for aligning audience sympathy is that, once again, Daisy's aggression can be judged positively by comparison. To begin with, Daisy never dresses down the hired help with such derision and condescension. Even in the early part of Hoke's employment, when she is most aggressive towards him, she does not resort to such negative practices. She acerbically reprimands Hoke for interrupting others who are working, but without implying that he is imbecilic. Further, the film has structured the event such that Daisy's point is less excessive than Florine's: Hoke *is* distracting workers, and there is a lot of work to be done. The scene is thus constructed in a manner so that Daisy's criticism, while aggressive, is somewhat justified.

The last of these scenes, the bombing of the temple, diminishes Daisy's aggression even further. This scene starts out with Daisy being driven to the temple. Before she can arrive, however, she and Hoke get stuck in a traffic jam. After Hoke investigates the cause, he informs Daisy that temple services have been canceled. When Daisy insists on knowing more about what is going on, Hoke tells her that the temple has been bombed. As he drives Daisy away from the scene, Hoke tells her a story from his past of a lynching.

Hoke's story serves an important rhetorical function within the plot: it renders Daisy as a coequal victim of bigotry through the act of the temple bombing. A key element to this rhetorical process is that the Afro-American character is the source of equating Daisy's victimhood with the violence of racism. The bombing of the temple is a deplorable sacrilegious act that strikes Daisy to the core. She becomes so upset that she tries to deny its occurrence, insisting that Hoke got the information wrong. Although the scene clearly attempts to align audience sympathy with Daisy, its central function is not to modify Daisy's character but, rather, to justify Daisy's aggression. Compared to the scale of violence involved in bombing the temple, Daisy's contemptuous treatment of people appears an insignificant matter of personal style, lacking in both violence and hatred. Daisy is self-righteous and overly proper, but she is not shown to be hateful.

In addition to its contrastive function, the bombing-of-the-temple scene functions to justify Daisy's aggression in another respect as it justifies her religious intolerance. The bombing of the temple is the culminating point for the rhetorical device of Daisy's Jewishness—a trait introduced in the first scene with Boolie when Daisy disparagingly comments about Florine that socializing with Episcopalians must be the daughter-in-law's idea of heaven on earth. This remark subtly introduces both Daisy's Jewishness and her religious intolerance. As mentioned earlier, by defining Daisy as Jewish, the film constructs her character as being a member of a minority, and as the bombing of the temple (and other scenes) evidences, a persecuted minority. This status of persecuted minority, as further discussion will demonstrate, is at the core of what is otherwise a negative character trait: Daisy's religious intolerance.

By setting itself (mostly) in the fifties, the period before the rise of black nationalism and the Nation of Islam, the plot represents Afro-American culture at a time when it can be closely associated with the majority religious culture of Christianity. In this respect, the black characters are part of the majority, and Daisy part of a persecuted minority. Daisy's religious bigotry is thus coded by the film as a protective response from a member of a minority community seeking ways of protecting itself. In this respect, Daisy's Jewishness provides the means by which the film can reverse the meaning of minority as it pertains to race by associating Afro-Americans with majority culture.

Furthermore, what the film makes clear is that protection of Jewish religion and culture is needed not just from outside attack, but from interior disintegration, which Boolie and Florine as eager assimilationists represent. Significantly, Daisy will quietly and subtly abandon her religious intolerance as the narrative reaches its goal, the sign that Daisy is personally rising above the limitations imposed on her by the culture of segregation. Her aggression, however, so thoroughly justified throughout the plot, is maintained right to the end, confirming the rhetorical function of justification through codes of idiosyncratic character traits.

In addition to justifying aggression, the bombing of the temple scene exercises other important rhetorical functions within the plot, chief among them is the justification of privilege and the denial of racism itself. The manner in which the scene is able to construct Daisy as a victim functions to mediate and contain her privilege: she lives in a world where it can all be quickly and violently taken away. With such potential for being a victim continually hanging over her head, Daisy no longer seems to be in a place of privilege. In addition, however, the bombing-of-the-temple scene is a complex ruse that uses anti-Semitism as a rhetorical device to deny the scope, if not the actual operations, of racism. Indeed, the plot insists on the coequal status of racism and anti-Semitism, but in a manner that consistently privileges the victimhood of anti-Semitism over racism.

The primary site of this privileging is the exclusive status the temple bombing is given by the plot. In a film so dedicated to historical detail—suspending production until the director could determine whether Daisy would eat fried chicken with her fingers, for example—the plot excludes important and corollary historical events from the narrative; the bombing of black churches. Indeed, not only are these historical events excluded from plot events, they are not even mentioned. When Hoke attempts to comfort Daisy he does not speak of church bombings, but rather, an individual lynching. As Hoke's discourse demonstrates, the function of that exclusion is to deny the scope and institutional operations of racism.

Before Hoke's story, Daisy rhetorically asks, "Who would do such a thing?" Hoke responds, "Now, you know as good as me, Miss Daisy, always be the same ones." Hoke's response, coming as it does from an Afro-American character, carries important implications. By consigning the violent act to a particular group of people, Hoke's discourse limits the scope of racism by locating it within a specific segment of society rather than in the very structure and operations of the social order itself.

Hoke's story thus works to define away racism. It implies, first, that racism is limited to a specific segment of society, but, furthermore, that those responsible for racism act out of a general hate and intolerance directed in several different places. In this rendering, race is simply one arena, along with religion and other social categories, that the group singles out for their hatred and violence. As a result, racism is limited to both its scope—it is only a segment of society—and its operation—it is acts of violence, aggression, or mistreatment. Indeed, segregation as a social operation is never actually shown in the film, only referenced by Hoke when he mentions to Daisy that he would not have been allowed to use the restroom at the gas station they stopped at. Helene Vann and Jane Caputi describe the rhetorical operations at stake in the scene when they argue: "This scene, charged as it is with a servant standing up for a basic human right, could have been played to some political affect. Yet, any political voice is muted as, once again, this interchange becomes part of the expected comic wrestling between the ever-patient Hoke and the ever-irascible Miss Daisy."[1] The scene thus evidences the manner in which racism and segregation as social dimensions are downplayed, if not ignored.

As a result, racism—limited in scope and operation—is then equated by the mechanics of plot with anti-Semitism. What is significant for the plot's justification of privilege is the manner in which the coequal status of racism and anti-Semitism is constructed. Anti-Semitism is without doubt an enduring mode of social oppression, and certainly it was virulently operative in the South during the period the film is set within. The point, however, is not so much which mode of social oppression is worse, but rather, the manner in which the film uses anti-Semitism to justify privilege. Here too the bombing-of-the-temple scene is significant for its placement within the plot, immediately following Boolie's award by the Atlanta Chamber of Commerce. As Boolie's small speech indicates, the award would have been unthinkable for a Jewish person in the pre–World War II era. By situating the temple bombing immediately next to Boolie's assimilationist achievement, the film points to the finality of Jew-as-signifier within the society it is portraying. No matter how non-Jewish Boolie attempts to be, within the society the film portrays he will always be seen as a Jew—a fact that is emphasized again in the prelude to the Martin Luther King dinner scene, when Boolie describes to Daisy what will happen to the family business if he attends.

Precisely what the film emphasizes, then, is the finality or permanence of that signifier within the society inhabited by the characters. Such status is first ironically and comically conveyed through Hoke's character, who, as a member of an oppressed group, informs Boolie that he does not mind working for Jews. More than a comic aside, Hoke's discourse serves an important rhetorical function since it articulates the bigoted stereotypes of Jewish people—stingy, cheap, dishonest—deployed by the anti-Semitic society in which Boolie and Daisy live. The film then draws from that bigotry to associate being Jewish with victimhood. The temple bombing, the police scene on the journey to Mobile, and the prelude to the King-dinner scene all underscore the constant potential for Jewish victimization.

As with the individual character of Daisy, the function of that constant potential for victimization is to mediate the place of privilege that the characters occupy, and the means by which they occupy it; the exploitation of Afro-American labor. The plot's repeated references of anti-Semitism mediate this exploitation by insisting on the victimization of Jewish people in the South but only at the expense of the oppression and victimization of Afro-Americans. Those historical details are repressed from the discourse of the film, only fleetingly depicted in the scene with the state police. The construction of the Werthan characters as Jewish does not function to reference the historical ties between Afro-Americans and Jewish people in their struggle against bigotry, but rather, operates within a more contemporary politics of victimhood, encouraging the spectator to equate anti-Semitism with racism, but only as a means of diminishing the latter. Anti-Semitism thus becomes the ruse through which the reality of racism can be naturalized and ignored.

Limiting racism in this manner allows the structure and operation of privilege, so fundamental for the process of racism, to fade from sight, and with it, the economic exploitation that occurs through its operations. Another textual operation that contributes to this disappearing act, especially with respect to economic exploitation, is Hoke's illiteracy. This character trait, significantly, is introduced in a scene at the cemetery, where Daisy attends to her husband's grave. The significance of the setting is the manner in which the scene thus starts off as another site for the plot to modify Daisy's character. Here, Daisy's exactitude, and the discipline that goes along with it, is shown to have a positive side it ultimately is directed towards caring. As the scene makes clear, Daisy could take the easy way out—as most people do—and simply pay to have the cemetery impersonally attend to the grave site. Daisy, however, has the discipline and devotion to care, not only for her deceased husband, but for others as well.

It is within the context of this modification to Daisy's character that Hoke's illiteracy is introduced. The significance of that context is that Hoke's illiteracy thereby functions not so much as a character trait for him, but rather, for Daisy. As a modification to Daisy's character, the scene functions to redirect Daisy's intolerance away from her earlier established religious bigotry and towards anything (like social systems that produce inferior educational systems) that promote ignorance and create obstacles for learning. Her response to Hoke is heated, but it is clearly not directed at him personally. Furthermore, and most significantly, the scene provides the means by which Daisy gives something back to Hoke, access to the world of written language, which the plot constructs as a profound exchange between the two characters that justifies the economic inequality that characterizes Hoke's servitude and the basis of their relationship. Within the rhetorical operations of the plot, Daisy is justified in receiving Hoke's servitude because she gives back something that has been denied to him, entry to the world of words. In this manner, the film represses the economic exploitation imposed on Hoke through segregation by focusing on what he receives through Daisy. It thus ensures that Daisy is not read as taking advantage of Hoke's economic vulnerability, while at the same time it represses the operative conditions that create and maintain that vulnerability. Thus it is that the plot provides the means by which Hoke learns to read, but refrains from suggesting the political and economic ramifications of that literacy. Hoke learns to read, but it does not provide him with economic mobility, or increased political power. Rather, the plot conveys this development in an abstract, aestheticized way, as Hoke being able to improve the quality of his life, thanks to Daisy.

Character traits and actions are not the only means by which the rhetoric of justification represses the economic dimensions of segregation. The film's appropriation of history is also a significant site for this operation. The manner in which the film renders the past—its position towards the events, characters, and places that it is presenting and the textual strategies employed for that presentation—is structured to promote audience identification with privilege.

The film's opening establishes this process of identification. The opening of the film fades up from black onto a window with the sun streaming in. Despite the strong light from the window, the rest of the room is not fully illuminated. The light is soft, having come through both Venetian blinds and lace. As a result, the rest of the room is presented in muted tones of beige and brown—the latter coming from classically antique bedroom furniture. The room is well furnished, but not extravagantly so. At the same time, however, it is clearly detailed. Before the spectator has a chance to dwell on these details, the figure of Daisy walks into the frame, stands in front of the camera as if in front of a mirror, places a hat on her head and adjusts it.

As Daisy turns to exit the frame, the film cuts to the next shot, the hallway she is going to enter. This shot picks up on the warm lighting and muted tones of the first shot, revealing places where the sunlight streams into the house. As Daisy moves through her house, clearly on a path towards leaving it, room after room is displayed in warm morning light, accented by the deep-colored wood molding that details every room.

As the film cuts to the outside, the light, still soft from the morning sun, gently illuminates the trees, the red brick of the house, and the slate roof. The camera pans with Daisy as she moves left of frame, revealing a car parked in a garage right before the shot ends. The significance of the car to this shot, and to this sequence in general, is that it confirms that the film is set in the past. Further, the camera pan integrates the object into the shot by maintaining the continuousness of space from the house to the garage. The car is not cut in to the film in order to present it as an important cue to be read, but rather is joined to the ongoing action as another detail to the presentation. It thus operates within a continual process of constructing detailed, historically accurate setting.

All these elements—soft, warm light, muted tones, simple but elegant setting, and attention to detail—combine to convey the film's nostalgic position towards the past it is presenting. As the rest of the elements within the film will confirm, this is an affectionate, if not longing, look at the past. This nostalgia for, of all things, the society of segregation, exercises a significant role for structuring spectator identification. In this respect, Vann and Caputi argue, "Movies such as *Driving Miss Daisy* are set in those mythic 'that's the way things were' times so that White audiences, without recrimination, can enjoy watching Black characters continually say 'Yassuh' with a smile."[2] Thus, more than with Daisy herself—who because of her cantankerousness is a difficult character to maintain identification with—the plot attempts to procure audience identification with an idealized image of the past. Moreover, this idealized image is created for spectators whose social existence is characterized by an increasingly complex, fragmented, and alienating society. *Driving Miss Daisy* offers them an image of a simpler but nonetheless elegant society that is endearingly civil, the result of the plot having pushed the social dimensions of racist segregationism out of the world of the story.

Through Daisy's character, the film constructs and maintains some of the values of its idealized image, but it is with the image of a simpler time itself—more so than with Daisy as character—that the film seeks to procure identification. Daisy provides the image of material comfort and security and an appreciation of simple elegance without the negative connotations of excessiveness and lavishness. Through Daisy as figure within that ideal world, rather than with Daisy as an idealized figure, the spectator can identify with a cozy image of wholeness and completeness—of a material existence free of demands and wants. In this manner, the film affords the structural basis for identification mediated through a specific social perspective, the point of view of white privilege. Indeed, the structures of identification in *Driving Miss Daisy* are based on the denial of Afro-American identification.

In his discussion of Afro-American spectatorship, Manthia Diawara describes the manner in which "the dominant cinema situates Black characters primarily for the pleasure of White spectators (male or female)."[3] The degree to which this convention is adopted in *Driving Miss Daisy* is evidenced by the manner in which the film constructs its Afro-American characters to provide pleasure for specifically White spectatorship, characterizations that Vann and Caputi reference in their earlier discussion. Diawara, for example, argues: "one may note how Black male characters in contemporary Hollywood films are made less threatening to Whites."[4] This is certainly the case in the construction of Hoke's character, which uses the connotations of elderly as nonsexual, and genial as domesticated, to provide a corrective to both the menacing black man of Hollywood convention who consistently figures as the threat of rape, and the more contemporary angry black male making his voice heard through hip-hop music. The same can be said of Idela's character, who, though endowed with sass, nevertheless is constructed as a familiar "mammy" figure, the only twist being, she is mammy to an elderly white woman, not a child.

The plot's characterizations thus structure what Manthia Diawara has described as an "impossible position" for Afro-Americans as spectators, who are compelled by narrative dynamics to identify with racist inscriptions of black characters, or can "circumvent identification and resist the persuasive elements of Hollywood narrative and spectacle" but forgo the pleasure inscribed in the text.[5] In her discussion of these dynamics, bell hooks has described the spectator identification of Afro-Americans as a position of negation where the Afro-American spectator must abandon his or her own Afro-American identity.[6] The film's duplicity in this absenting of Afro-American spectatorship is inscribed within the narrative itself—imaged in the scene of Hoke and Idela glued to a television screen and absorbed in the drama of soap opera populated by white upper-class characters.

The contrast between hooks's description of preintegration black spectatorship, and that portrayed in the scene could not be more striking. hooks argues, for example, that:

> Before racial integration, Black viewers of movies and television experienced visual pleasure in a context where looking was also about contestation and confrontation. . . . Then, one's enjoyment of a film wherein representations of Blackness were stereotypically degrading and dehumanizing coexisted with a critical practice that restored presence where it was negated. Critical discussion of the film while it was in progress or at its conclusion maintained the distance between spectator and the image.

In the soap opera–watching scene in *Driving Miss Daisy*, however, the discussion between Hoke and Idela is not about critical distance or contesting a presence where it is negated, but rather is focused on narrative information about the soap opera. Rather than critical distance, it functions to bring the characters more fully into identification with negation.

This negation of Afro-American identification is reinforced through the structure of plot through narrative point of view. The affectionate look into the past that the film provides not only derives from the point of view of white privilege, but restricts itself to the world of white privilege. The film never strays from representing Afro-American characters unless they are in the company of white characters. Vann and Caputo thus argue, "Hoke speaks of a daughter, and for about ten seconds we see the side of his granddaughter's face inside a car; this is all we ever learn about Hoke's life outside his job."[7] This restrictive point of view is partially disguised by the film's realism and attention to detail; the film is so full of history that it conceals its highly one-sided view of the past. And yet, it is precisely by focusing exclusively on the world of privilege that the film denies the economic exploitation on which privilege depends: the film never portrays what it is like for Hoke and Idela after they leave Daisy's house. It represses, in fact, the other world that segregation created and that was present during this time. There is no view of the living conditions of Idela and her neighbors, of Hoke and his neighbors, of the schools their children attend, of the health care they receive, and so on; rather, the film represses images that might threaten the cozy world of material comfort that it creates.

Instead, the film consistently implies that Hoke and Idela, if not most blacks, are doing well. In this respect, the film makes a point of Hoke being able to purchase the cars Daisy owns when she gets a new one. Although they are used, the cars are nonetheless luxury cars in good condition. The film makes clear, in fact, that Hoke initially paid *above* market value when he bought the Hudson—portraying his willingness to do so as an issue of independence, but endowing him with the financial ability to make such choices and such personal stands. Indeed, the one glimpse the film provides of the other world of segregation, the black church during Idela's funeral, does little to speak of economic exploitation. The condition of the church and the characters' costumes—most notably those of the choir—all function to erase any sign of the degree of economic exploitation that segregation exacts from the black community.

This erasing of the social structure and operations of racism is crucial for the film's resolution. By removing the operations and effects of economic exploitation that racism maintains, the film provides the means by which Hoke can be defined as Daisy's equal. The give-and-take between the two characters throughout the narrative—especially the scenes in which Hoke has to hold his ground against her (the trip to Mobile, and the King dinner)—function to establish the equality between the two characters. As a result, Daisy is able to finally see through the obstacles that stand in the way of their relationship, and see instead all that they have been through together. This allows Daisy to understand that their relationship is not professional, but rather, personal. Hoke is her friend—indeed, her best friend.

The problem with this resolution is twofold. To begin with, it comes through an ambiguous, if not mediated, plot device. Daisy's realization comes only through the haze of a confusing moment in her very old age. Alone, frightened, and completely disoriented, Daisy then comes to see

Hoke as her friend, not her servant. The result is that Daisy can come to this realization but not have to be responsible for its actual implications—social and economic. The narrative's inability to acknowledge the social and economic dimensions that such a resolution would actually entail are demonstrated by the manner in which the plot shifts to Daisy in a nursing home after her realization; the shift serves as a means of avoiding how problematic (and improbable) it would be for the plot to maintain a relationship with Hoke that is defined personally rather than professionally.

Furthermore, Daisy's realization still denies the structures of privilege that mediate the relationship. The very basis of their friendship depends upon the institutionalized economic exploitation of Afro-Americans. For Daisy to see Hoke as a friend, she has to ignore that he serves her—and serves her in the menial capacity he does—because of the real effects of segregation on the lives of Afro-Americans: the low wages, the limited education made available, and the restrictions on career opportunities that are imposed. Daisy can see past these social realities, if she chooses, precisely because she is above them and does not have to suffer them. Hoke, by contrast, has to live with them as part of his everyday existence.

The closing image of the film further denies the social reality of privilege and exploitation by showing Hoke feeding Daisy, not because he is hired to, but because of their friendship. As he does, an image of the car driving down the road slowly dissolves into the image of the two friends at the table. The images remain fused together as the film ends, confirming that racism is something that people can transcend through friendship.

The choice of cars that the closing image uses emphasizes this point. Of all the cars that Daisy and Hoke shared, the one in which they drove to Mobile is chosen for this closing image. The car thus references the journey they shared, and at the same time, reinforces that Daisy is a member of an oppressed group too. This is the car over whose image the State Police officer earlier characterized Hoke and Daisy as "an old nigger and an old Jew woman taking off down the road together." In this manner, the film renders Daisy and Hoke as equal victims who came together as friends despite the obstacles society imposed.

The closing image thus concludes a process of attempting to persuade its audience that racism is about people and their behaviors, not an oppressive, pervasive, and largely invisible social structure rooted in privilege. Indeed, the final scene in which Hoke and Boolie visit Daisy suggests that the social reality of race, like the story itself, is a thing of the past. Hoke arrives at the house driven by his granddaughter, who, he informs Boolie, is a college professor. The educational and professional opportunities not afforded to Hoke are now available to his grandchildren. The social structures that the film worked so hard to conceal are now consigned to the past in any case. In this manner, privilege is first justified, then made to disappear, an effective strategy for maintaining its operation.

Driving Miss Daisy thus organizes its signifying elements to downplay the social in favor of the individual as a means of persuading its audience of the power of individuals to rise above the social structures imposed on them. Tellingly, however, that ability to rise above social structures never translates into resisting or transforming those very structures of oppression that the film is supposedly against. Instead, *Driving Miss Daisy* consistently organizes its rhetoric to cover over and ignore the operations of white privilege and the real effects it has on the lives of Afro-Americans. Such willful neglect is an easy perspective for people possessing privilege to adopt, less so for those who bear the burdens privilege imposes.

Within that rhetorical process, however, some elements resist the grain. The film works too hard, for example, to justify and limit privilege. Audience identification with Daisy depends on her humble past, having to do without, and being a victim herself. The contrast with Florine emphasizes this point. Florine's character goes from being positively evaluated by the film to negatively portrayed as a result of her relationship to privilege: in the beginning of the film, she is presented as Boolie's wife; later in the plot, she is defined almost solely as the overindulgent recipient of privilege. Her character thus places on privilege a degree of unacceptability. The fact that Daisy and Boolie "do the right thing" with privilege fails to contain completely the repulsiveness at the core of privilege that Florine reveals. In this respect, the film does not attempt to *defend* privilege, but to *deny* it through Daisy and Boolie, and disguise it through Florine, where it can be read as personal excess. Through the process, however, the film gives voice to the unacceptability of the very structure of privilege it so cunningly reinforces. Thus, however unwillingly, the film acknowledges the objectionableness of privilege by the very operations it employs to deny its operations and effects.

In addition to a troubled presentation of privilege, the film's attempt to individualize race as a means of denying the social processes through which it is conducted also runs into discourses that resist this process. The film reduces social structures to the status of abstract (and inert) context, the backdrop through which characters (individuals) move, and define themselves for having transcended (a not too difficult process given the inert status of such social backdrop). Within the construction of that social context, however, the film articulates discourses that work against privilege and towards egalitarianism. These discourses can be seen in the film's contrast of the internal relationships within the white and Afro-American communities. Within the white community, the plot organizes internal relationships around Daisy, the main character. A character of privilege, she is consistently concerned with what the neighbors, as well as the women at the temple, think about her, a trait that will be contrasted with the Afro-American characters. She is mortified, for example, when Hoke parks the car out in front of the temple, fearing that others will think she is taking on airs.

Daisy's concern is replicated in Boolie's character, although through the prism of assimilationism. Boolie strives not to stand out as different, as an object upon which the contempt and vindictiveness so prevalent within the white community can be heaped. Indeed, as was discussed earlier, there is an uneasy moment in the Man of the Year–award scene when the film implies how unthinkable it would have been to present the award to a Jewish person a couple of generations ago. The implication fails to function as a measure of how far Atlanta has come, and instead, gives measure to how much bigotry it still possesses. Boolie's withdrawal from the Martin Luther King dinner then emphasizes this point; the white community is plagued by the degree to which "what people think" has real consequences.

By contrast, the Afro-American community is rendered as free from these social ills. The film's nostalgia clearly extends to its idealized look at the Afro-American community from the point of view of privilege. Nonetheless, what that perspective values is the solidarity and mutual respect that can be found in the Afro-American community. Though inscribed within the justifying discourse of privilege that suffering makes for good people, the portrayal, as with the discourse itself, is nonetheless rooted in the historicity of Afro-American solidarity, what bell hooks has described as "the chitlin circuit," "where black people (though contained) exercised power, where we were truly caring and supportive of one another" and formed "a network of black folks who knew and aided one another."[8] Though it may look down contentedly at the chitlin circuit, the film nonetheless articulates how a radically egalitarian society would conduct itself. Freed from a preoccupation with who is doing what with how much they have—which is the concern of the white community and its society of surplus wealth and inequitable sharing of resources—the egalitarian society can focus on individual well-being and mutual support—on enjoying each other's presence and company.

Even at the point at which it is closest to this ideal, the white community seems to lack the warmth and depth capable of sustaining it. The scene in which Daisy's friends play mah-jongg conveys this. Daisy's apology is greeted with acceptance and support, and a friend offers to drive her to temple, but there is an uneasiness to the scene, articulated through primness of dress and manners, that give motivation to Daisy's concern that the gossiping and backbiting she so fears is just below the surface. By contrast, Hoke and Idela's conversation about a soap opera, condescending as it is in its portrayal of Afro-Americans, nevertheless portrays a higher degree of involvement between the two characters. In this respect, the film constructs privilege as antithetical to allowing sincere human interaction.

As bell hooks notes, the chitlin circuit has long been broken—and this historical fact certainly helps *Driving Miss Daisy* encode Afro-American solidarity as an apolitical and quaintly cultural phenomenon. Resistant readings to that depoliticization, however, allow such representations to "function as a way of knowing and learning from the past."[9] In this respect even though it is contained by being encased within the past, the message of the film is still articulated: What the white characters in the film can learn from Afro-American culture is the same lesson necessary to form a liberationist egalitarian society—the lessons of solidarity.

Notes

1. Helene Vann and Jane Caputi, review of *Driving Miss Daisy*, *Journal of Popular Film & Television* 18(2) (Summer 1990), 80.

2. Ibid.

3. Manthia Diawara, "Black Spectatorship: Problems of Identification and Resistance," in Manthia Diawara, ed., *Black Cinema* (New York: Routledge Press, 1993), 215.

4. Ibid.

5. Ibid., 211.

6. bell hooks, "The Oppositional Gaze," in Manthia Diawara, ed., *Black Cinema* (New York: Routledge Press, 1993), 293.

7. Vann and Caputi, *Driving Miss Daisy*, 81.

8. bell hooks, *Yearning: Race, Gender, and Cultural Politics* (Boston: South End Press, 1990), 35, 36.

9. Ibid., 40.

5
Mississippi (and History) Burning

In addition to being a good object lesson in how discourses of justification can operate to reinforce structures of privilege, *Driving Miss Daisy* also demonstrates that being opposed to racism is not enough to prevent participation in the process of racism; not enough, that is, to prevent one from generalizing and finalizing meanings, and naturalizing, justifying, or legitimizing privilege or aggression. The last film to be discussed in this section, *Mississippi Burning*, is an even more vivid example of this involuntary participation, and as such it demonstrates the necessity of consciously applying a more complex definition of racism.

Mississippi Burning is decidedly opposed to racism—far more so than *Driving Miss Daisy*, which subtly criticized malevolent racism but restricted this criticism to certain points in the narrative. By contrast, *Mississippi Burning* is a much more explicitly antiracism film; its narrative centers around the fight against racism during the early years of the civil rights movement. In this respect, *Mississippi Burning* provides another example of the issues that are involved in the appropriation and representation of history in dramatic narrative. In addition to these issues, this chapter analyzes *Mississippi Burning* as a means of demonstrating how abstract concepts like privilege can be related to formal properties of representation, in this case the relationship between privilege and narrative point of view.

The film's opposition to racism is stated with the opening image. The film begins by fading up from black onto the image of a wall holding two water fountains. As the image comes up, the voice of a woman sings a spiritual. The image is distinct for several reasons, the first of which is its rejection of stylistic conventions. Hollywood cinema frequently employs certain stylistic conventions of lighting, scenic arrangement, and focal properties to provide the illusion or at least impression of depth, a quality the opening image in *Mississippi Burning* lacks. A primary principle to scenic arrangement is avoiding flat backgrounds because they emphasize the flat, two-dimensional properties of the image. Even when such backgrounds are used, they are seldom filmed with the camera directly facing them—what is referred to as "head-on." In its opening shot, however, *Mississippi Burning* pointedly rejects that convention, shooting the wall from head-on and providing little depth between the wall and the camera.

The flatness of the shot gives added compositional impact to the elements within the frame, particularly the water pipe that enters at the top of the frame and bifurcates the frame vertically into two halves. Each of these halves contains a water fountain, which is joined to the pipe through a junction; each of the fountains has a sign over it, the one on the right reading Colored and the one on the left reading White. The two fountains are distinct from each other in that the one on the right is ceramic and mounted on the wall, while the one on the left is made of metal and is free standing. The two fountains are so different, in fact, that it is a misnomer to call the one on the left a water fountain; it is actually a water cooler, constructed of metal because it contains a refrigeration unit. The fountain designated Colored, by contrast, merely draws the water from the water pipe.

As the shot continues on the screen, a white man enters from left of frame, takes a drink from the water cooler and exits. Shortly afterward, an Afro-American boy enters from right of frame, takes a sip from the water fountain, and exits. The similarity between the two actions, combined with the manner in which the shot's composition draws attention to the water pipe that feeds both water units, underscores the irony of what is being represented. It is the same water, but social conventions—specifically the laws of segregation—require that it be separated for each race.

What the irony of the shot articulates is that more is at stake than merely separating the water into two distinct spaces: something happens *after* that separation to more clearly differentiate white water from colored. Here too the shot's rejection of cinematic conventions for rendering space works to underscore the point. In addition to emphasizing the composition within the frame, the shot's rejection of stylistic conventions draws attention to itself *as* a presentation, a discursive operation. In other words, it attempts to foreground itself as engaged in representation for a rhetorical point. This degree of self-consciousness functions to allegorize the shot itself, to emphasize that there is more to the shot than the literal denotation of two water units. Rather, the shot works to emphasize connotation, that the film invokes a history of meaning attached to the separation and difference of the two water fountains. In this manner, the shot functions as a reference to and an embodiment of the issues at stake in legalized segregation, drawing into its discourse the landmark Supreme Court rulings of both *Plessy v. Ferguson*—the decision that legalized segregation—and *Brown v. The Board of Education*—the ruling that outlawed segregation.

The shot emphasizes that although the water comes from one source, what happens to it after separation is anything but equal. In this respect, the shot functions as a critical assessment of the manner in which the South consistently failed to meet the standards of legalized segregation. Emphasizing itself as discourse, but maintaining codes of realism nonetheless, the shot evokes a cultural milieu in which even the most basic public amenities were seldom, if ever, made to be equal, but rather constructed separation as a means to maintain racial hierarchy. In leveling that criticism from the vantage point of history, the shot also inscribes the legacy of *Brown v. The Board of Education* as the symbolic position from which it speaks.

The Brown decision exercised a significant role in the history of civil rights, and the evolution of the law in American society. In addition, however, Brown represents the court's most active engagement with the fundamentals of semiotics. The court was lead to this theoretical engagement by the issues that it struggled with earlier in *Sweatt v. Painter*. In that decision, the court had to discern the ambiguities surrounding the issue of separation of public facilities based on race. The case revolved around Herman Sweatt being denied admission to the University of Texas Law School solely on the basis of being an Afro-American. The Sweatt case, like the opening shot of the water fountains, demonstrated the degree to which the culture of Southern segregation was fundamentally unwilling and unable to acknowledge the inequalities it imposed and created.

With the Sweatt case, for example, the State of Texas argued, and its courts affirmed, that the separate law school created for "Negroes" offered "privileges, advantages, and opportunities for the study of law substantially equivalent to those offered by the State to white students at the University of Texas."[1] "Substantially equivalent," however, was clearly in the eye of the beholder. In its decision against Texas, the Supreme Court argued:

> The University of Texas Law School, from which petitioner was excluded, was staffed by a faculty of sixteen full-time and three part-time professors, some of whom are nationally recognized authorities in their field. Its student body numbered 850. The library contained over 65,000 volumes. Among the other facilities available to the students were a law review, moot court facilities, scholarship funds, and Order of the Coif affiliation. The school's alumni occupy the most distinguished positions in the private practice of the law and in the public life of the State. It may properly be considered one of the nation's ranking law schools.

In contrast to the University of Texas Law School, the Supreme Court found that the separate school for Afro-Americans: "has a faculty of five full-time professors; a student body of 23; a library of some 16,500 volumes serviced by a full-time staff; a practice court and legal aid association; and one alumnus who has become a member of the Texas Bar." As a result, the court concluded that "we cannot find substantial equality in the educational opportunities offered white and Negro law students by the State. In terms of number of the faculty, variety of courses and opportunity for specialization, size of the student body, scope of the library, availability of law review and similar activities, the University of Texas Law School is superior." The Sweatt case is thus significant for confronting the manner in which the enormous disparities imposed by segregation would be justified: it confronted the reality that sixteen does not equal five—that somehow, Afro-Americans should be content that they have the five law professors rather than none.

In addition however, the Sweatt decision also marked a decided movement of the court in the direction of semiotics—of recognizing that entire networks of meaning and value are engendered in the creation and operations of social institutions. Indeed, the court concluded that far more is at stake there than the actual brick and mortar of social institutions, when it argued:

> What is more important, the University of Texas Law School possesses to a far greater degree those qualities which are incapable of objective measurement but which make for greatness in a law school. Such qualities, to name but a few, include reputation of the faculty, experience of the administration, position and influence of the alumni, standing in the community, traditions

and prestige. It is difficult to believe that one who had a free choice between these law schools would consider the question close.

The court's emphasis on qualities that escape "objective measurement" is a recognition of the network of meanings that circulate from the operation of social institutions, which will exercise a more significant role in its later decisions. Further, the court's conclusory remark clearly chastises the culture of Southern segregation for its denial of inequality. It was a warning that would not be heard.

As a result, when *Brown v. The Board of Education* came forward the Supreme Court was not only well aware of the degree to which the South would ignore inequality, it was also prepared to understand fundamental principles of semiotics, of what is at stake in the creation of difference. In reaching the Brown decision, the court reasoned that difference itself will engender inequality, arguing "separate educational facilities are inherently unequal."[2] The court's conclusion finds its foundation in the principles of semiotics, that the meanings assigned to difference will themselves have value. The court recognized this function of assigning meaning when it argued: "To separate them [Afro-American children] from others of similar age and qualifications solely because of their race generates a feeling of inferiority as to their status in the community that may affect their hearts and minds in a way unlikely ever to be undone."[3] *Mississippi Burning* thus begins with a shot that references the key issue that was at stake in the Brown decision, the perpetuation of difference for the purpose of inequality. The separate and unequal water coolers function to convey the social dimensions of this process, itself a key principle for semiotics: that linguistic value resides ultimately *only* in difference. Saussure went on to demonstrate that there is no such thing as a stable, inherently meaningful sign, up to and including the signifier of race (see Chapter 1). The function of segregation, as the water-cooler shot demonstrates, is to maintain the "meaning" of race as itself a signifier of inequality.

The *Brown* decision thus fundamentally confronted the social contingencies constructed around difference, and the inequalities engendered and maintained there. The disruptive and shattering effect of confronting those contingencies is imaged in the film by the shot that follows the opening image. In stark contrast to the relative stasis of the opening, the following shot is a small clapboard church engulfed in flames, a shot that will conclude the opening credit sequence. As the narrative begins, it maintains that violently disruptive context by building itself around the violent murder of three civil rights workers.

Within this dark, violent world of segregation that the narrative establishes, the plot introduces, in the light of day, the FBI agents sent to Mississippi to solve the murder case. As it does, one of the agents, Anderson, begins mocking the Ku Klux Klan by singing one of their anthems, and concludes by joking that the Klan is better at lynchings than lyrics. Anderson's song confirms what has been a consistent narrative operation since the beginning of the film, the plot's alignment on the issue of race: against inequality and for civil rights. The conversation between Anderson and Special Agent Ward then further defines the film's position. The plot constructs Ward's character as one of the agents involved in a historically significant event in the dismantling of segregation, James Meredith's attempt to enroll at Ole Miss (the University of Mississippi). Meredith was the first Afro-American to enroll at the all-white public institution, but he did so only with the assistance of the U.S. government.

The plot fictitiously establishes Ward's character as an agent who helped protect Meredith in his attempt to enroll. It further defines his character by his conversation with Anderson, who sums up Ward's experience with Meredith with the remark, "At least you lived, that's important." Ward, however, corrects him by stating, "No, Meredith lived, that's what's important." The response functions to establish the degree of dedication Ward's character possesses to the cause of civil rights and equality, to the point of self-sacrifice.

The significance of the scene, however, goes beyond confirming the film's opposition to racism. Antiracist position notwithstanding, the characters and conflict introduced in the scene move the narrative forward in such a manner as to participate in the process of legitimizing and maintaining privilege. The introduction of Ward and Anderson puts in place a complex plot device that dispenses with a simple narrative structure of good guys (pro–civil rights) against bad guys (racists and Klansmen). Rather, the introduction establishes conflict between Anderson and Ward, a conflict that initially centers on the proper way to conduct the investigation. As Thomas Doherty describes it, the conflict becomes structured around "the familiar tango between the avuncular pragmatist [Anderson] and the callow idealist [Ward]."[4]

As the story progresses, this conflict enlarges to the point where it competes with the crime drama itself (solving the murder of the three civil rights workers), clearly expanding beyond the practical question of how best to conduct an investigation in a hostile environment and becoming an ideological conflict over how best to defeat the culture of segregationist racism. This ideological conflict, however, becomes the principal means by which the film legitimizes privilege; as with *Driving Miss Daisy*, the view of history that *Mississippi Burning* presents is structured from the position of privilege, and its gaze is directed at the same place, privilege. The struggle for civil rights, a largely black social phenomenon rooted in collective action, is cast aside and replaced with the film's history of how the FBI won the battle against segregationist racism.

The film's distortion of history is significant for several reasons, but chief among them is the manner in which the Ward-Anderson conflict inscribed there functions to displace the struggle for civil rights, and thus privilege the perspective and position of majority white culture over the perspective and position of minority black culture. The film's choice of events in the history of the FBI's involvement in the civil rights movement is highly selective, to the point of being a distortion of history. The repressive function of this selection is significant. To begin with, it extracts a specific event—the Chaney, Goodman, Schwerner murders—from the struggle for civil rights (the movement itself is not actually depicted) and places it within a distorted picture of FBI involvement with civil rights. Through the character of Ward, as will be discussed further, the film tries to make clear that government, specifically the law, can be a lever with which to change society for the better—using the discourse of history to make that argument. The conflict between Ward and Anderson functions as allegorical history: as a microcosm of the conflicts going on within the FBI between the Kennedy Justice boys, and the freewheeling good old boys of J. Edgar Hoover.

This allegorical function is significant for the film's legitimization of privilege, because it operates to generalize about the FBI as a participant in the struggle for civil rights. The conflict between Ward and Anderson, which resolves itself in favor of Anderson and the good old boys, functions to assure its audience that the excesses of the Hoover boys are directed only against "known" bad guys slipping through the law, and thus ultimately are for the greater good. Such a rendering, however, is a gross distortion of the FBI's involvement with the civil rights movement, a history that shows far more activity against the civil rights movement than in support of it. Indeed, what history documents is that the freewheeling— that is, lawbreaking—activities of the FBI were directed *against* the civil rights movement, not for it, in order to impede, harass, and contain it.

This distortion of history is done not so much for its own sake, but functions rhetorically to legitimize privilege. The history of the FBI is sanitized by the plot because the film's rhetoric is structured around the argument that racism is such a large and complex problem that it can only be solved from the place of privilege. The film's consistent refusal to depict Afro-American collective activism functions within this rhetorical mode, since such depiction would speak to the opposite.

The principal function of the Ward-Anderson conflict and its appropriation of the buddy-film genre is to structure identification with the place of privilege. Indeed, as further analysis will demonstrate, the film achieves the displacement, and subsequent repression of Afro-American history and voice through the manner in which plot operations are structured to procure identification at the site of the crime story and the conflict between Anderson and Ward.

Establishing identification with that narrative trajectory allows the film's repression of Afro-American activism to seem natural. The demonstration down Main Street illustrates this operation. In this scene, the Afro-American population of the county, accompanied by some whites, is shown in an organized march through the town. Many in the demonstration carry hand-sized American flags. The scene is a fairly faithful reenactment of an event in the history of the civil rights movement, drawing on the powerful iconography of news footage of the time. As the demonstrators march, outraged white policeman start confiscating the flags.

This entire scene, however, is intercut with shots of Anderson poking through town. Furthermore, its screen time is less than a minute and a half before it is abandoned in favor of Anderson entering the beauty parlor to conduct his investigation. When he does, the demonstration is reduced to the background, audible, but visible only through the window of the beauty parlor, where it is framed and placed behind the characters. The march returns only briefly, and even then it is motivated by and reduced to a point-of-view shot from the perspective of Pell's wife as she watches the deputy conducting crowd and traffic control.

The scene therefore demonstrates the narrative's unwillingness to leave the confines of privilege and tell the story of Afro-American culture's collective transformation of white racist society. Rather, the story privileges the Ward-Anderson conflict, and the need to resolve it, as fundamental to solving the crime and winning the battle against racism. Thus, in a manner similar to *Driving Miss Daisy*, the film privileges the white point of view over Afro-Americans' place in history.

The conflict between the two white FBI agents displaces the role of collective Black action in the Civil Rights struggle.

This narrative abandonment of Afro-American history and culture for the space of privilege is dependent upon the text's ability to procure identification with the Ward-Anderson conflict. Within the operations of the text, spectators will give up interest in Afro-American collective action precisely because they are already aligned with the conflict between the two white agents.[5] This conflict, which has several dimensions, centers on the efficacy and liabilities of the federal government as a vehicle of social change, but takes its shape from, and structures itself around, an oedipal drama. It thus attempts to engage its spectators not only through a social dimension but through the structure of individual identity.

The film mobilizes the first of these identifying processes—the social—by creating parallels between contemporary social conflicts and the conflicts within the film. The principal site through which this social dimension is enacted is the Ward/Anderson conflict. *Mississippi Burning* is set in the period of history during which the growth of federal bureaucracy facilitated the shift from local to mass society, a process that the film makes a point of articulating at several junctures. *Mississippi Burning* was released in 1989, however, and thus during a long period of reactionary struggle against both a large activist federal government and a progressive, more equitable society. The role of the federal government in achieving social change was the central point of organization for this reactionary movement—a movement that achieved its hegemonic dominance with the election of Ronald Reagan to the presidency of the United States. During this period, reaction against progressivism successfully portrayed large federal government as the *cause* of social problems, not the solution. So successful was this ideological shift that shrinking the size of federal government, and more importantly the taxes that pay for it, became a central concern not only of the Republican administrations, but of the Democratic administration that followed them. The process of redefining government as a problem was carried out through a restructuring of the nation's economy that directly affected a majority of individuals within U.S. society. Government support for the poor and working poor was curtailed, as was support for education and health care. Government spending was dramatically shifted to subsidize an incredible expansion of the military-industrial complex, with a predictable economic dependence on such expenditure being the end result. This dependence was so acute that by the mid-1990s Congress would actually give the Pentagon *more* money than it asked for as a means of maintaining defense contracting jobs within key congressional districts. At the same time that the government began its military buildup, the private sector of the economy was also facing turbulent times. Many individuals in the manufacturing and middle-management sectors of the economy were displaced through either corporate relocation or downsizing, as companies strove to achieve greater profits through increased productivity. The economic vulnerability of what turned out to be large numbers of people was made to seem a symptom of a society in decline: a decline that was blamed on a massive federal bureaucracy and liberal political philosophy. The issue of the size of the federal government, and its economic consequences, was thus a more vital issue than it might at first appear.

The conflict over the efficacy of the federal government to affect social change, and the ideological dimensions attached to that conflict, are a central motivating element to the Ward-Anderson conflict. In this respect, Special Agent Ward's character comes to represent the overly confident technocrats of 1960s government and their naive faith in social engineering, bureaucracy, and, in general, the power of government to solve problems. The cue to this definition of his character occurs when Anderson calls Ward a "Kennedy boy," a reference to the Kennedy administration's infamous group known as the "best and the brightest," whose overconfidence in the government's and their own abilities led to such disasters as the Vietnam War. On the other side of the conflict, Anderson's character is defined as a good old boy who has escaped from the intellectual restrictions of growing up in the South. He is therefore constructed as an individual who understands the South and appreciates it, but no longer holds its racist beliefs. Anderson's appreciation of Southern culture is a primary motive for his opposition to the bureaucratic approach to solving the problem. In contrast to the by-the-book method of investigation identified by the characters as "Bureau procedure," Anderson takes a personal approach that is rooted in his understanding of the society and the context within which the crime was committed.

Anderson's consistent focus on solving the crime conveys his belief that crime-solving itself is the limit of what law enforcement (and by extension the law itself) can accomplish. For Ward, however, solving the crime and bringing the guilty to justice is part of a larger battle in the war against racism. An exchange between the characters at a crucial point in the plot functions to express this conflict. In trying to dissuade Anderson from personally seeking revenge against Deputy Pell, Ward argues that vigilante justice is precisely the difference between the FBI and the Klan culprits they are pursuing, between them and "us." Anderson replies: "That's the difference between them and YOU." The following exchange then occurs:

WARD: You're not any more like them than I am.
ANDERSON: Wrong! What do you care what I do with some son-of-a-bitch hiding behind a sheriff's badge? Don't you have the whole world to change?
WARD: That's right. And I'm changing it.
ANDERSON: Awwh. You're just as arrogant as you are stupid.

The exchange between the two characters significantly articulates the key signifiers that function for a site of recognition and identification for spectators: the efficacy of the federal government to change society, the arrogance associated with that kind of exercise of power, and the place of the law within that process.

The ideological conflict between Ward and Anderson over the efficacy of federal bureaucracy thus held for its spectators the promise of providing a symbolic resolution to one of the largest social debates/conflicts confronting them. As the narrative trajectory progresses, spectators are in the position of witnessing and judging the dynamics engendered by the federal government as a vehicle for social change. The film images the enormous resources the government can bring to bear on any situation: money (the FBI simply buy the hotel when the owner becomes a problem); manpower (the town is flooded with FBI "suits"); and media attention (the film makes clear that the government turned the crime into an "event"). In contrast to those images, however, the film represents the liabilities of the federal government as a vehicle for social change. The FBI men are shown to be completely out of place and fairly ineffective in accomplishing anything—their activity is shown to be impersonal, if not incompetent (as they tromp through swamps and farmland in their suits and black dress shoes) and their approach arrogant (as when Ward shuns the codes of segregation and sits next to an Afro-American at a diner without recognizing what the consequences would be for the young man he speaks to). Further, as Anderson makes clear, the increase in violence is due directly to the government's escalation of the investigation.

The resolution to this conflict, however, demonstrates that the form and structure of the social dimension are nonetheless organized around the structure of individual identity, itself a means of procuring spectator identification. As the introductory scene with Sheriff Stuckey indicates, the conflict between Ward and Anderson is not wholly an ideological conflict: the two struggle over the issue of authority. Anderson is the older of the two agents, has much more experience as an FBI agent—especially in the field—and is far more adept at interacting with the citizens of the town, having grown up in Mississippi himself and thus being knowledgeable about the culture. Yet despite these qualifications, Ward, the "Kennedy boy," is put in charge of the case through the workings of the Justice Department.

This conflict over authority, occurring through the context of an age difference between the characters, finds its structure in an oedipal conflict. The trajectory of the narrative will confirm this structure. Early in the film, the younger Ward occupies the place of authority largely through his desire (the desire for a better world). The older Anderson resents Ward's authority over him because it is, as demonstrated by outcomes, incompetent (and hence illegitimate). As the investigation continues unsuccess-

fully, however, the younger Ward realizes that he must renounce his
youthful idealism and accept the reality of how things are done; he must
not only accede to Anderson's knowledge, but grant Anderson his authority in order to achieve anything. The narrative trajectory, therefore, inscribes the oedipal trajectory, where desire (the pleasure principle) must
give way to the reality principle and the authority of the social symbolic
system incarnated in the figure of the father.

Precisely what spectators recognize within the narrative trajectory is the
structure of their own identity; the successful resolution of their oedipal
drama. This structural similarity provides the means for identification
with which the social dimensions are then associated—as is usually the
case in mainstream narrative film. In this manner, the film provides a
symbolic resolution to the ideological conflict of federal government as
agent for social change by constructing it around an oedipal trajectory.
The conflict is resolved when Ward "comes of age" and recognizes the
limits of idealism and accepts the "reality" of the way things are done—a
highly rhetorical construction of reality that allows the film to affirm the
reactionary, nontransformational agenda of its social context. As a symbolic structure, the film deftly allows both sides of the conflict to resolve
themselves without vanquishing the other. Ward's character will come to
see that idealism and bureaucracy are not enough to win the battle—that
the enemy must be fought on its own turf—while Anderson's character,
though vindicated on that front, must begrudgingly come to see that the
law and law enforcement should be a lever for changing society; if not
used by the righteous, they will be appropriated by the immoral, like
Stuckey and Pell.

In a manner similar to *Driving Miss Daisy*, these plot conflicts and resolutions function to direct identification towards privilege at the expense
of Afro-Americans having a place in the story—and in history. Although
Afro-Americans can find the structural basis to identify with the narrative
trajectory, the symbolic mode of identification that mediates that process
falls into the pattern of creating an "impossible position" for Afro-
Americans, who find their social position absented from the screen. Their
place in history, and within the story, is removed through a process
whereby the struggle for civil rights is told only from the perspective of
privilege; what whites think should be done to solve the problem of
racism.

This repression of Afro-American society, collective Afro-American
struggle, and Afro-American perspective/voice functions within the film

to deny a position of identification for Afro-American spectators, as it maintains the structure of privilege, especially through a process of legitimization. Although *Mississippi Burning* presents itself from its very opening as a film that is antiracist, it organizes its opposition to racism around the character of Agent Ward. Ward's character explicitly wants to change the world, to end racism. Nonetheless, by structuring the narrative around Ward, the plot is structured through the point of view of privilege. Racism, perpetuated by whites, becomes a problem for whites to solve.

Unlike *Driving Miss Daisy*, the film does not hide from showing either the violent manifestations of racism or its malevolent and economic effects. It will, however, fundamentally deny the place of Afro-American collective action to change a racist society. The degree to which the film centers on white dominant culture at the expense of Afro-American experience is demonstrated in a small moment of exposition late in the film, in which Ward and Anderson walk through the burned-out remains of a farm the Klan has recently torched.

This scene comes immediately after a depiction of the actual event and its violence: the Afro-American family is terrorized, the father lynched despite the brave son's attempts to save him. The next scene opens with medium shots of animals that have been burned to death, their skin taut from bloat and baking, their lips burned away. This scene soon cuts, however, to reveal that these shots have been Anderson's point-of-view shots. With this cut, there is a permanent shift from the Afro-American family's story (which was structured around their victimization, powerlessness, and ultimately, a dependency on whites) to the world of privilege. As Anderson and Ward survey the charred remains of the farm, Anderson begins describing how cows do not have the sense to flee from fire. The focus of the plot shifts however, when Ward, rather than respond, states, "I have relatives in Detroit." In terms of the film's exposition, the dialogue functions to insert the social into the film's articulation of history; it references the riots going on in Detroit, and thus adds specificity to the time frame of the story.

Within the film's overall operations, however, the dialogue functions to assert the point of view of privilege over the Afro-American perspective. Ward's statement is followed by Anderson asking, "Are they gonna go?" to which Ward replies, "I didn't give them any choice." In a concise piece of dialogue the plot works to convey that racism is everyone's problem, but it does so in contradiction to the image track. The image track depicts the violent effects of racism, and the economic effects of that violence as it pertains to specific Afro-American characters—who in turn stand in for poor, rural, Southern Afro-Americans in general, to whom the devastating consequences of racism are a constant threat. Ward and Anderson's dialogue, however, functions to displace that focus and generalize race as a problem that affects and endangers everyone: it not only expands the boundary to the north (Detroit) but to whites as well (Ward's family). Tellingly, it also functions as a justifying discourse of the white flight that would occur after the Detroit riots—a discourse authorized through the antiracist character of Ward, who orders the family to go.

Furthermore, that the scene then escalates into another clash between Ward and Anderson over their ideological orientations indicates the manner in which the narrative fundamentally structures itself around the point of view of privilege. The burning and lynching, rather than having value in themselves as an indication of Afro-American suffering under racism, become only another narrative event that contributes to the ongoing evolution of how Ward and Anderson interact with each other to solve the murders.

Other scenes within the plot exercise two important rhetorical functions for legitimizing the privileged place within the narrative that Ward and Anderson possess. The first of these are the scenes involving the media. The plot associates the media with the mass society that is being ushered in with the help of the enormous federal bureaucracy. The media is thus aligned with the impersonal, arrogant, and alienating forces that constitute the negative dimensions of Ward and the army of suits he brings into the conflict. This critique is delivered at several points, but articulated by Anderson when he argues that "this whole thing was fucked up the moment we turned it into a show for the newsmen." Anderson's statement ties the escalation of the investigation, an escalation the film has coded as a mistake, into the actions and operations of the media. In this manner, the film evaluates the role of the media negatively.

The film's negative position towards the media, however, is bound to the narrative's rhetorical function of legitimizing the privileged position of the FBI, and the federalist bureaucracy it represents. The narrative trajectory consistently affirms that this operation of privilege is the most capable of solving the complex problem of racism. The media, and its role of creating and shaping public opinion, constitutes a site of potential control against that privilege. The film renders the media as illegitimate by having them replicate the worst of Ward's traits: arrogant, intrusive, alienating, and not a little incompetent (as Frank's brutalization of a cameraman demonstrates). The media are thus rendered more as part of the problem and not the solution, a position reserved for the FBI.

A similar site for such legitimization is the trial scene in the state court, which emphasizes the local court's inability to handle the problem of racism as a result of their own xenophobia and racism. The men on trial, the scene clearly establishes, are guilty, but the judge refuses to punish them because of his own bigotry. The later scene of Ward and Anderson in the rain as the special operative flies off affirms this position; they have to prosecute the culprits in federal court if they are to succeed. In this manner, the film structures the FBI (albeit through a distorted history) and the federal bureaucratic system as the guarantor of the Civil Rights movement's success, and thus legitimizes its privileged place within the narrative.

The film's ending confirms this rhetorical position. The film closes with the scene of an integrated congregation singing a spiritual in the burned-out remains of a church next to the cemetery. The image suggests that while the building may be gone, a new church will arise, a church built of racial harmony and understanding. Ward and Anderson look on, then turn to leave, their work done. What the sequence implies is that this racial harmony is the result of Ward and Anderson's success—their ability to bring to justice the murderers and end the tragedy of violent racism. Their earlier failure in state court and the subsequent rioting in the black neighborhood stands in contrast to this image of unity and harmony that comes after the success of the investigation. The film closes by craning and panning away from the congregation and over to a battered tombstone upon which a partial inscription can still be read:

1964
gone but not forgotten.

What the film's rhetoric ironically demonstrates, however, is that although the struggle for civil rights, especially in the deep South, is not forgotten, it can be distorted to legitimate the very privilege that caused it.

The repression of Afro-American participation in the history of the civil rights movement, along with the decidedly inaccurate rendering of the FBI's role in the struggle, functions not only to legitimize privilege, but also to repress collective transformation of society. As Anderson's criticism of Ward makes clear, Ward's attachment to the movement as such makes him arrogant and stupid; it is not until he hunkers down into the ways of the good-old-boys lawmen that he becomes effective. The film's rhetorical operations, then, serve to repress collective transformations of society in favor of privilege controlling that process.

Within the process of the narrative, however, some elements resist that rhetorical operation. The first such site of resistance occurs when the film figures the process of racism. The term "figures" refers to the process by which cinematic narration allows abstract social processes to take form or shape in such a manner that they can be readily seen by the audience. Early on in the story, *Mississippi Burning* engages in just such a process with respect to racism, giving form to its operations and causes.

This figuring occurs in the scene of Ward and Anderson's first night in Jessup. Here, the two agents sit in their hotel room discussing the case in terms of its social dimensions. Ward is looking at photographs contained in the files when he comes upon one of a lynching. Struck by the graphic violence of the photo, he asks, "Where does it come from, all this hatred?" In response, Anderson tells a story about his father, and a "Negro" neighbor named Munro. In the story, Anderson's father spitefully (and hatefully) kills Munro's mule, by poisoning the water. Ward, however, does not quite understand the nuance of the story, and misinterprets it as a broader discourse of justification for the racism of the South. Anderson attempts to clarify by saying, "The old man was just so full of hate that he didn't know that being poor is what was killing him."

Precisely what the narrative does within this scene is create a figure— Anderson's father—who embodies the social process of racism as it operates on the level of the individual. Through his father, Anderson is able to convey how individual actions were shaped by and conducted through an abstract social process—racism. As a result, racism can be seen and understood as something more complex than individual moral inadequacy. Rather, racism is shown to be rooted in the effects on individuals of a social system of inequity and privilege. Furthermore, Anderson's story starts to indicate the manner in which racism operates as a process of diversion that keeps economically disenfranchised whites from recognizing the structure and operations of privilege and inequity.

This economic dimension of racism is then referenced throughout the film's iconography, which consistently draws attention to the poverty of Jessup County, Mississippi: its dusty and unpaved main streets, its prevalence of shacks, and its backward working conditions. This last point is dramatically emphasized with the arrest of Clayton Townley, the leader of the Klan. Prior to his arrest, Townley is defined as a "businessman," and is shown to be of an economic class higher than the other members of the Klan. His arrest by the FBI, however, qualifies his position within privilege. As he is escorted from his business by the FBI, the camera reveals the primitive conditions of his business, where Afro-Americans labor to bundle raw cotton.

The plot's portrayal of these decidedly undeveloped working conditions performs several functions. First, it emphasizes how poorly Townley treats his workers, and thus further defines his racism. In addition, the scene demonstrates the irony of the narrative's racist leadership depending on exploited Afro-American labor for his living and his wealth, as the medium shot of one black employee's reaction to Townley's arrest makes clear. Lastly, however, the setting deflates Townley's own position of wealth. He is not the modern industrialist, like Boolie Werthen in *Driving Miss Daisy*, but a backwoods cotton processor who will sell his raw cotton to someone up the economic ladder like Boolie.

What these operations make clear is that racism, especially the violent Southern racism of segregation, is deeply imbricated in the North's economic exploitation of the South. In this manner, the film critiques the overly simplistic moral arrogance (attached to Ward's character) with which the North so naively judged the racism of the South—a judgment that ignored both the racism in the North and the vital role exercised by the economic exploitation of the South in maintaining racism. Although the film's rhetoric functions to render privilege as the most legitimate site for creating social change, these elements nonetheless articulate the operations of inequity and privilege and thus point out the direction of collective transformation.

The image of that transformation is found in the film's ending, first with the deputy's wife, and then with the church congregation. In the first scene, Anderson comes to the ransacked house of Gilly Pell, the deputy's wife. The house is in shambles, and Pell's wife stands alone in the kitchen, still bruised from her beating. With a husband whom she did not love in jail and her home in ruins, Gilly has strong motivations for leaving to find a better life. She tells Anderson, however, that she is going to stay, arguing that there are enough good people who know what she did is right. Although the film has made little reference to these good people, and has not given image to them, Gilly's conviction asserts the reality of their existence.

This conviction is an important lesson in collective transformation. Gilly does not argue that *most* people think what she did was right; rather, she asserts that there are *enough* people who think so. Her discourse thus asserts that a majority is not the essential requirement for social transformation, but rather, a collective united in their ideals. The film then gives image to this collective in the closing scene, in which the racially integrated congregation stands together in harmony at the burned-out church.

Further, the film suggests that this harmony is achieved because the collective are united, in this case by their common faith in the ideals of Christianity. Within those Christian ideals of building the egalitarian community, strife and suffering—the themes articulated in the spiritual they sing—have meaning and purpose. The image thus testifies to the power of the collective united in their ideals to withstand the forces against them and to prevail in social transformation. That the film attempts to persuade its audience that this situation was made possible by the actions of privilege fails to contain the powerful potential of the collective that the scene articulates. Beyond the film's rhetoric, then, lies an image of creating the egalitarian society in which race has neither purpose nor power.

Notes

1. *Sweatt v. Painter,* 339 U.S. 629 (1950). All Supreme Court quotations in this section are extracted from this case.

2. *Brown v. The Board of Education of Topeka,* 347 U.S. 483 (1954).

3. Ibid.

4. Thomas Doherty, review of *Mississippi Burning, Cineaste* 17(2) (1989), 48.

5. Here the term "spectators" refers not to the actual individuals sitting in the theater, but to the position that the operations of the text addresses.

Part Three

Confronting Racism and Representation

6
A World Apart
(from the World of Privilege)

Chapters 4 and 5 (on *Driving Miss Daisy* and *Mississippi Burning*) demonstrate that a film's being "against" racism does not prevent its signifying practice from participating in the process of racism. Rather, a film's incorporating and upholding the very structures and forms through which racism is conducted can counteract whatever antiracist message a specific signifying act might convey. Thus, both *Driving Miss Daisy* and *Mississippi Burning* end up reinforcing privilege by appropriating its structure and by articulating discourses of justification or legitimization. Each film looks at privilege from the position of privilege and thereby excludes the disenfranchised (in this case Afro-American culture).

The process of appropriating the structure of privilege within the text can also be described as using the language of the dominant. Language of the dominant refers to a specific culture's established and preferred system for representing reality. Here, language represents more than just words, expressing instead the whole range of signifying practices, styles, and forms by which dominant cultures represent themselves as a means of maintaining their positions of dominance, prominence, and/or influence through discourses of naturalization, justification, and legitimization. The manner in which both *Driving Miss Daisy* and *Mississippi Burning* speak through the language of the dominant and end up participating in the process of racism despite their opposition to it raises an important theoretical issue. Is it possible to speak from the place of privilege about privilege without maintaining privilege, or does using the language of the dominant in and of itself support the process of racism?

This theoretical issue was the central critical concern with the release of the film *A World Apart*. As Karen Jaehne describes it, the film's story is "about a mother/daughter relationship set in South Africa of 1963 against the backdrop of political arrests and accusations of treason toward those who raised their voices against White Supremacy in support of the African National Congress."[1] The story centers around the conflict of a mother trying to balance political activism with child-rearing, and a daughter's growing into consciousness as a result of her parents political activism and commitment. As the story progresses, the mother is imprisoned by the government for her political activities, leaving the preteen daughter without her most crucial role model as she struggles with her growing consciousness. Because the story is constructed around white characters, however, the ideological role that privilege exercises within the film becomes a crucial critical concern, as was the case with the film's entry in the Cannes Film Festival.

In her summary of the competition, Jaehne points out that critical reception of *A World Apart* was split along gender lines, with female critics largely appreciative of "the portrayal of a mother caught between absolute political commitment and her role as solely responsible parent."[2] Male critics of the film, however, raised precisely the issue of privilege speaking about privilege, arguing "against another 'white man's burden' film" and chastising "the film for not addressing apartheid through a black protagonist."[3] This particular criticism is similar to that leveled against another South African film, *A Dry White Season*. bell hooks, for example, points out that the latter film "disturbed many progressive viewers who did not want to see another film about a white man becoming radical."[4] hooks, however, cautions against the quick dismissal of such narrative structures, arguing, "a compelling story line centralizing white folks does not diminish the radical subversive element in the film."[5] Such possibility for subversiveness was ignored, however, by both critical groups at Cannes. Each group evaluated *A World Apart* without examining the manner in which the film is centered around privilege for the purpose of critique. Rather than naturalize, legitimize, or justify privilege, *A World Apart* exposes each of these modes of discourse in order to criticize privilege and social systems of inequity. That each group misreads the film is significant because of the manner in which they limit the focus of their analysis to the visible signs of race and gender within the film at the expense of the film's discourse about those very signs; the rhetorical position the film takes with respect to dominant cultural signifying practices. Just as *Driving Miss*

Daisy and *Mississippi Burning* are antiracist in their discourse, but justify, naturalize, or legitimize privilege in their signifying practice, *A World Apart* demonstrates that a film can be about privilege in its discourse but resist, obstruct, or expose privilege in its signifying practice.

The film conducts its critique of the naturalization of entitlement by constructing its narrative around the character of Molly, the preteen daughter of Diana and Gus Roth. As further analysis will demonstrate, this narrative strategy functions precisely as a means of appropriating privilege in order to make visible its operations. The film begins this process in its opening scene, which depicts Molly's father, Gus, preparing to leave South Africa because of his work against apartheid. As the scene ends, he drives off in his car under cover of darkness, and never returns to the narrative.

This plot device exercises a significant role in the film's rhetorical strategy of exposing the operations of exclusion and entitlement because of the manner in which it dismisses patriarchy from the story world as a means of establishing the story itself. An important site for the concentration of power within privilege, patriarchy becomes one of the sites from which the film problematizes the structure and operation of entitlement. By absenting Gus, the film announces that it is not going to construct another "white *man's* burden film." It will not naively construct itself around white patriarchal privilege.

In and of itself, of course, this narrative strategy does not constitute a critique of the politics of exclusion. *Driving Miss Daisy*, for example, also refrained from constructing its narrative around the figure of a white male, yet still endorsed and justified entitlement. Within the narrative organization and trajectory of *A World Apart*, however, the dismissal of the father from the narrative functions to construct a complex position towards privilege. As a plot device, it works to transfer the narrative to a more compromised place within the entitled world of white South Africa; the character of Molly. With the removal of the father, the narrative is left with Diana, the wife and mother, and Molly, the eldest child. As the narrative trajectory progresses, the film concentrates on neither character to the exclusion of the other, yet does organize itself around Molly over the mother; much of the film is rendered through her eyes—as further discussion will demonstrate—and prison scenes with the mother are frequently introduced through Molly's character.

Organizing the narrative around the character of Molly performs several functions for the film's rhetorical goals of exposing the operations of privilege. As a preteen, Molly is in a position in which she inherits the benefits of entitlement (exclusive schooling, dance lessons, expensive homes with house domestics) but, as the film makes clear, does not yet possess it. She is still subject to the authority of the adult world, an authority that rests upon, among other things, the physical superiority of adults—as Molly's humiliating confrontation with Yvonne's father demonstrates. The film thus organizes itself around the character of Molly as a principal means of exposing the structure and operations of privilege. As Diana Sippl argues, "*A World Apart* presents the viewer with a white world of which Molly [as a result of her upbringing by antiapartheid parents] is no longer a part. . . . Convertibles, pool parties, and Bossa Nova; class paranoia, race phobia, and slander."[6]

Molly's character allows the film to figure privilege—to make visible an abstract social process through the operation of individual character. As the film brings out the operations of exclusion and privilege for examination, the oppression at stake there is made visible too, no longer seeming natural or neutral, but contrived and exploitative. Several plot devices structured around Molly's character perform this exposing function. Many of these devices are constructed around Molly's age. As mentioned, Molly is a white preteen who inherits the benefits of apartheid. What the film makes clear, however, is that this is not the only thing Molly inherits, she also receives the social-justice, egalitarian, antiapartheid values of her parents—which sets her apart from the world of privilege. It is not simply that Molly is taunted by schoolmates and abandoned by a friend who previously stood by her. More significantly, the film makes apparent that Molly is not accepting of the ways and values of privilege. She stoically resists singing the white national anthem at a school assembly, chastises her friend Yvonne for calling a black waiter "boy," and demonstrates her preference for the company of the black kitchen staff to that of the white guests.

By organizing itself around Molly, then, the narrative trajectory does not merely build itself around a coming-of-age process (one that can also include the mother's conflict between the necessity of political action and the demands of raising a family without her husband). Rather, what is significant for the film's rhetorical strategy of exposing the operations of entitlement and exclusion is that the coming-of-age trajectory functions to figure those repressive operations, not naturalize and cover them. In this respect, the film works against the normative model of the Hollywood cinema. As Colin MacCabe demonstrates in his discussion of *American*

Graffiti, the coming-of-age narrative can be an effective structure for de-politicizing the social by transforming it into the personal.[7] This depoliticizing process, an important ideological practice of the Hollywood cinema, functions to repress or erase the power relations at stake within a social system by insisting on individual initiative and desire as determining outcomes. *A World Apart*, however, does the opposite: it politicizes the social by demonstrating its impact on the personal.

One plot device in particular functions to articulate the ways in which the film politicizes both the process of coming of age and the operations of discourse in general. Throughout the film, Molly is associated with the pop tune "Let's Twist Again." At first, Molly and her friend Yvonne are dancing with hula hoops as they play the tune on a record. The song thus becomes the occasion for innocent preteen fun. Later, Molly requests the tune from the band playing at the party for her mother, extending the song's function as a mode of entertainment and source of fun. In both cases, however, the song becomes a point of contact between Molly and Solomon, the African political activist and brother of Elsie, the domestic who works in Molly's house. The point of contact is established first by Solomon entering the narrative as Molly and Yvonne are dancing to the music, then by his presence and affectionate reaction when the tune is played at the party.

Throughout the narrative, the song as a point of contact between Molly and Solomon will be maintained by the latter consistently greeting Molly by referencing the song. Because of this association, the meaning of the song begins to change, not only for Molly, but within the meaning system of the film itself. It changes from an "innocent" pop-culture tune used to display Molly's preteen innocence to a more politically resonant reference to Molly's increased involvement with the struggle for freedom and equality through her ongoing relationship to Solomon.

The meaning of the song is transformed a third time when Molly goes with her family to visit her mother in prison. As she walks through prison corridors, Molly hears white Afrikaner women saying, "C'mon. Let's twist again." As she looks, Molly sees black African prisoners polishing the floors of the corridor by dancing on polishing cloths as the guards goad them with references to the song. Rendered through Molly's perspective, the association of the song with a dehumanizing prison routine brutally demonstrates not only the operation of power within privilege but also the political-social dimensions at stake when the powerful appropriate discourse: the song has lost all innocence when Molly hears it this time.

Rather, appropriated by a specific site of white concentration of power (the police and prison system) the song is distorted into an insidious prop for the exercise of power.

Furthermore, the prison scene is significant for making clear its rhetorical strategy of organizing itself around Molly. The film allows much of the plot to be rendered through Molly's eyes precisely because she lacks the introjection of those social discourses that naturalize the concentration of power and exclusion—and the necessary oppression that creates it. Molly is not only surrounded by that exclusion and entitlement, but also the discourses that naturalize and justify them. Molly's position within the film and within the story world, however, is that of not having fully adopted the signifying strategies that deny and make invisible the oppression at stake in creating entitlement and privilege. She is therefore confronted with the brutally repressive operations and effects of a social system that concentrates power. Without the necessary discourses to contain the operations of privilege, she witnesses its violence and repression in its most visible and repulsive forms: blacks being run over in the street by white motorists and receiving no aid; black children forcibly kept apart from their parents (a fate Molly will share); police breaking up parties with attack dogs, stopping white motorists who have black passengers, and breaking up black church services. Rather than coming to accept these events as natural, Molly is confronted with how severely unjust privilege is, how it fronts for hideous exercises of power, and how enormously difficult it is to resist—as the fate of her mother and father demonstrate.

Rendering the plot through Molly's eyes serves another important function within the film's rhetorical operations since it motivates the adoption of different narrative points of view. By constructing its narrative around a preteen and her struggle for identity, the plot provides the means by which to transfer its perspective to other characters—the characters that Molly identifies with. These characters take on the narrative and its trajectory independent of Molly precisely because the plot has established the importance of their activities for Molly to model herself upon. This kind of narrative motivation allows the plot to open itself out and away from Molly and the exclusive world of white South Africa. As a result, the narrative is taken up from the point of view of nonwhite characters, focusing on the effects of the politics of exclusion, and giving voice to the disenfranchised. Thus, Molly's identification with Elsie and Solomon allows the black African perspective to consistently enter into the plot. The film makes frequent reference to the effect of forced separation on Elsie, the housekeeper, and gives voice to black collective struggle through the character of her brother Solomon. The concept of voice here is significant. It is not just that the film shows Solomon leading black African workers in an industrial strike, but more that the narrative provides the space by which he can speak of repression and the need for revolution.

The need to cut these references short and get back to the main plot structured around white people—as was the case with *Driving Miss Daisy* and *Mississippi Burning* is significantly lacking in *A World Apart*, as is evidenced by the length of Solomon's speech, and the other sites at which the plot gives voice to black Africans (the speech for resistance at Solomon's funeral, Elsie's grief over her children). Furthermore, these sites of black African voice are not rendered as events whose purpose is solely defined by how they effect white characters. Elsie's grief is not portrayed as a means for showing how badly Molly feels about it. Neither is Solomon's arrest and torture conveyed as a means for showing its effect on the main characters. Indeed, none of the principal characters witness what happens to Solomon. Rather, representations of black voice and perspective are allowed to stand as the source of the narrative, not a colorful backdrop through which principal white characters will move. In this manner, the film avoids the process of representing privilege at the exclusion of black voice and perspective.

Instead, as the film's title suggests, black voice and perspective are shown in order to demonstrate that they are a world apart from privilege, and in the process, make the concentration of power, exclusion, and entitlement visible. Molly's character likewise functions in this respect, as she comes to occupy an unbearable position that exposes the many dimensions of privilege. Because she has accepted her parents' values, Molly is estranged from the world of exclusion, and will be unable to bring herself to join it. Having come to her parents' consciousness, she cannot occupy the place that ignores the operations of privilege. Harold's visit to Molly at school articulates the almost impossible position that Molly comes to occupy. Harold arrives at the school to inform Molly of the crushing news that her mother has been reincarcerated under the 90 Day Detention Act, a law that was originally used to imprison Diana in the first place. In discussing the devastating setback—Molly had been counting the days for her mother's release—Harold tries to remind Molly of the importance of continued struggle against the apartheid state. Molly, however, voices the temptation of taking up the far easier position of complicity—as the rest of the world of white South Africa that surrounds her has. When Harold asks her, however, what she really thinks of the people who take up that position, Molly has no response, silenced by her knowledge of how much she has already come to resent complicity with apartheid. Ill equipped to handle the vindictive retribution that accompanies resistance, and unable to take up a position of complicity, Molly has no place.

Molly's lack of a symbolic position is further articulated in the film by her visit with Elsie to Solomon's house. The scene makes clear that as a white Afrikaner, Molly cannot just simply join the world of nonprivilege. Her status as a white will not allow her to assimilate into the world of the disenfranchised blacks of South Africa, despite her affection for and identification with them. Her introduction to the township makes clear that despite her affinities she cannot erase the signifier of whiteness, as the exchange of glances between Molly and the two black South African young men demonstrate. Later, as one of only a few whites in the black church, Mollie is shown facing the awareness that although she may share in the struggle, she is not a part of the group. Molly listens self-consciously as Solomon describes the process by which whites invaded and confiscated both land and freedom. The editing of the scene emphasizes her increasing awareness that she cannot deny her status as white. Lacking a place in which to position herself as a full participant of a social group, Molly makes visible the divisions that the operation of privilege creates.

The scene in which Molly tries to contact Yvonne gives image to the sociopolitical dimensions of these divisions. Running to Yvonne's house because she cannot get through to her on the phone, Molly sees Yvonne playing with friends in the family pool. As Molly runs around to the front of the house, she is confronted by a large security gate, on which a sign warns that a guard dog protects the property. The entrance of Yvonne's father will make clear that Yvonne's sequestration results from her parents' indignation at Molly's parents and their antiapartheid social activism. Even before that exposition, however, the iconography makes clear that the divisions that privilege creates require enormous resources for their maintenance: houses with stone fences, steel security gates, intercoms, guard dogs.

Furthermore, as the scene also shows, the construction and operation of Molly's character make visible how these divisions depend on constructing themselves through a series of oppositions that become justified and naturalized. Yvonne's father demonizes Molly because of her parents, who, as he observes to others at a party, are communists. The necessity for those in power, such as Yvonne's father, to vilify communism is repeated elsewhere in the film by Diana Roth's interrogators in the prison. The repetition of the term and the contempt with which it is used by characters of exclusion and power make clear that the maintenance of privilege depends on the creation of an enemy that can justify its existence.

Another site of opposition is made clear in the text in the scene in which Molly visits Elsie's family. The stark contrast between the opulence of the world of privilege in which Molly and Yvonne live and the destitution of the village in which black South Africans live evidences the very real effects that privilege creates based on division by race. Further, as Solomon's speech at the church gathering will make clear, privilege—and the maintenance of privilege—is the *cause* of the poverty, and not just an unrelated and innocent counterpart within the social system of South Africa that coincidentally happens to be white.

In addition, the film also articulates the manner in which narrative itself functions as an important operation to the justifying process of this privilege. The history-lesson scene at Molly's school shows Molly's alienation from her peers as a result of her parents' activism, but it also shows the necessary internalization of narratives that justify the politics of exclusion upon which white South Africa is built and maintained. The history lesson Molly drifts away from is not an antique, random lesson on the civilizations of Greece or Rome, but rather covers the creation of the South African state by white settlers. The lesson the history teacher imparts to the students is the struggle of the white settlers—the Afrikaners—against the British empire, a struggle the Afrikaners won against considerable odds. Further, the lesson includes the suffering of Afrikaner women and children who were rounded up by the British and concentrated into refugee camps, where they would be poorly kept and exposed to diseases.

The function of the history lesson within the rhetorical operations of the film is to make visible the discourses of justification used in the creation of the white-minority ruled South African state. Because the scene is rendered through Molly's character, however, the function of the lesson is not to give validation to these discourses, but rather, to expose them as an ideological process whose function is the maintenance of exclusion and entitlement. Molly drifts away from the lesson because the history teacher imparts a narrative structured around the process of justification: of how the Afrikaners struggled against the world's superpower and won, and in the process suffered enormous—and unfair—consequences. The lesson's comparison to the American revolution completes the narrative by adding legitimization to the process of the narrative. The lesson is thus very much about justifying and legitimizing the taking of land from the indigenous African peoples and maintaining that appropriation through force. Within the scene, Molly's attention does not wander away solely because of her concern for her mother, but because she already rejects the ideological grounding of the lesson. Molly's character reveals that this history (and by implication, history itself) is not objective information, but rather narratives people accept to justify and legitimize specific social formations—in this case, white privilege.

Furthermore, rendering the scene through Molly's character reveals that this acceptance of narratives is not just an intellectual process, but occurs through the process of identity. Throughout the trajectory of the narrative, Molly is shown—literally and figuratively—constructing her character. She is shown imitating her mother at the mirror applying makeup (twice, in fact), taking dance lessons, sneaking wine at a party, and accompanying her mother to a demonstration. Molly is depicted as drifting away from the history lesson precisely because she has no basis for identification with it. Rather, her attention is drawn to a butterfly at the window seeking to get past an invisible barrier. The editing of the scene works to create a parallel between Molly and the butterfly by showing that rather than the history lesson, Molly is identifying with the butterfly. Like the butterfly, Molly seeks to get past the confines that the politics of white exclusion and entitlement imposes—frequently through such invisible processes as the discourses of legitimization, justification and naturalization. By comparison, the conduct of Molly's peers demonstrates that they are readily identifying with the narrative of the lesson and will grow to accept the operations of privilege and its maintenance.

It is through this process of illustrating Molly constructing her identity and trying to get out from her unbearable position that the film seeks to procure audience identification. The narrative trajectory that is organized around Molly is structured around the drive for wholeness: a primary drive of the ego that results from an individual's incompleteness, what Lacan describes as "lack in being." As discussed in the introductory chapter, part of the response to this incompleteness, or lack in being, is the introjection of traits, norms, values, and beliefs that structure an identity—an identity that will need to be continually reaffirmed. By structuring the narrative trajectory around Molly's drive for wholeness, the film establishes the means for a structural identification with its spectators, who can recognize in Molly's character their own desire for wholeness.

The plot establishes this structure within the narrative trajectory by absenting Molly's father, which constitutes a severe loss for Molly. As the narrative progresses, Molly suffers another significant loss when her mother is arrested and taken to prison. Molly's desire to be reunited with her parents functions to signify her incompleteness and gives form to her drive for wholeness. As the earlier discussion of Molly indicates, however, other plot elements also contribute to this structure, particularly her status as preteen and the manner in which it leaves her in a vulnerable and fragmented position: she is neither child nor adult. Throughout the narrative, the plot makes clear that Molly's separation from her mother is an obstacle to her desire for a less fragmented identity because of her dependence on Diana for identification.

The structural basis for Molly's identification is thus constructed around the desire for wholeness she seeks via reuniting with her parents, receiving her mother's support and affection, and being able to assume her mother's place in the struggle—to take up the symbolic mantle of her mother. It therefore affords to the spectator the opportunity to see their own desire for completeness with the character of Molly and her position within the narrative.

Furthermore, the film attempts to enjoin that structural basis for identification with a more specific symbolic identification with the struggle against apartheid. Within the trajectory of the narrative, Molly's struggle to achieve a stable identity is joined to the struggle against apartheid. The film thus affords its spectators with the opportunity to symbolically identify with the struggle, to recognize their own assumption of the values that Molly is struggling to adopt. The narrative is structured to provide the opportunity for spectators to have their individual commitment to social activism and the struggle for racial justice validated and confirmed. This confirmation and validation was especially in need given the status of both social activism and the struggle for racial justice within the broader social arena in which the film was seen.

A World Apart was released in 1988, a significant time in the history of both South Africa and the United States. South Africa in 1988 was only beginning what at the time was an imperceptible decline in maintaining the politics of exclusion and entitlement—its ability to do so closely bound to its relationship to the United States. During the 1980s, the U.S. government adopted a position with respect to South Africa that was termed "constructive engagement," which translated into the U.S. government adopting no sanctions against South Africa despite its repressive policies and gross violations of human rights. Under this policy, U.S. corporations doing business in South Africa, including such Fortune 500 companies as Ford and IBM, did not have to worry about facing financial repercussions from the government for their business activities in South Africa. As Jennifer Davis notes, U.S. companies had reason to be engaged in business activities in South Africa, having reaped large profits there. Thus she argues: "By 1981, U.S. direct investment totaled more than $2.6 billion, nearly triple the book value of investments made during the previous decade. U.S. investors, like other foreign investors, had been drawn to South Africa by very high rates of return—29 percent in 1980 and 19 percent in 1981, several percentage points higher than the average rates of return worldwide."[8] The economic benefits that American companies gained by doing business in South Africa were of great significance for that country's system of white exclusion and entitlement. Davis, for example, points to the manner in which throughout the 1960s and 1970s the U.S. consistently used its vote on the UN Security Council to veto economic sanctions against the country.[9] With momentum for sanctions growing in the 1980s, the U.S. government's support became vital to maintaining the system of racial stratification.

With such strong economic and political forces backing South Africa's system of apartheid, white privilege and aggression seemed very much able to entrench and fortify themselves. Not surprisingly, reaction against freedom for blacks in South Africa was exercised by both the government and nongovernmental paramilitary groups that the government did little to control. Although the struggle for a free South Africa intensified during this period, the forces of reaction seemed far superior and destined to prevail. As with social activism in the United States, the causes may have been morally superior, but made to seem ultimately hopeless.

The identificatory structures of the film are centered around defeating that hopelessness, and providing instead the means by which spectators can see the struggle for racial justice as both vital and valid. The film's setting points toward one of its strategies of identification. The film sets itself in a period of time that corresponds to the events and the situation of 1980s political activism. The film is set in the early 1960s, when the government of South Africa had been able to crack down on the struggle for freedom with near impunity and in gross violation of international human rights, with little international recrimination. Throughout the film, the coercive force of the state is shown to be well armed, far-reaching, and enormously powerful. Its mobilization against the demonstration at the funeral, for example, evidences an ability and resolve to put down large-scale protest with whatever means necessary.

In the face of such overwhelming advantage of power and coercive force, however, the film demonstrates the resolve of the collective to resist and dismantle such power. Through the characters of Molly and Diana, the film offers a site for identification affiliated with the commitment and perseverance of the collective, offering an image of hope for the struggle. Further, the film resolves its narrative conflict without having to dispense with either social activism (the struggle for freedom) or individual responsibility (love and care of family). With respect to the identity of its implied spectators, the film's discourse functions to confirm the belief in the moral virtue of the struggle. In addition, however, the film also encourages its spectators to see their own political situation with respect to social activism within the plot's setting. The narrative's appropriation of the past is not limited to a historical function but also functions allegorically as an object lesson in how resilient the collective can be in resisting a powerful and entrenched political system. Through allegory, the film attempts to expose the aura of invincibility that surrounds the maintenance of the status quo of inequity—to reveal its vulnerabilities and contingencies. In this respect, the allegorical function of the film's appropriation of the past is significant for the manner in which it encourages its spectators to identify with political activism: to see within the past their own current situation and keep up the struggle.

Such a strategy of identification is very much against the grain of Hollywood norms, which seek identification with complacency for the status quo, and the kind of complicity within it that *A World Apart* so devastatingly critiques in scenes like the pool party at Yvonne's house. The degree of this opposition can be evidenced by comparison to other contemporary films that appropriate the past such as *Driving Miss Daisy* and *Mississippi Burning*. Rather than taking an allegorical view, *Driving Miss Daisy* examines the past through nostalgia, whose function is to persuade its viewers that the issues of racism that it raises are consigned to the past (see Chapter 4). Spectators can thus identify with a rhetoric of complacency that exonerates them for their complicity in a social system of inequity that conducts itself through, among other things, the process of racism. *Mississippi Burning* does not adopt such a nostalgic view of the past, but still structures its identification with maintaining the status quo, positing racism as a problem for white society to take care of. *A World Apart* constitutes an alternative to these modes by structuring its identification against the status quo and against complacency and aligning it instead with active resistance to the status quo—an active resistance whose source is not white leadership, but rather the black African collective that conscientious whites like Gus and Diana—and later Molly—take up.

As with most narrative film, moreover, the symbolic identification that *A World Apart* seeks to procure is not confined to the social identities of its own society. Indeed, the structure of the narrative conflict between social activism and individual responsibility carries strong international resonance. As discussed earlier, the 1980s was a period of intensive reaction and containment against the activism and progressivism of the 1960s. In the U.S., this reaction galvanized around and was advanced by the Reagan presidency. In Britain, it took on political manifestation in the prime ministry of Margaret Thatcher. Both in the U.S. and in Britain, this period of reaction was advanced politically through conservative political parties obtaining and exercising power, and economically through market-friendly fiscal policies. In the U.S., this period was characterized by a government hostile to protecting the environment, workers, children, women, minorities, and public health, and eager for opportunities to showcase its exponentially increasing military spending.

With the working and middle classes far more vulnerable to financial instability—this was also a time of industrial downsizing—social activism and progressivism found themselves without the sympathetic audience they had cultivated in the 1960s, and with far fewer participants in their causes. Indeed, the powerful containment exercised against progressive social activism effectively isolated and marginalized it. The result was precisely the conflict that Diana Roth faces in *A World Apart*, as increasingly small numbers of people had to devote themselves to their causes with increasing energy and devotion to keep those causes alive. Furthermore, part of the ideological containment strategies of this reaction was the propagation of the myth that social activists sacrifice their home life, relationships, and general happiness by trading it for infatuation with their causes. The "angry feminist" and "angry young black man" were stereotypes that helped promote this myth.

Through its narrative conflict and resolution, *A World Apart* provides the means by which spectators holding on to progressivism in such a reactionary period can recognize themselves and receive validation. Further, it encourages spectators less inclined to be progressive and/or activist to abandon complacency because of its moral insufficiency. One of the means by which the film articulates this position is by confronting the myth of the conflict between social activism and individual responsibility. Through the trajectory of the plot, the film demonstrates that an important cause of such conflict is the willed ignorance of those within privilege: the consequences and costs of activism would be far less extreme if not for the willed complicity of those receiving the benefits of inequity and exclusion. Moreover, the symbolic resolution that the narrative provides to the conflict allows spectators to maintain both their progressivism and their personal relationships/individual responsibilities.

What is significant for the rhetorical operations of *A World Apart* and its making visible the politics of exclusion is the manner in which the film's identificatory structures, and its narrative conflict, refuse to subordinate the collective struggle against privilege and aggression to the figure of the individual. Molly and Diana are not only of privilege, but as main characters, hold privileged positions within the narrative. Nonetheless, the struggle for racial justice is not reduced to a dramatic backdrop through which Diana and Molly move, act, and enhance themselves. Quite the contrary, the struggle against exclusion and the violence that maintains it forms the basis for the narrative. Indeed, the continuing struggle is the basis by which the main characters are defined and constructed over their traits of privilege and wealth—it is the means by which they become main characters over the rest of the characters of entitlement. As such, the manner in which the narrative moves forward is structured around activism and resistance more than any one individual character goal or desire. The struggle for racial justice itself becomes the means by which the narrative goes forward.

The film's resolution of the narrative conflict confirms the central place of the struggle to the narrative, and the manner in which the struggle shapes, indeed pervades, the operation of character. Prior to the film's ending, opposition and resistance to privilege consistently advances or holds the narrative itself, as with the demonstration in the factory/industrial district, the numerous references to Elsie's children, Solomon's speech at the church, and the eulogy at his funeral. Even though the massive strike within the factory/industrial district is introduced through the characters of Diana and Molly, the narrative resists subordinating the event to their characters. The principal function of the strike within the plot is not to provide backdrop to the ongoing development of Diana and Molly's relationship, but rather, to advance the struggle itself—to foreground its place within the narrative. Indeed, within the dynamics of the plot Diana is there—in her role as reporter—to narrate the strike: to emphasize its role in advancing the ongoing struggle. Thus, the role that the strike plays within the narrative is to enhance the vitality of the struggle far more than it is to provide opportunity to embellish Diana's character. Unlike *Mississippi Burning*, the struggle for racial justice is not reduced to a theme or a dramatic backdrop whose function is to ennoble specific characters. Rather, *A World Apart* constructs the struggle as primary by defining the characters through it.

In addition to foregrounding the struggle for racial justice, the actual maintenance of exclusion and entitlement is made visible and prominent within the narrative, as with the police actions at the party and at the demonstration, their disruptive violence at the meeting in the church, their torturing of Solomon, and their interrogation of Diana. Within the narrative dynamics, the operation of privilege through the coercive power of the state functions not so much as obstacle, but rather as powerful and pervasive cause for a narrative—the means by which a narrative trajectory structured around the struggle propels itself. As a result, the narrative makes visible the function of government and police forces within a social system of inequity to maintain the power of the vested interests that benefit from structured entitlement. Further, the narrative dynamics make clear the moral ramifications of complacency within a social system of inequity: willed ignorance of the maintenance of exclusion through force is the means by which the violence is allowed.

The film's ending, in which the narrative conflict between social activism and individual responsibility is resolved, further evidences the centrality of the struggle against privilege to the narrative. The resolution to the narrative conflict begins with Molly attacking a police officer searching the house in order to protect her own previous invasion of Diana's privacy. When later reprimanded by Diana for her actions, Molly confronts Diana by revealing her knowledge of her mother's suicide attempt in prison. This confrontation brings to a climax the conflict between Diana's social activism and her responsibility to Molly. Molly comes to see that her exclusion from the struggle is not solely the result of her age—indeed, her mother waits for her to join the struggle—and Diana comes to see that Molly's inclusion is important for their ongoing relationship. The significance of this resolution is that it provides the symbolic means by which both Diana and Molly can choose political activism and participation in the struggle and not have to be coerced into complacency as a result of family responsibility. Indeed, precisely what the film repeatedly articulates is the necessity of participating in the struggle because of family responsibility: that parents are failing their children if they allow an unjust society to exist as a result of their own complacency.

The extension of this resolution into Solomon's funeral then functions to reassert the centrality of the struggle over individual characters—especially characters of privilege (as discussed previously, Molly and Diana are not only of privilege, but as main characters, hold privileged positions within the narrative). Solomon's funeral makes clear that Molly achieves a measure of wholeness by taking her place beside her mother in the struggle. She achieves her desired unity with her mother when she takes up the symbolic mantle of Diana, raising her fist with the others at Solomon's gravesite as she sings the black nationalist anthem *N'kosi sikelela I-Afrika*.

The plot defines this moment as Molly's taking up of her mother's position by structuring Molly's participation as a progression. When the collective begins singing at the grave, Molly joins in—having carefully learned the song from Elsie. It is only when she sees her mother singing with fist raised, however, that Molly raises her own fist. The parallels with Molly's gaze and her reactions from the earlier scene in the black church convey the manner in which Molly's action of the raised fist signals a move from affection and sympathy for Solomon (and for black South Africa) to joining the struggle and assuming a position of resistance alongside her mother. In the earlier scene Molly's reactions and gaze upon the blacks within the church convey her sense of being an outsider. Though sympathetic to Solomon's point of view, she is shown to be acutely aware of her status as white South African. In the latter scene, however, Molly's gaze provides the means by which to resolve her outsider status through the figure of her mother's activism. Molly comes to see that although she cannot shed her status as white South African and simply become a member of black South African society, she does not have to be an "outsider" either—in a world apart from both black and white societies in South Africa. Rather, as her mother demonstrates, she can find a place for herself within the struggle for freedom and racial justice. The narrative conveys Molly finding that place through Diana's unifying gesture of putting her arm around Molly, an action signifying her recognition of Molly's new place within the struggle.

Ending the film in such a manner might seem to subordinate the struggle against privilege to individual character—reducing it to dramatic backdrop through which mother and daughter are ultimately able to find each other. *A World Apart* resists such a subordination, however, by transferring Diana and Molly's unity and position in the narrative to the struggle itself. The film cuts from the medium shot of Diana and Molly to a wider shot of the two as they stand within the collective. The film then zooms out even

Molly finds her place in a deeply divided and violent society by joining her mother in the struggle for equality.

further to confirm Diana and Molly's position within the collective. As it does, the sounds of rifle-fire and helicopters are heard out of frame.

As the camera continues to pull back, the sound increases and the image of the helicopter can be seen landing in the background. While the collective continues singing at the gravesite, the film cuts to a shot of military trucks and another helicopter advancing towards the funeral. More closely framed shots of the militarized police deploying themselves are then intercut with shots of groups of blacks demonstrating, while the anthem continues to be sung. As the narrative progresses, the government forces begin firing tear gas against black demonstrators. With the song's concluding notes, the film zooms in to a single demonstrator picking up a rock to throw at the armed forces, while it progressively slows the rate of projection. The film ends with a freeze-frame of this act of defiance against the forces of privilege—immortalizing the act by taking it out of time, and asserting the centrality, necessity, and dignity of the struggle. The narrative significance of Diana and Molly's place within this struggle—out of frame and now out of site—has clearly been transferred and subordinated to the struggle itself.

Just as the funeral collective ends it chant, the film places a subtitle over the closing image of defiance. It states:

Ruth First (Diana Roth) was
assassinated on the 17th of August, 1982.
This film is for her and
for the thousands who have died
in the struggle for a free South Africa.

Placing the subtitle over the film's closing image of defiance does not, however, function to assert Diana's place over that of the conflict itself. Rather, the information of the subtitle operates to argue for the necessity of continued struggle by solemnly warning of the enduring (and vindictive) aggression of privilege. At the time of the film's release, South Africa was still under white minority rule. Within that context, the subtitle functions as a somber coda: emphasizing how persistent, violent, and vindictive the politics of exclusion and entitlement are, waiting for nearly twenty years to kill Diana (Ruth) for her involvement in the struggle. The subtitle, while expressing individual information, is thus no less a discourse about the social—articulating the necessity for continuing struggle against such a vindictive, violent, and morally bankrupt social system.

A World Apart concludes its strategy of making visible the structures and operations of privilege by asserting the central place of the struggle within its own signifying practice. As a result, the film demonstrates that the appropriation of the forms and structures of the language of the dominant does not in itself constitute reinforcing privilege. Indeed, appropriating the language of the dominant in order to expose and reveal its relationship to ideological and hegemonic processes can be an effective site of resistance. *A World Apart* thus goes beyond giving image to the struggle against privilege—it attempts to expose the invisible means by which privilege conducts itself, and the moral complacency necessary to maintain that invisibility.

Notes

1. Karen Jaehne, "The Press and Politics at Cannes '88," *Cineaste* 16(4) (1988), 9.
2. Ibid.
3. Ibid.
4. bell hooks, *Yearning: Race, Gender, and Culture Politics* (Boston: South End Press, 1990), 187.

5. Ibid., 188.

6. Diana Sippl, Review of *A World Apart, Cineaste* 17(1) (1989), 34.

7. Colin MacCabe, "Theory and Film: Principles of Realism and Pleasure," in Philip Rosen, ed., *Narrative, Apparatus, Ideology: A Film Theory Reader* (New York: Columbia University Press, 1986), 191.

8. Jennifer Davis, "Squeezing Apartheid," *Bulletin of the Atomic Scientists* 49(9) (November 1993), 16–20.

9. Ibid., 18.

7

School Daze and the
Politics of Appropriation

The 1980s was a complicated period for the marketing of Afro-American culture. As Ed Guerrero notes, the decade began with a trend of effacing and repressing Afro-American culture. He argues, "the 1980s saw a steady reduction of films with black narratives and leading roles as black actors found themselves increasingly pushed into the margins or background of the cinematic frame."[1] Guerrero also observes, however, there was a paradox to this effacement, for as Afro-Americans as a group and as a culture were losing ground, Eddie Murphy "emerged as Hollywood's most popular box-office draw."[2] As the decade came to a close, however, a dramatic shift had occurred with respect to the mass media and Afro-American culture. Among other things, the decade ended with the rise of hip-hop music, the expansion of television programming centered around Afro-American characters, and the emergence of several Afro-American film directors, led by Spike Lee. Though far from being the first Afro-American film director, Lee was one of the first whose films not only developed an "Afro-American aesthetic" but drew attention to the commercial viability of Afro-American culture.

As Sharon Willis demonstrates, Lee's work did not so much cause this commercial viability as function within it: his films coincided with a broader cultural shift from "repressing race" to "consuming it."[3] Nonetheless, the relationship between Lee's films and dominant culture's interest in reducing black culture to the status of commodity—a means of maintaining privilege—involves a complex confrontation between antagonistic signifying practices. Chapters 7 and 8 analyze two of Lee's films,

School Daze and *Do the Right Thing*, as a means of delineating the parameters of that confrontation.

The primary site of that confrontation is the previously discussed language of the dominant—a specific culture's established and preferred system for depicting reality—and its consistent striving for invisibility as a conduit for the operations of privilege. Several film scholars, including Jean-Luc Comolli and Jean Narboni, have discussed the manner in which the specific stylistic elements that make up the norms of classical Hollywood cinema function within this preference for invisibility.[4] Such cinematic elements as continuity editing, three-point lighting, and staging in depth, as well as nonimage elements such as sound fidelity and character-centered, goal-oriented narrative, contribute to a very unobtrusive story-telling system that seeks to convey its meanings without reference to its source. This system is both shaped and valued by the goals and objectives of dominant culture for its ability to function inconspicuously as a site for reducing the structures and operations of privilege and inequity. Character-centered, goal-oriented narrative, for example, corresponds to dominant culture's insistence on the individual's ability to achieve their goals through hard work and effort—the result of the freedoms that society affords. This discourse seeks to minimize, if not erase, the social barriers like class, gender, and race that restrict certain freedoms and impede and prevent an individual from achieving economic and social mobility. The repetition of character-centered, goal-oriented narrative that consistently ends with the obtainment of goals and desires participates in that process of denying the role of social barriers.

School Daze and *Do the Right Thing*, however, both intervene in that process; the films offer different but related approaches to confront the inconspicuous operations of the language of the dominant. In the case of *School Daze*, this approach can be characterized as appropriation and intervention; with *Do the Right Thing*, as subversion and transformation. These two approaches, while different, nonetheless constitute processes that seek to expose and critique the language of the dominant and its maintenance of privilege.

The first of these films, *School Daze*, does not at first seem to offer much critique of the language of the dominant. The narrative, and the cinematic style that presents it, are very much within the norms of classical cinema: realist mise-en-scène, characters with consistent traits, clear motivations, and goals, editing patterns that conform to character actions and interactions, and clearly defined narrative transitions. At several important junctions, however, the film foregrounds its appropriation of classical style and exposes the structural operations at stake there. The film's opening introduces this rhetorical practice.

After the studio, and a series of production attributes, the film opens with a title logo in the middle of the frame. The style of the logo is dynamic and contemporary, and prepares the audience to enter into the story world that is about to unfold. Instead, the next image, which coincides with the soundtrack spiritual "I'm Building Me a Home," goes back into history, portraying the layout of slaves on a slave ship as rendered in the antebellum period itself. As the spiritual continues, the images progress chronologically, each portraying a particular stage in black history. As the credits at the end of the film will indicate, each of these images can be situated within a progression of "uplifting the race."

In many respects, the opening can be characterized as self-conscious. The scope of the images is fairly wide, including education, entertainment, sports, politics, and social movements. The transitions between images and areas is frequently based on graphic similarity and/or visual metaphor with the lyrics of the soundtrack. Furthermore, the pace of the sequence, moving as it does from poor shanties to successful black leaders, is studied and deliberate. All these factors work to articulate the centrality of race within the upcoming narrative. Thus, although the film begins within the conventions of contemporary Hollywood production, it quickly shifts to a more self-conscious style. The function of that style is to make clear that, unlike the Hollywood system it appropriates, this film is not going to subordinate, set aside, or ignore the issue of race within the narrative.

The opening scene confirms this sense by using a student-led protest against South Africa as a means of establishing the story world—or diegesis. The editing of the scene, while not as self-conscious as the opening or other moments in the plot, nonetheless functions to build the space of the story, while organizing itself around the narrative action of Dap, one of the main characters, as he leads the protest. Within the dynamics of plot, however, the protest quickly evolves into a complex confrontation between different Afro-American constituencies over issues of cultural/racial integrity. Cinematically, the title sequence and the opening are fairly conventional, functioning within established norms of contemporary film. Narrative operations, however, begin a process of exposing those conventions. By making clear that the film is going to focus on race, and confirming that focus in the plot's opening and dynamics, the film begins the process whereby the appropriation of the classical cinema functions in service of exploring issues within Afro-American culture, rather than the far more conventional marginalization that it has been used for.

As the narrative progresses, the film will create a dialectical relationship between narrative and cinematic style, where each will appropriate the classical style but function to transform the other. In order to analyze this appropriation and its transformation accurately, a degree of definition is necessary. In their discussion of classical Hollywood cinema, Bordwell, Staiger, and Thompson argue that:

> The Hollywood cinema sees itself as bound by the rules that set stringent limits on individual innovation. . . . Telling a story is the basic formal concern. . . . Unity is a basic attribute of film form. . . . The Hollywood film purports to be 'realistic' in both an Aristotelian sense (truth to the probable) and a naturalistic one (truth to historical fact). . . . The Hollywood film strives to conceal its artifice through techniques of continuity and 'invisible' storytelling. . . . The film should be comprehensible and unambiguous.[5]

Focusing on Hollywood's perception of itself as bound by rules, Bordwell, Staiger, and Thompson define the classical film as playing out a dynamic normative system that operates on three levels: devices, systems, and relations of systems.[6] By devices, Bordwell, Staiger, and Thompson refer to individual technical elements, such as close-up camera framings, dissolves, or three-point lighting. Because individual elements themselves do not comprise film style, Bordwell, Staiger, and Thompson define two more levels of classification. Systems refers to what they describe as "a set of functions and relations" for individual technical elements. This refers to the manner in which individual technical elements are organized to perform specific tasks like denoting the passage of time, creating space for the story, conveying cause and effect relationships. Finally, Bordwell, Staiger, and Thompson point to the necessity of being able to examine how different systems relate to each other in a specific film, which they describe as the third level, the relations between systems.

The significance of these different levels is that it allows film analysis to delineate the manner in which a particular technical element functions to convey meaning without having to argue that individual film techniques have an inherent meaning or even an inherent function. Rather, as was discussed previously, it is through a dynamic relationship between elements and systems that meaning is constructed. This distinction is particularly important to the study of racism and film because it prevents analysis from inaccurately concluding that individual cinematic techniques themselves—like close-ups or narrative point of view—inherently participate in the process of racism. Previous discussions of narrative point of view in *The Birth of a Nation, Driving Miss Daisy,* or *Mississippi Burning* demonstrate this point. The discussion in these films demonstrate the manner in which narrative point of view functions as a means of engendering and reinforcing privilege. The narrative point of view in these films is the point of view of privilege as a means of sustaining its position. A film like *A World Apart,* however, demonstrates that conjoining narrative point of view with the position of privilege does not in and of itself reinforce privilege—indeed, it can be used to criticize and expose privilege. Likewise, a film like *The Gods Must Be Crazy* indicates a kind of reverse danger of simply condemning narrative point of view as being inherently racist. By switching points of view, but nonetheless naturalizing and justifying privilege in the process, *The Gods Must Be Crazy* demonstrates that narrative point of view can be aligned with nonwhite and/or nonprivileged cultures but still articulate the ideologies of privilege.

The levels Bordwell, Staiger, and Thompson discuss places an emphasis on delineating the process by which meanings are both constructed and validated as a result of dynamic relationships between elements. How a film participates in the process of racism depends on its particular modes of signifying on all three of the levels they describe.

The significance of *School Daze* (and, as Chapter 8 will illustrate, of *Do the Right Thing)* is the manner in which it confronts classical norms and their participation in the process of racism on all three of the levels Bordwell, Staiger, and Thompson describe.

The primary site for *School Daze*'s appropriation of classical narrative is the level of system, particularly with the system of narrative logic. *School Daze* appropriates the structure of binary opposition within narrative conflict and foregrounds its role within the narrative logic of the Hollywood cinema. In their discussion of narrative, Bordwell, Staiger, and Thompson argue, "here in brief is the premise of Hollywood story construction: causality, consequence, psychological motivations, the drive toward overcoming obstacles, and achieving goals. Character-centered . . . causality is the armature of the classical story."[7] In other words, classical narrative is character-centered, goal-oriented narrative: conflict between the character's goals, and obstacles to achieving it, functions to move the narrative forward. Within this structure, the conflict that drives the narrative forward is usually organized around two competing, indeed opposing, characters. Bordwell, Staiger, and Thompson argue, "Melodrama's formula of hero versus villain, never too hoary for Hollywood, depends upon the clash of opposed purposes."[8] As several film genres like the western demonstrate, the competing characters frequently engender opposing values or ideologies. Thus, as Thomas Schatz has pointed out, the hero of the western often represents one site in a conflict between civilization (with laws and normative behavior) and frontier (where the only law is strength, will, and competence—in short, survival of the fittest).[9]

It is precisely this binary opposition within narrative conflict that *School Daze* appropriates. In a film that announces its focus on race, the plot establishes its conflict within that context—as an antagonism between two competing views on how best to uplift the race. This conflict is introduced when the character Julian (also known as Dean Big Brother Almighty) along with the members of his fraternity (Gamma Phi Gamma), their pledges (the Gammites), and their Little Sisters (the Gamma Rays) disrupt the South Africa protest led by Dap and his followers. The argument between Dap and Julian makes clear that the interruption of the protest was not coincidental—Julian ideologically opposes what Dap is doing. That the conflict is ideologically charged is made evident by the manner in which Dap and Julian, and their followers, nearly come to blows, and by the way in which the narrative will return to the conflict at several junctures.

As the narrative progresses, this conflict is defined as an opposition of black solidarity or cultural integrity on the one hand, and assimilationism on the other. In the language of the film, the conflict is expressed as the antagonism between the jigaboos and the wannabees. In establishing this narrative conflict, the film appropriates a convention of the classical Hollywood cinema, where the binary opposition between two competing interests engenders two antagonistic ideologies. According to that convention, the resolution of the conflict in classical cinema involves the narrative validating—and therefore privileging—one ideological position over the other. Thus it is that in classical westerns, the figure of law and order wins out over lawlessness and anarchy.

By appropriating such a conventional narrative form, *School Daze* holds out the promise to its spectators of resolving Afro-American ideological conflict and in the process reveals the truth about Afro-American cultural identity—defining once and for all (in other words, finalizing) what it means to be Afro-American. Moreover, following another convention of classical cinema/narration, the narrative trajectory adds to the complexity of the conflict by heightening and delaying its resolution. The elaborate, and outside of the story, musical-dance scene at Madame Re-Res Beauty Salon is an example of this convention.

The scene begins with a confrontation in the hallway of the women's dorm between the Gamma Rays, led by Jane, and the unaligned women led by Rachel. As the confrontation escalates into name-calling, the film makes clear that the two groups are defined by the already established opposition between assimilationists and cultural purists. As with the earlier confrontation between Dap and Julian, this standoff progresses to the point where violence could be imminent. Before it manifests, however, the film cuts to a space outside the actual world of college—Madame Re-Res's salon. There, the women do ideological battle through the choreography of singing and dancing. The function of the scene is made clear by the manner in which the film returns to the space of the standoff in the hallway; the space of the beauty parlor and the action that occurs there allows the confrontation to express itself physically yet without actual violence.

The scene thus functions in several different dimensions. The first of these is within the operation of plot: the number allows the film to heighten and delay the conflict's resolution. It heightens the conflict by extending it beyond Julian and Dap (and the men they would lead) to Jane and Rachel (and the women they would lead). It also heightens the conflict by reestablishing the brinkmanship that this clash of ideologies engenders—the conflict is consistently on the verge of creating violence. In this respect, the musical-dance scene functions to delay the conflict's resolution by displacing the violence to a symbolic space, where it is then removed from the story world itself. As a result, the plot avoids, at this juncture, the kind of culminating violence that frequently characterizes conflict resolution in classical narrative. Without that kind of culmination, the conflict can continue to move the narrative forward.

In addition to this temporal dimension of plot, however, the scene operates within another dimension, which could be described as an intertextual dimension. The highly self-conscious scene, which bursts into the narrative with no stylistic motivation, is clearly modeled on the genre of the lavish Hollywood musical. The scene's self-consciousness, however, allows spectators to see the manner in which the film is not simply mirroring but *displaying* the form of the Hollywood musical. Thus in addition to expressing the dimensions of its own narrative conflict—the themes of the confrontation from the dorm are expressed within the music and choreography—the film attempts here to show its audience the manner in which musical numbers function to express the ideological positions of their narratives. In this respect, the film tries to expose the "innocence" of the musical's "entertainment" and demonstrate its participation in ideological warfare.

In addition to this intertextual dimension with respect to the musical, the scene also operates within a more specific dimension of race and representation. To begin with, the musical number articulates the manner in which the narrative conflict is expressed through image: each camp espouses a different aesthetic of hair based on their concept of race. Even further, though, each camp references—and attempts to expose—the role of cinematic representation in the construction of race. At a certain point, each group holds up a photographic image of a face from the Hollywood cinema as the ideal image of their counterparts. Even before this highly reflexive plot device, the wannabees strike an intertextual pose of Hollywood's image of the smiling jigaboo. All these elements work together to articulate the manner in which the construction of race is dependent on a hegemony of ideal social images.

The complexity of the scene thus indicates that in addition to appropriating the conventions of classical Hollywood cinema, *School Daze* is intent on exposing those conventions as they relate to racism and the construction of race. This subversive agenda is further evidenced by the manner in which the plot renders its evaluative position ambiguously—and uses that ambiguity as a mechanism for heightening and delaying the conflict's resolution. This evaluative ambiguity manifests itself within the plot by the manner in which narrative operations render each group within the conflict both positively and negatively.

Dap and the cultural purists are evaluated positively for their solidarity with the struggle against apartheid, but more than once the plot indicates that Dap can place ideals above individuals. He turns on his friends when they cannot share in his absolute commitment, and has to be corrected by them for being too dismissive of their relationship. Furthermore, he is accused by his girlfriend Rachel of being attracted to her because of his ideology of racial purity. Even here, however, the plot does not render Dap's trait of ideals over individuals as absolute, since Dap is supportive of his cousin Half-Pint and the latter's attempt to join the Gammas. Despite his intense loathing of the fraternity, Dap supports his cousin out of family solidarity.

In the highly stylized musical dance number, each side of the conflict appropriates images from the classical Hollywood cinema to degrade the other.

Conversely, the plot does not render Julian and the assimilationists in consistently negative terms. Rather, they are shown to be very much concerned with black cultural integrity. From the beginning, when Julian expresses his solidarity for the South Africans, the film demonstrates that the position of the assimilationists is not necessarily a *denial* of Afro-American culture. Indeed, as Julian's later argument with Dap makes clear, the assimilationists see themselves as dedicated to uplifting the race—and Afro-American cultural identity—just as much as the black solidaritists. Their position is lent support through Dap's own girlfriend Rachel—the leader of the jigaboo women—when she points out to him that Afro-American cultural integrity cannot be based on racial integrity, which is a myth. If for no other reason, Rachel points out that the scope of racial inmixing that occurred during slavery, when the rape of black slaves by their white masters was a widespread cultural phenomenon, eliminates any plausibility for an appeal to racial integrity as a basis for black cultural integrity. In addition to his expressed solidarity with South Africans, Julian derides the manner in which Dap's pan-Africanism displaces and devalues Afro-*American* culture. As he states proudly, he is from Detroit—Motown—one of the rich cultural centers of Afro-American life.

Within the contours of the plot, *School Daze* consistently demonstrates that this evaluative ambiguity is not just an aesthetic function—a way of fashioning the kind of "well-rounded" characters to which film critics would give a hearty "thumbs up." Rather, characters and characterizations are consistently constructed around ideological complexity as a means of subverting the simple binarism of the classical cinema. The excessive materialism of the Gamma culture demonstrates this point. As opposed to other students in the film, students associated with Gamma society—the brothers, the pledges, the Gamma Rays—are consistently associated with upscale material objects, especially clothing. There seems to be no end to the amount and styles of clothing that Gamma society possesses, as evidenced by the stunning costumes of the Gamma court. Even the sweatshirts they wear are multicolored, highly styled, and emblazoned with Gamma iconography.

Even here, however, the film does not construct this association with upscale materialism as a completely negative and one-dimensional ideological trait that demonstrates assimilationist desires. Rather, in a manner that parallels the refusal of Dap's friends to risk their college education for the cause, the film articulates the ideological complexity that is at stake in the possession of upscale material objects. Lack of access to material comfort is precisely one of the economic barriers racism imposes; and breaking through such barriers, no matter how co-opted by the status quo, consequently becomes a form of resistance (albeit a limited one). In this manner, *School Daze* subverts the simple binarism of classical cinema, and creates a sense of ambiguity out of ideological complexity.

Ideological complexity is also created by the manner in which the film constructs each side as sharing the same negative traits as the other. This is particularly the case with the sexism of both the Gamma Men and the unaligned men led by Dap. Each group repeatedly reduces women to the status of sexual objects for male gratification. The repetitiveness of their sexism, and its unquestioned acceptability within both groups, makes clear that each group sees both sexism and sexual gratification as a means of compensation for the burden of racism.

The film renders this ideology of black sexism as naturalized—it comes readily to males in each group—and largely unchallenged—its only interior critique comes from "the nerd" who is immediately put down. Its critique is thus not as visible as other criticisms the film levels. Two interrelated narrative elements, however, work to convey the film's critique against sexism. The first of these is the overemphasis on Half-Pint's virginity. By raising this character trait to the level of subplot, the film makes visible the sexist trope of intercourse as a right of passage. Accordingly, within the context of the film, this emphasis on Half-Pint's right of passage articulates the manner in which the right to a woman's body is seen as compensation for living in a racist society.

The second narrative element that advances this critique is Jane's submission to Julian's request to have sex with Half-Pint. As further discussion will indicate, the plot refrains from having a culminating narrative action. Nonetheless, it is Jane's liaison with Half-Pint that comes closest to functioning as culminating device, and as such the scene is invested with significance. The stark contrast between Jane's reaction to this demeaning, dehumanizing encounter and the congratulatory attitude of the fraternity brothers functions as pointed critique of sexism. Further, by having this sexism shared by both groups, the film refuses to limit its critique to Gamma society, but indicts all the men in the film. This critique of both groups, then, creates an ideological complexity that subverts the simple binarism of the classical style, and works to expose its role in validating ideologies of exclusion (like race and gender).

The most pronounced subversion of classical norms, however, comes at the film's resolution, or denouement. In their discussion of classical narrative, Bordwell, Staiger, and Thompson argue that the classical narrative ends "with a definite action which resolves the chain into a final effect (the climax) and which lingers to establish a new situation of stasis at the end."[10] This ability to end with a new form of stasis the authors refer to as "classical closure."[11] An analysis of *School Daze* demonstrates that the film not only subverts this classical structure, but fairly rejects it.

To begin with, *School Daze* does not provide the "definite action" that resolves the causal chain of the plot. Half-Pint's sexual liaison with Jane is motivated only by very minor subplot: Julian's desire to end his relationship with Jane, and the issue of Half-Pint's virginity. Its impact on the narrative is out of proportion to its motivation, and thus its function as culminating event is unexpected. Precisely what the narrative subverts, then, is the resolution of causal chains. The conflict that has been set in motion by the ongoing ideological tension between the assimilationists and the cultural purists is not resolved by Half-Pint's "actions" or Jane's "sacrifice." Their coupling does not even join the two sides of the narrative conflict, since they are both from the assimilationist side.

Rather than being resolved, then, the narrative conflict is dissolved. There is no culminating action that validates one side of the conflict over the other and provides spectators with the expected answer as to the essence of Afro-American identity. Instead, it is the effects of the subplot around Julian, Half-Pint's actions, and Jane's sacrifice that motivate Dap to dissolve the narrative conflict. The film does not validate either Dap's ideological position nor Julian's, but rather, through Dap's actions, discards each as part of the problem and not of the solution.

In the film's ending, Dap begins ringing the bell on the main lawn and urgently yells at the other characters, and by extension, the spectators, to "Wake up." The level of stylization in this scene clearly indicates that Dap's urgent request is to be read as figurative and not literal: though characters who have appeared throughout the narrative stumble out of their beds, houses, and dormitories and walk to where Dap is standing, the use of slow motion, direct address to the camera, high-key lighting, extreme camera angles, and other elements work to create a highly self-conscious narration. The function of this self-consciousness is to distance Dap's message from the story world itself: it is of the story world, but is not limited to it. Demonstrating an awareness of itself, the film's conclusion provides the means by which the message can transcend the story world, and thus be read allegorically.

It is through the allegorical meaning of Dap's message that *School Daze* dispenses with the very conflict it has established, heightened, and delayed through the progression of the narrative. As the final scene reaches its ending, Julian comes into the space of the lawn. He slowly takes his place next to Dap, the two stare into each other's eyes, then they turn towards the camera. Dap, looking directly into the camera with Julian beside him, urges, "Please, wake up." As he does, the film freezes the frame, and slowly fades the image from color to black and white. With such a conclusion, the film decidedly refrains from validating either Dap or Julian's previous ideological position. Instead, the narration makes clear that Dap and Julian abandoned their ideological conflict, and instead, reached some sort of unity.

The source of that unity is articulated by the plot through its emphasis on the look into each other's eyes by Dap and Julian. Several elements of plot work to create this emphasis on the look: camera framing, gesture, makeup, and lighting. The camera frames the two figures tightly, as a means of focusing on the painful searching in the exchange of looks. Further, a subtle acknowledgment of each to the other is conveyed through facial expressions. The acknowledgment at stake in the exchange of looks articulates the manner in which the two characters come to see beyond the limitations of their ideological struggle and instead, see the other for who he is: an equal in the struggle to uplift the race. In this respect, Dap and Julian share in the same humanity, a point that the film privileges over the ideological conflict in which they had been engaged, and which the narrative has abandoned.

This abandonment of the conflict is thus a significant rejection of classical style and the ideological framework of domination it articulates. *School Daze* establishes but then dispenses with the manner in which the classical style engenders the structure of conflict/competition, and through the repetition and resolution of that structure, renders domination as a natural structure.[12] Precisely what *School Daze* rejects, then, is the structure of validating an ideological position based on the successful outcome of conflict/competition. In so doing, the film asserts that uplifting the race will not occur through the resolution of conflicts over what defines Afro-American identity, but rather, will be accomplished through solidarity and respect for the humanity of all. In this respect, the narrative trajectory functions as an intervention against black liberation struggle adopting the very structures of domination it works against. As bell hooks argues: "Assimilation, imitation, or assuming the role of rebellious exotic other are not the only available options, and never have been. This is why it is crucial to radically revise notions of identity politics, to explore marginal locations as spaces where we can best become whatever we want to be while remaining committed to liberatory black liberation struggle."[13]

Moreover, by dispensing with the narrative conflict that the plot has built up so complexly, *School Daze* attempts to make visible how the structure of narrative works. Lacking narrative motivation, the abandonment of the conflict is a startling development that functions to foreground the very structure of the narrative itself. This foregrounding of narrative structure reveals how specific ideological positions are validated through the structure of successful conflict resolution. Given its self-announced concern with uplifting the race, *School Daze's* rejection of classical style demonstrates an unwillingness to passively adopt the norms and style of classical Hollywood cinema, a cinema that exercised an enormous role in promoting and maintaining the process of racism, not only through stereotypes, but through several cinematic conventions, among them, as discussed here, the naturalizing of domination politics through narrative form. The ending scene's rejection of several realist techniques—rate of projection, lighting, camera angles—points to the complicity of other conventions as well. Through these technical elements, for example, the classical system renders American society—a social system of inequity—as stable and orderly; a stability that depends on, among other things, complacency with racism and willed ignorance of both the injustices it causes and the struggles against it. Recognition of either of these social operations undermines a view of society as "stable."

In its attempt to critique this politics of representation, *School Daze* is not, to be sure, without limitations. Indeed, while the film consistently subverts Hollywood cinema, the visibility of the narrative's rejection of classical style and its ideological underpinnings may come too late, recognized only at the ending. As a result, the rejection is counterbalanced by a narrative trajectory that has so much momentum it creates potential for overwhelming its own planned derailment—inviting misreadings that provide the clear resolution the plot itself rejects.

Prior to the ending, the film's stylistic flourishes also work against accurately reading its pointed critique of Hollywood and domination ideology. This is certainly the case with the musical-dance number in the hair scene. The lyrics of the song insist that what is being talked about is "good and bad hair," despite the fact that other lyrics within the song, as well as the choreography itself, demonstrate otherwise that there is a larger conflict at stake. The scene is thus self-consciously aware of how aesthetic and stylistic flourish can bury critique just as much as they can effectively disguise it. For all its self-consciousness, however, the scene is still too easily read as the film (and/or director) flaunting stylistic prowess, and the sophisticated critique and commentary engendered within the music and choreography can be readily overlooked.

This seems particularly the case with one of the film's more popular scenes: the dance in the gym to the EU Band number "Da Butt." In many respects, the scene is important to the rhetorical operations of the film because of the manner in which it is a space where the binary conflict between the two sides is not only suspended, but absent. Furthermore, and as a result of that abandonment of the conflict, the scene models collective unity: though each individual must dance to the same beat, they can do so with a high degree of individuality. Despite these important rhetorical functions, however, the scene was predominately read for its "hipness." Houston A. Baker, Jr., for example writes that the scene made "'Da Butt' a national dance" that "ran far ahead of the film's general popularity." He further mentions that "I remember a Philadelphia deejay asking one of his call-ins to discuss Lee's movie. All the young man could say was: "Did you check out that dance, man? Did you see it? Da Butt is hip."[14] The film's potential for misreading is of significance because of the manner in which, without recognition of the ideological critiques the film levels, the film itself can function to reinforce the very system of representation it is trying to dismantle, as Amiri Baraka's reading of the film demonstrates. In his synopsis of the film, Baraka criticizes the manner in which "the light-skinned/dark-skinned conflict eschews actual class analysis. It is dealt with as 'a number,' a bit of music, ahistorical and cartoonish, reduced to the beat of a sorority competition." This leads Baraka to conclude that the film "is not a real wake-up; it's a buppie on the way up."[15] Such a reading, however, itself "reduces" textual operations by overlooking the manner in which the film is engaged in critiquing the norms and conventions of representation, rather than merely passively adopting them. Not coincidentally, the film urges it spectators to "wake up" at the moment in which the film most visibly exposes these conventions and their relationship to ideology.

The potential and realized complications of misreading are thus fundamental for *School Daze*'s ability to function as critique of the politics of representation as they relate to racism. As Ed Guerrero argues: "The issue is that the shift toward, and refinement of Lee's big-screen, glossy images . . . subtly but effectively betray the insurgent possibility of rendering the nuances of black life in a fresh cinematic language."[16] While opposing the passive adoption of the norms and conventions of the classical cinema, the strategies of representation employed in *School Daze* nonetheless depended on such conventions for their meaning, and thus did not articulate what the alternative would be—what an emancipatory cinema would look like. As the next chapter will demonstrate, that project would be taken up, and boldly articulated, in *Do the Right Thing*.

Notes

1. Ed Guerrero, *Framing Blackness* (Philadelphia, Pa.: Temple University Press, 1993), 114.

2. Ibid.

3. Sharon Willis, *High Contrast: Race and Gender in Contemporary Hollywood Film* (Durham and London: Duke University Press, 1997), 159.

4. Jean-Luc Commolli and Jean Narboni, "Cinema, Ideology, Criticism," in Bill Nichols, ed., *Movies and Methods,* vol. 1 (Berkeley: University of California Press, 1976). See also, in the same volume, J. A. Place and L. S. Peterson, "Some

Visual Motifs of Film Noir"; Brian Henderson, "Toward a Non-Bourgeois Camera Style"; and Bill Nichols, "Style, Grammar, and the Movies."

5. David Bordwell, Janet Staiger, and Kristen Thompson, *The Classical Hollywood Cinema: Film Style and Mode of Production to 1960* (New York: Columbia University Press, 1985), 3.

6. Ibid., 6.

7. Ibid., 13.

8. Ibid., 16.

9. Thomas Schatz, *Hollywood Genres: Formulas, Filmmaking, and the Studio System* (Philadelphia, Pa.: Temple University Press, 1981), 30.

10. Bordwell, Staiger, and Thompson, *Classical Hollywood*, 175.

11. Ibid., 370.

12. What marxist critical theory demonstrates is that rather than a natural structure, competition and conflict are two organizational modes that are valued and encouraged by the various forms of capitalism, and its commodification of people and objects.

13. bell hooks, *Yearning: Race, Gender, and Cultural Politics* (Boston: South End Press, 1990), 20.

14. Houston A. Baker, Jr., "Spike Lee and the Commerce of Culture," in Manthia Diawara, ed., *Black Cinema* (New York: Routledge Press, 1993), 167.

15. Amiri Baraka, "Spike Lee at the Movies," in Manthia Diawara ed., *Black Cinema* (New York: Routledge Press, 1993), 148.

16. Guerrero, *Framing Blackness*, 147.

8

Do the Right Thing:
Style as Confrontation

In 1989 *Do the Right Thing* lit up both movie screens and controversy, as an indignant media immediately criticized the film's representation of violence as a call to action. By representing Spike Lee as the stereotypical angry young black man, the media created an interpretative context that made *Do the Right Thing* one of the most misread and misunderstood films of the late-twentieth century. Thus, in her discussion of the film, Sharon Willis describes the manner in which the mainstream (and mainly white) press overemphasized and misinterpreted the violence within the film. Willis argues: "In the weeks following *Do the Right Thing's* release, the film's 'message' became a site of struggle as journal after journal set up the debate in terms like these from *U.S. News and World Report*: 'Doing the Controversial thing: A provocative discussion of race relations in the 1980s or a racist incitement to riot?'"[1] As Willis suggests, the controversy over *Do the Right Thing* reflected the white press's discomfort over a black director confronting the issue of race; hence the media's consistently implying, when not outright arguing, that the film was a call to violence.

What this chapter demonstrates is that *Do the Right Thing* not only confronts the issue of race relations in its urban milieu, but also constitutes a sustained confrontation of Hollywood norms and style and the ideological meanings these norms and style engender in relation to racism. For a film to confront an institution and mode of experience (like the Hollywood cinema) to which dominant culture is powerfully attached would in itself provoke reaction. To combine such a confrontation with the delicate issue of racism, which dominant white culture has steadily tried to suppress as an issue and ignore as a social reality, constitutes a significant challenge to the comfortable invisibility of the operations of privilege.

Do the Right Thing begins this process of confrontation and appropriation before the narrative even begins. The credit sequence begins with a slow and easy jazz melody playing over the studio logo. The image then transfers over to the logo for the production company, followed by the film's title. Both the music and the title fade to black. The music, however, is replaced immediately with the uptempo and complex music of Public Enemy's *Fight the Power*. The image fades up to fast-paced cutting that follows the beat of the music; this editing technique has the effect of giving motion to a female figure (Rosie Perez) standing in different positions in front of brownstone apartment buildings. The camera zooms in and the woman begins dancing to the song as the lyrics start.

In some respects, this sequence can be said to adhere to the norms for Hollywood credit sequences (a part of the plot to which the system grants a large amount of stylistic flexibility). It has become standard practice for the credit sequence, in some way, to begin to establish the story world. This can be achieved through a variety of means. The music in *Driving Miss Daisy* and *Mississippi Burning*, for example, worked to convey not only the period of the films, but the tone by which the films would examine these periods. Films about Robin Hood or other chivalric heroes will frequently use Old English styles of type to evoke the period, whereas in the 1980s films that had plots dealing with the advancement and abuse of computer technology frequently used fonts that replicated the LCD lettering of computer monitors or print-outs. The opening to *Do the Right Thing* fulfills this particular stylistic norm. By having Rosie Perez dance in front of different apartment buildings, the opening begins to establish the story world as one that will take place in the contemporary inner city, as can be judged by the spray-can style of graffiti on one of the buildings.

In contemporary film, however, the credit sequence is commonly used to introduce and even advance certain aspects of the plot (again, as with *Driving Miss Daisy* and *Mississippi Burning).* This practice is decidedly rejected in *Do the Right Thing.* While the sequence uses a character who will later appear in the plot, it does not *introduce* her as a character. Further, the sequence lacks any plot causality or time. Rather, the sequence is organized solely around the relationship of the image and its choreography to the music and lyrics of the song. As a result, the song and its lyrics hold a privileged position along with the setting, as opposed to serving the kind of background supportive role to which music and lyrics are usually assigned.

The opening can thus be described as a confrontational appropriation precisely because, although it adopts certain aspects of the Hollywood style, its does so only as a means for dramatically rejecting others. Rather than introduce the main characters or construct the specific story world that will become the backdrop for the characters, the opening to *Do the Right Thing* places emphasis on the dynamics of the setting through its stylized editing, dramatic lighting, and the nondiegetic commentary of the music. Furthermore, the tenor of Public Enemy's commentary is both confrontational and analytical, working against the invisibility of the process of racism, and articulating what will be one of the film's evaluative norms: fighting the powers that be. Combined with the choreographed dancing of Rosie Perez, the intense lighting, and the close-ups, the opening also works against the invisibility of film style, clearly announcing that the last thing *Do the Right Thing* is going to be is escapist entertainment.

In one respect, however, the opening of the film (along with other scenes) has been criticized as being escapist in terms of its stereotypical representation of females as adjuncts to both the narrative and the issue of black liberation. The opening scene in particular is justifiably in need of such feminist analysis, since it encourages its spectators to gaze upon the body of a woman, frequently in sexual display. Feminist analysis, then, seeks to determine whether the film's provocative discussion of racism is not used as a justification for sexism, which would then provide precisely the kind of "escape" from the complexity of social issues that *Do the Right Thing* seems to confront—especially with respect to race.

Justifying sexism through racism is a process that is exposed and critiqued in Lee's earlier film *School Daze* (albeit, not as successfully as might have been wished). What this chapter will demonstrate is that the critique continues and is expanded in *Do the Right Thing.* The opening of *Do the Right Thing* continues the discussion of the relationship between racism and sexism in several ways. The primary manner in which it does so involves the relationship between the figure of the woman, the setting, the lyrics of the song—which boldly and repeatedly advocate to "Fight the Powers that Be"—and the context created by the plot's self-conscious narration. The latter of these elements functions to ensure that audiences do not read the appropriation of Public Enemy's music as a merely aesthetic choice, limited to an inexplicit meaning like mood or beat. Too many elements of plot—intense lighting, setting, editing, choreography—interact with the music in such a manner as to establish what has earlier been described as the dynamics of setting. The self-conscious narration in particular works to foreground the lyrics as an important part of understanding the dynamics of setting. As a result, the opening, as well as the rest of the film, is structured to be read through the value of fighting the powers that be.

It is within this context that the figure of woman—Rosie Perez— dances through different costumes and settings. Here too, the changing settings, clearly not causally or temporally linked, work to create the very self-conscious narration through which these settings are structured to be read. Within such a context, the display of woman's body as eroticized object is juxtaposed to the image of her body dressed in boxing gear, and to the image of a woman dancing a physically demanding choreography. These juxtapositions undermine the ability of the sequence to naturalize the display of the body as eroticized object. Further, these juxtapositions work to situate the display of woman within the self-conscious discourse of fighting the powers that be. Rather than subordinate sexism to racism, the opening of *Do the Right Thing* features the discourse of sexism as precisely one of the powers that be that must be confronted.

In addition, the opening's subversion of gender roles functions within the film's stylistic commitment to confrontational appropriation. By incorporating Public Enemy's song and establishing an urban setting, the film has provided the means by which to construct one of the more popular and politically significant fantasies of dominant white culture: the angry black male (a white fantasy, Sharon Willis points out, that structures the dominant modes through which Lee himself is represented in mainstream discourse[2]). The opening of *Do the Right Thing* confronts that fantasy by delivering everything but the corporeal figure of the angry black man—a fact made glaringly evident by the boxing costume Rosie Perez wears. The boxing costume functions not only to amplify the message of the music by presenting an associative image of fighting, but also references the figure of the angry black male athlete—most notably Mohammad Ali, who refused to stay quiet about racism in sports and in broader culture.[3]

By referencing the fantasy of the angry black male, the film's opening raises the specter of this fantasy in order to critique it. The blaring, self-conscious advocacy to fight the powers that be insists on racism as a social reality, as a blanketing and oppressive force that has very real social effects—as the settings' backgrounds attest. It thus works against dominate white culture's obsessive intent to ignore racism by designating it as merely a fantasy of angry black men in need of an excuse for their own individual failure. The figure of Rosie Perez, desperately trying to perform what the opening advocates, suggests instead that racism is a social reality against which all people of color struggle. Furthermore, the individualism that dominant white culture insists upon with its discourses of self-help, merit, and equal opportunity is referenced—and exploded—by Perez as a solitary figure representing the wholly inadequate possibility that alone she can fight the powers that be.

This subversion of the myth of individual power is carried on through the rest of the narrative by one of the primary narrative sites of confrontational appropriation, the film's main character Mookie, who functions in the plot as an antihero. Several of the criticisms leveled at the film imply that the casting of the film's director as the main character is a textual strategy that endorses or validates the character, his actions, and his ideological position within the text. The problem with such an interpretation—which goes outside of the text itself to find meaning—is that it is both unsubstantiated by the text, and inconsistent with the role that the casting exercises in other Lee films—especially with respect to the casting of Lee himself. Willis, for example, argues,

> Lee always emerges in his films as both a slippery, ambivalent, and slightly shady character, who is often the object of implicit critique, and as an extradiegetic resistance interrupting the narrative texture. As a textual figure, then, Lee circulates his own body and image through his films as he does those of many of his regular actors, whose roles from film to film vary dramatically. Such an effect interrupts any easy correlation between on-screen and off-screen realities.[4]

Willis's argument brings up several important points for reading *Do the Right Thing* accurately. To begin with, the casting of Lee as a character does not provide for a consistent evaluative position on character. The position of Lee's characters (those he plays) with respect to the normative system of the text is not static, any more than is the position of the characters played by actors featured regularly in his films. The characters played by Giancarlo Esposito provide a clear example of Lee's tendency to cast actors in greatly divergent roles. In *School Daze*, Esposito played the ultimate assimilationist; in *Do the Right Thing*, he plays a character who espouses black neonationalism. In *School Daze*, the narrative's evaluative system was complexly ambivalent about Esposito's character; in *Do the Right Thing*, the evaluative system is far less ambiguous, as it holds back validation of almost every aspect of Buggin Out's position.

In terms of textuality, the film's most significant cue to Mookie's status as antihero is the absence of goal-oriented narrative to begin with. In their discussion of classical film, Bordwell, Staiger, and Thompson argue that, "Psychological causality, presented through defined characters acting to achieve announced goals, gives the classical film its characteristic progression."[5] This structure is decidedly deemphasized, if not altogether lacking, in *Do the Right Thing*. Rather than a tight, linear, goal-oriented trajectory organized around a specific hero's quest, *Do the Right Thing* is organized around the relationships among characters, their points of view/ideological positions, and the space they all occupy, the Bedford-Stuyvesant neighborhood of Brooklyn. Thus, rather than a linear trajectory, the narrative seems to move circuitously—investigating the different groups within the neighborhood and their relations to each other.

Within this investigation, Mookie's character stands out as a go-between. Narratively motivated in part by his job delivering pizzas, Mookie is well liked and rather seamlessly moves between and within constituencies. Mookie thus functions as mediator in the friction between racial and ethnic groups, most notably mediating between Sal, the white pizzeria owner, and Buggin Out, an Afro-American friend of Mookie's from the neighborhood. Yet even though the film evaluates this mediating role positively, the plot still resists fully validating Mookie as character. Indeed, the plot makes clear that there are deep character flaws in Mookie, among them being a failure to face up to his responsibilities.

This evaluative ambivalence with respect to Mookie's character (and indeed, almost every character) is another significant site for the film's confrontation with classical narrative. Rather than being organized around the binary opposition of a central conflict that would give clear evaluative cues to reading each individual, the characters in *Do the Right Thing* share no such organization and no such clear evaluative positions. Sal, for example, is an important site for the plot's evaluative system, as is Radio Raheem. Each character embodies important values for the film's normative system (doing, respect for individuals, fighting the power) but they each are significantly constructed with negative aspects to their characters as well.

Sal, for example, comes to embody much of the film's evaluative norms. As the film makes clear several times, Sal is a "do-er": he built his pizzeria with his own hands, and having built it, he works with his hands to feed people—something he takes pride in. In addition, he looks after the less fortunate of the community—like Da Mayor and Smiley—with compas-

Mookie and Sal stand in front of "The Wall of Fame," which will function as a catalyst for conflict in the tension-filled setting.

sion and dignity. Sal consistently does the right thing. The film withholds complete validation from Sal, however, by assigning negative traits to him as well. While well meaning and well intentioned, Sal nonetheless ignores or hides from his own racism, and as the narrative trajectory will bear out, this self-imposed blindness has disastrous consequences. In addition, the narrative will judge negatively Sal's subdued attachment to the politics of confrontation—an evaluation that is in part conveyed through the disproportionate effects the politics of confrontation exercises at the narrative's culmination.

Disproportionate effects are not limited to Sal, but are shared by Radio Raheem as well. Radio Raheem is recognized by the characters as a moral voice within the community. He is granted almost spiritual status, as the fire-hydrant scene testifies: all playful activity must temporarily be suspended to allow him to pass untouched. The four teens and Mookie all show deference to him, and his narrative soliloquy in direct address to the camera further defines him as a privileged moral voice within the narrative. Despite his articulation of the necessity of love over hate, however,

Radio Raheem also functions as a destabilizing presence in the film. It is his character who introduces off-angle camera framing when he comes upon the four teens hanging out, a stylistic element that will be consistently associated with his character. Further, the politics of confrontation—in apparent contradiction to his view of the necessity of love over hate—is also associated with Raheem, first with the battle of the boom boxes, then with Sal. Here too the effects of Raheem's politics of confrontation will be disproportionately tragic in the film's conclusion.

The pervasive evaluative ambivalence with respect to character is a principle means by which the plot rejects the norms of classical style, particularly the norms of narrative organization. Rather than being structured around a central conflict that organizes the characters, the narrative is built on the dynamics of shared space and the different orientations that create conflict within that space. Here too, however, Lee has been criticized for appropriating stereotypical characters—especially the characters that white audiences want to see.

As with most of his work, however, Lee's appropriation is not so much a naive reliance on form as it is part of a political aesthetic. The use of familiar character types is part of a narrative strategy of highlighting and confronting the continuing discourse on race and racism. Within the plot of *Do the Right Thing,* characters do not so much advance a specific narrative trajectory as represent a particular discourse about race and/or racism, discourses that the film is reluctant to endorse overtly and that are frequently in conflict with each other.

One of the clearest examples of this is the scene involving the four teens who are hanging out and Da Mayor. When the group comes upon Da Mayor, the character Ahmad takes the opportunity to ridicule the old man in what starts out as typical teenage put-down dynamics—the insult functions to enhance the sense of self of the individual delivering the criticism. Da Mayor at first attempts to walk away from the group, but when the haranguing continues, he confronts the behavior as inappropriate, attempting to critique the teens' shallow evaluative position and lack of empathy. Da Mayor's confrontation, however, only motivates Ahmad to become even more vocal and angry, dressing down Da Mayor more vehemently and getting so worked up that his friends have to drag him away.

The significance of the scene to the evaluative system of the film is twofold. To begin with, the scene makes clear the importance of discourse in defining a group. Conflicts within the film are structured around discourse just as much as they are around race. The teens and Da Mayor belong to the same group in terms of race, but they are defined by two conflicting discourses from two different eras. Ahmad articulates the discourse of self-determination so prevalent in 1980s America, and so valued by dominant white culture, thus showing his own political naivety. Da Mayor articulates the discourse of black male emasculation of the pre- and postwar era, when Jim Crow society and segregation created severe obstacles to self-sufficiency for large numbers of black males. Their confrontation is thus a confrontation between discourses on race and the individual's relationship to the social institution of race.

Another significant aspect of the scene, however, is the manner in which the plot withholds explicit validation from either discourse, and indeed, undermines both. Ahmad too readily aligns himself with an untenable position—the discourse of "self-sufficiency" so important to white reaction against racial justice. Although he readily adopts the position to insult Da Mayor, the late-night scene in the pizzeria suggests he would just as readily abandon it when he himself is confronted with racism. Further, his argument is not as historically valid as he thinks it is, since Da Mayor's justification addresses a different historical context of self-determination and self-sufficiency. Da Mayor speaks of and is defined by a period of even less accessibility to the labor market than the current one, a period that Ahmad seems completely ignorant of. And yet, as the discourse of Mother-Sister makes clear earlier in the scene, neither is Da Mayor's position fully credible; black male emasculation is not adequate justification for a retreat into self-centered do-nothingness.

As a result, neither of the discourses is validated, and the film remains ambiguous about what, if anything, the conflict between the two resolved. This dynamic of conflict between discourses and ambiguous resolution is the dominant mode of the film's narrative organization. As Willis argues: "Organized by collisions among competing discourses, Lee's films present contradictions that are highly resistant to resolution as a clear assertion or statement—precisely the form required by a dominant discourse that seeks to place them as examples in its ongoing story of race relations."[6] As Willis makes clear, the film's evaluative ambiguity, especially as it relates to the structure of conflict-resolution, is a significant site of narrative misappropriation. By refusing to validate particular discourses on race and racism, the film resists the ideology of domination that undergirds privilege, and also rejects the kind of simple solutions and resolutions on which the mass media has come to rely.

In her reading, however, bell hooks criticizes the film precisely for its simplistic examination of the discourses on race and racism, faulting it for not challenging "the conventional thinking about the 'meaning' of race and its relation to identity formation."[7] Such a criticism, however, does not fully account for the critique that the film's evaluative ambiguity articulates against conventional thinking about race. In a highly visible and cinematically self-conscious scene that suspends the narrative and narrative temporality (creating, significantly, its own temporality and causality), members of specific groups hurl racial/ethnic slurs directly at the camera as if to each other. Narratively motivated, but operating outside of the temporal and spatial continuity of the narrative, the sequence functions as if it were a nondiegetic insert, creating commentary on the narrative world. The sequence begins with Mookie, out of narrative time, insulting Pino's Italian identity. Pino then hurls a string of racial slurs against Afro-Americans. This is followed by a Hispanic male (introduced earlier in the narrative) rendering a list of insults against Koreans, followed by a white cop deriding Hispanics. The causal string concludes with the Korean grocer insulting Jews through the figure of Ed Koch. The sequence itself comes to an end by the plot cutting to the character of Love Daddy in his radio studio, who moves in quickly toward the camera and yells for "time out." Like the characters before him, Love Daddy speaks in a direct address to the camera. Unlike the others, however, he does not participate in the string of racial slurs, but seeks to end it, admonishing the characters that they need to chill and to "cut that shit out."

Love Daddy's ending to the sequence is significant for several reasons. To begin with, it is one of the few moments in the narrative in which the plot's evaluative system is clear, explicit, and unequivocal. Love Daddy leaves no room for interpretation that what the characters are doing is wrong, and that it needs to end. In this respect, Love Daddy provides a critique of what is a highly visible rendering of the operation of racism and the conventional thinking about race that goes along with it. The self-conscious narration functions to remove the action from the narrative trajectory in order to provide it with a level of abstraction. Extracted as it is from the specifics of individual character within the narrative, the sequence can be read more allegorically as a generalized manifestation of how racism operates through a debased but nonetheless conventional and uncritical thinking about race.

Furthermore, the self-conscious narration and its strategy of abstraction work to delineate the politics at stake in conventional thinking about race and its relationship to the operation of racism. Precisely what the sequence shows is how readily and completely groups are willing to think negatively about, and put down, other groups as part of a complex, interrelated, and effective means of maintaining privilege. The common denominator of each group represented in the sequence—including the white working class cop, a figure of the state's coercive force—is that none of the characters can be described as "the powers that be." Instead, they are the objects and the means by which the powers that be maintain their privileged position by engaging oppressed groups in a spurious conflict that distracts them and deflects them from fighting the powers that be.

The success of this mode of social control results from the manner in which different groups define themselves through negative comparison to another group. The "meanings" that result from the comparison then becomes the source of conflict between them. Locked in conflict, these groups fail to form precisely the kind of collective that would bring down the powers that be and create a more just and equitable society where race and the meaning of race are extricated from power relations. Thus, rather than endorsing conventional thinking about race, *Do the Right Thing* constitutes a strong indictment against it.

Indeed, the narrative's organization as a conflict between discourses, and its unwillingness to validate specific discourses, is another means by which the film challenges conventional thinking about race. By withholding validation, the film allows discourses that are bound to the conventional thinking about race to clash aimlessly and constantly, without resolution, or achievement. In the end, these discourses are exhausted by their impotency, and invalidated by their disproportionately negative effects. This is particularly the case with Buggin Out, whose conflict with Sal and with the white bike rider lacks what Mookie's sister Jade will ultimately define as doing something positive for the community. It is not that the discourses of positive role models and gentrification are without value, but the film makes clear that they too easily become the ends in themselves. Through the character of Buggin Out, the positive role model becomes a site of conflict in and of itself, the larger purpose of which—doing something positive for the community—gets overshadowed. The film subtly invalidates Buggin Out's position by having an enormous picture of Mike Tyson loom in the background as Buggin Out stakes the claim for more pictures. The film is thus critical of this discourse precisely because it has become an end in itself that has lost site of doing something positive in the community.

That conventional thinking is on display for the purpose of critique is further evidenced in the discourse of sexism within the film. In addition to the previously discussed opening, Jade's visit to the pizzeria appropriates the iconography and discourse of sexism and its relation to racism. Preceded by Mookie's late return from a delivery, Jade's presence turns Sal from his anger at Mookie to visible infatuation (to the point of reverence). As Sal affectionately talks to Jade, the camera pans across the glowering faces of first Mookie, then Pino, both of whom are angered—though for opposite reasons—by what they interpret as Sal's obvious desire for Jade.

The plot cuts from this scene to other character-development scenes, but when it returns, Sal continues talking affectionately to Jade while the two share a booth. After Sal pays Jade a compliment about her eyes, Mookie comes into frame and drags Jade outside, where he confronts her about Sal's sexual motives and prohibits her from coming to Sal's anymore. As the argument between Mookie and Jade continues, however, the plot works to undermine Mookie's position, and to call into question his interpretation of the interaction between Sal and Jade.

To begin with, Jade confronts the hypocrisy of Mookie's machismo by pointing out that his authority is severely undermined by his financial dependence on her. She further undermines Mookie's position by confronting his crudeness, and by asserting her own position as grown woman no longer in need of oversight and regulation. She then diminishes him even more by demanding that he start to take control of his own life. By casting the conflict within these terms, Jade starts to underscore the issues of power and control that stand behind Mookie's machismo and attempt to regulate her sexuality.

Furthermore, the film offers no other support to Mookie's and Pino's interpretation of the event as sexual, rendering it instead as ambiguously affectionate. The function of this ambiguity is to emphasize the lack of discourse or cultural signifying practice for communicating affectionate human interaction that is independent of gender, sexuality, and race. The heavily overdetermined sexual-racial interpretation of Mookie and Pino is offset by the fundamental ambiguity to the scene, and this produces a self-consciousness that foregrounds the scene's resistance to the codes that conventional thinking about race, gender, and sexuality would impose on it. Prior to the scene, Sal has conveyed to Pino his pride in watching children grow up on his pizza. Jade's presence within the pizzeria thus functions as an individual manifestation of what Sal is talking about: she has grown up into an independent, together, beautiful, young woman. Sal not only admires Jade for this, but takes pride in how he has contributed, in however small a way, to this development. The self-consciousness of the scene, however, flaunts the manner in which the iconography created around the conventional thinking about race, gender, age, and sexuality is fundamentally unable to convey that.

The most important scene for articulating the limitations that conventional thinking about race imposes on human interactions and community is reserved, not coincidentally, in the narrative's culminating scene, the confrontation at the pizzeria. Here too the film maintains its stylistic commitment to confrontational appropriation, constructing a culminating scene that resists the kind of resolution and denouement that the classical narrative demands. Rather than being structured along classical norms, the scene is organized around conflict and contradictions between discourses. And rather than offering resolution in the manner of the classical norm of culminating action, the scene misappropriates this norm to heighten these conflicts and contradictions.

The first manner in which the scene achieves its heightened sense is with dramatic reversals and turnarounds. The scene begins by announcing itself as an ending. Sal and the boys are closing up the shop, the darkness of night further suggesting that things are coming to an end. As he closes the shop, Sal reflects on the day and on the future, but as the plot makes clear, he is alone in his affection for the business—Vito, Pino, and Mookie gaze at him in disbelief and irony. The moment is interrupted by the four teenagers who have been hanging out all day banging on the door for pizza. Mookie immediately jumps up and announces that they are closed. The teenagers beg to be let in, and Sal, still within his affectionate mood, tells Mookie to let them in.

The reversals that the plot is constructing begin here. Sal opens his doors out of affection and pride, and the teenagers convey their gratitude to him while insulting and cursing out Mookie. Mookie responds by telling them to sit their black asses down. Their small confrontation is suspended when Ahmad asks Sal for four slices to go, beaming with appreciation for what Sal has done for them. As they begin talking again, there is another interruption. A thud is heard out of frame, followed immediately by the blaring lyrics of Public Enemy's "Fight the Power." The teens look to the source of the sound, and the plot cuts to first a reaction shot of Pino and Vito, and then to the unlocked door, where Radio Raheem, Buggin Out, and Smiley now stand.

The disrupting presence of Radio Raheem, Buggin Out, and Smiley is emphasized first with off-level and low-angle framing, then with the camera pulling back from its medium shot. The characters, however, walk into the camera position, reframing them again up close. Dramatic camera framings are then repeated through the scene, as when the film cuts to Sal, reversing its camera angle from low to high, and having Sal walk into the framing as well—his face slightly distorted from the lens proximity. As Sal and Buggin Out engage in a shouting match, the reaction shots of the other characters are all rendered through dramatic and nonclassical camera framings.

These intensive and highly stylized camera framings work to enhance the sense of destabilization that results from the clash of discourses present in the scene. Buggin Out, Raheem, and Smiley are there to push an agenda about role models and the economic relationship between races (black consumership-white ownership) as constituted at Sal's Pizzeria. Sal's demand to shut the music off comes from his commitment to and belief in self-determination. Having built the pizzeria with his own hands, Sal wants its general ambiance to reflect on him as a testament to self-determination. Mookie, in his last act of mediating, adds to the fray out of self-interest, wanting Buggin Out to stop so that he can go home. That the confrontation is about conflict between discourses is articulated by the characters themselves, when they argue over what their confrontation is about. Buggin Out confronts Sal's racism, asking Sal why his derogatory remarks about the music contain references to the jungle and Africa, he insists that this confrontation is about racism, in the form of the pictures on the wall of fame. Sal, however, refuses to accept Buggin Out's premise, and insists on the literal: the confrontation, he claims, is merely about the music. What the intensity of the scene suggests, however, is that the conflict between discourses is about several things: control, privilege, racism, and the relationship between the individual and the community.

Further, the narrative trajectory demonstrates the limitations conventional discourses impose on complex interactions. Locked into a confrontation between conventional discourses, the characters are without hope of resolution, limited in their options, and thus subject to the effects of language. This is first seen in the reaction shots of the supporting characters: neither Mookie, Vito, Pino, nor the teenagers knows exactly what to do. Further, the rapid reversal of the teenagers' position within the conflict displays how powerful the effects of language on individual identity can be. When the confrontation first begins, the teenagers are aligned with Sal, despite their previous expressed deference to Raheem. Ahmad, for example, urges Vito to help quell the disturbance. After Sal uses the word "nigger," however, the teenagers shift their allegiance and verbally enter into the fray against Sal.

The inability of the discourses to relate to each other or resolve themselves articulates their limiting effects. Locked as they are in the politics of confrontation, the characters are ill served by the discourses they appropriate, which cannot provide them with options or resolution. Instead, the discourses inscribe the characters into a trajectory whose goal is destruction and violence. That this violence leads not to resolution but to more violence not only demonstrates the limitations these discourses impose, but confronts the myth of classical narrative's culminating violence as precursor to resolution.

The film's critique of this classical norm is evidenced in the effect that Sal's act of violence has on the narrative space. With Sal's destruction of the radio, a quiet calm pervades the pizzeria; the cacophony of music and shouting has been replaced by utter silence, and an uneasy peace settles over the space. The reactions of the characters makes clear that they are all stunned and unsure of how to react or what to do—even, and especially, Radio Raheem, who does not know what to make of this assault on the extension of himself. In this respect, the film briefly appropriates the order that is supposed to be restored by the classical hero's justified and purging violence.

Radio Raheem's reaction and the unsteady calm of the pizzeria are not, however, the result of the resolution violence achieves. Quite the contrary, they function as a means for the plot to emphasize the limitations that the discourse of confrontation imposes, and its profound failure to achieve resolution. In the unsteady tranquility of the pizzeria, the reactions of the characters express their searching for the meaning of their situation. Vito in particular looks from side to side as if someone might have an answer that will allow everyone to escape from where their discourses have led them. In a space looking for a solution, a way to transcend what has occurred, Sal, understatedly but tragically, reappropriates the discourse of confrontation, stating to Raheem: "I just killed your fucking radio." Sal's discourse will engage a trajectory that leads to violence, expanding both its scope and its effect. The whole neighborhood is drawn into what will ultimately lead to the death of Radio Raheem. Mainstream media criticism that focused on the destruction of the pizzeria thus overlooked the complexity of the film's critique, reading that particular point as the plot's culmination and ignoring the other culminating points of violence. In doing so, the film's critics, as Willis points out, obscure the distinction between property crimes and murder.[8] Furthermore, such critiques overprivilege the manifestation of violence, and thereby fail to see the plot's pointed critique against both violence and the limitations that conflicting discourses impose on the complex issue of racism.

As with most of the plot, the pizzeria scene fails to validate Buggin Out, Sal, or Radio Raheem. Indeed, it undermines the position of each. Withholding validation from all of the characters, the plot creates a confusing atmosphere full of reversals and the clash of conflicting discourses, rejecting the ideological clarity of classical narrative and the conventions that render it. Radio Raheem's attack on Sal is an example of this reversal and rejection. Given Raheem's earlier soliloquy on Love and Hate, Raheem's attack on Sal is neither validated nor justified, but rather, portrayed as a reaction to Sal's discourse of confrontation.

Raheem's lack of justification is the important site of a plot reversal whose function is critique. Raheem's attack consists of choking Sal; as the brawl spills out to the sidewalk, the image track shows Raheem maintaining his choke hold and striking Sal's head onto the sidewalk. Raheem's violence is not only disproportionate, it also threatens death. Rather than temporarily disabling his opponent with the knockout punch, which is the norm for Hollywood film, Raheem's choke hold is far more limited in what it can accomplish, far more locked into killing the opponent—as later events will confirm.

The plot, then, renders Raheem's violence as excessive and dangerous. When the police arrive, expecting to break up the fight, the plot reverses the direction of the violence. The police enter the fray, extricating Radio Raheem and putting him into a choke hold. Through the soundtrack, the plot makes clear that the Italian-American cop Gary takes advantage of the situation and uses undue force to kill Raheem, ignoring his partner's warning of "That's enough!" In this manner, the plot structures a symbolic reversal of violence that levels a significant critique against the structure of classical cinema and its politics of identification.

Prior to the police entering the fray, an Afro-American violently chokes an Italian-American in the heat of anger. With the arrival of the police, an Italian-American chokes an Afro-American, only this time, the signifier of death, so closely related to the action, fulfills itself. This plot reversal, engendering as it does Radio Raheem's tragic death, functions as a rejection of the classical cinema's norm of the hero's purifying and justified killing. Despite Raheem's choke hold on Sal, the violence of the police comes across as unjustified, but given the politics of race, not necessarily unexpected. Indeed, the plot makes clear that the basis for the killing was not the protection of Sal, nor even the confusion and violence, but the racism of the cop. As the characters themselves conclude, Raheem was murdered, creating, once again, a culmination that brings no resolution. The character's death, much like the pulverizing of the radio, creates instead an uneasy suspension of the frenetic violence. The tension within that vulnerable stasis is a stark opposition to the order and stability that a hero's righteous, justified, and culminating violence achieves in classical narration.

The plot's rejection of classical cinema's reliance on the myth of violence-and-resolution is thus significant for the film's critique. The rejection attempts to expose the ideological underpinnings of classical norms and their justification of violence and death through a process of aligning spectator identification with the hero who performs it. Radio Raheem's death serves as a reminder that the politics of identification are such that in the classical cinema, nonwhites are typically assigned to be the subject of the hero's salvific violence.

Further ideological critique articulated by the scene occurs through the misappropriation of another classical norm, the recurring motif. The scene is structured around several recurring motifs, not the least of which is the previously discussed rejection of culminating violence leading to resolution (it occurs three times in the scene: the destruction of the Radio, the death of Radio Raheem, and the destruction of the pizzeria). In addition, however, the scene repeats one of Sal's earlier motifs, relating it to the film's ideological critique and to the evaluative system of the narrative. Bordwell, Staiger, and Thompson argue that the function of a motif is to "reinforce the individuality and consistency of each character."[9] Furthermore, they argue that, "For major characters, the motif serves to mark significant stages of story action." These functions—reinforcing consistency and marking stages of story action—are appropriated in Sal's recurring motif of "you do what you gotta do."

When Sal first speaks this line, he is directing it at Mookie, who is trying to get paid early. The line is meant to silence Mookie by indicating to him that he has no bargaining position in the matter—especially given his reputation for possessing a poor work ethic. As a remark, the line functions to reinforce Sal's individuality and consistency. Throughout the film,

as previously mentioned, Sal is defined by the discourse of self-determination—that doing (working hard, making your own place, and so on) affords individuals their just due: being the boss, deciding what pictures to
hang, and so on. The motif thus continues an association between Sal and
"doing." Furthermore, the motif articulates and reinforces another trait to
Sal's character, his reliance on the discourse of confrontation. Similar to
Mookie, Sal frequently plays a mediating role between groups and individuals; however, he also consistently appropriates the discourse of confrontation when his right to self-determination is challenged, as with
Buggin Out and Radio Raheem earlier in the film. Though understated
when directed at Mookie, Sal's statement can nonetheless be rooted
within the discourse of confrontation.

In this respect, the motif lays the groundwork for marking stages of
narrative action. When Sal repeats the line "you do what you gotta do" to
the crowd in front of the pizzeria, the statement is much less understated—the result of the explosive narrative events—and much more
clearly situated within the discourse of confrontation—the result of a
standoff with the crowd. The disastrous consequences of the statement—
it incites the crowd against Sal and his sons—emphasizes the manner in
which consistency of character is precisely what is being criticized. An
overdependence on the discourses of confrontation as they are related to
conventional thinking about race is at the core of the situation to begin
with. Like the moments just after the destruction of the radio, the unsteady stasis after Radio Raheem's death—imbued as it is with uncertainty—is in desperate need of *unconventional* thinking: of discourses and
interactions that can transcend the traumatic effects of the violence.

Far from constituting advocacy for violence, as many of the mainstream
critics fantasized, the scene articulates instead the tragic and destructive
limitations to the discourse of confrontation. Indeed, the cycle of violence
ends only when the discourse of confrontation is abandoned for the discourse of conciliation. The crowd refrains from ransacking the Korean
grocery upon being stunned by the grocer's declaration that he is not
white; rather, as he claims, he is "black." In the moment afforded him by
their uncertainty over how to interpret his discourse, the grocer abandons
trying to fight and asserts to the crowd, "You . . . Me . . . Same . . . We
Same." Although his discourse does not persuade the character M.L., it
does provide the means for others in the crowd to recognize the conciliation being offered—a conciliation further emphasized by the Korean extending his hand in friendship. As a result, the crowd turns away without
destroying the store.

The ensuing melee between the crowd and the police and fire department then further contrasts the politics of confrontation with the politics of conciliation. Upon returning to the neighborhood, the police immediately adopt the discourse of confrontation, ordering people away from the scene. Their orders, however, only serve to reinvigorate the crowd towards violence and confrontation. Rather than culminating, the plot makes clear that violence does not bring resolution and ideological clarity, but leads to more violence. Indeed, it is only by cutting away to a shot that isolates the figures of Mookie and Jade mutely contemplating the melee before them that the plot escapes from the continuum of violence.

In organizing the narrative trajectory around the conflict between discourses and the groups that appropriate them, the plot comes to reject a narrative structured around the resolution of a binary conflict. Instead, the plot disseminates conflict and the potential for conflict throughout the narrative space—indeed, as the dynamic of the narrative space. Binary structure is appropriated by the plot at the site of the film's evaluative system, which renders "doing" as positive, and evaluates anything that substitutes for doing—like talking—negatively. The film does not completely discredit the verbal, but it clearly places its emphasis, as the title suggests, on doing the right thing. Further, as the repetition of Public Enemy's signature song articulates, doing the right thing can be determined by the degree to which an action constitutes fighting the powers that be.

Within that evaluative system, the film pointedly asserts that Buggin Out's request, and the destruction of the pizzeria, fall far short of fighting the powers that be, another point that mainstream critics persistently ignore. The film repeatedly articulates its evaluative norm about "fighting" the powers that be, but seeks to redefine the term as it relates to racism and the black community in particular. As the opening sequence suggests, fighting is an action frequently associated with black males and the myth of their penchant for violence—whether in the boxing ring or on the streets. Through the trajectory of the narrative, however, the plot dissociates fighting the powers from violence. The film asserts instead that doing something positive in the community itself constitutes fighting the powers that be—since the powers that be depend on the disenfranchisement of the community to maintain their status. Within this process of redefining an evaluative concept, acts of conciliation, of doing for others, of making contact with individuals, all take on a new political dimension rooted in the potential for creating human community beyond the conventional thinking of race. In the politics of the film, realizing such potential would be to defeat the powers that be.

Notes

1. Sharon Willis, *High Contrast: Race and Gender in Contemporary Hollywood Film* (Durham and London: Duke University Press, 1997).

2. Ibid., 160–165.

3. Indeed, one of the reasons that Muhammad Ali is the only man to win the Heavyweight title three times is that he was stripped of his title by the boxing commission for his refusal to participate in the U.S. war in Vietnam.

4. Willis, *High Comtrast.*, 165.

5. David Bordwell, Janet Staiger, and Kristen Thompson, *The Classical Hollywood Cinema Film Style and Mode of Production to 1960* (New York: Columbia University Press, 1985), 17.

6. Willis, *High Contrast*, 168.

7. bell hooks, *Yearning: Race, Gender, and Cultural Politics* (Boston: South End Press, 1990).

8. Willis, *High Contrast*, 164.

9. Bordwell, Staiger, and Thompson, *Classical Hollywood Cinema*, 15.

9

Daughters of the Dust and the Figurative as Mode of Resistance

In the cold winter of 1991, the Sundance Film Festival was ignited by Julie Dash's entry, *Daughters of the Dust*. The film won the festival's award for best cinematography, and critics were quick to praise the accomplishments of a new and emerging directing talent. In hindsight, their comments demonstrate how little attention had been paid to Afro-American independent cinema: in her article on *Daughters of the Dust*, for example, Toni Cade Bambara makes clear that Julie Dash is anything *but* a "new" directing talent. Indeed, according to Bambara, Dash was among a group of black UCLA film students who, from the 1970s on, committed themselves to challenging the Hollywood cinema and its participation in a broader process of racism. As Bambara notes, "Their views differed markedly with the school's orientation," which was very much structured around preparing students to take their place within the industry.[1]

Instead, the "Black insurgents," as Bambara designates the group, developed an alternative set of filmmaking principles, among them their belief that "accountability to the community takes precedence over training for an industry that maligns and exploits, trivializes, and invisibilizes Black people." In order to contest industry practices, this group of filmmakers "engaged in interrogating conventions of dominant cinema, screening films of socially conscious cinema, and discussing ways to alter previous significations as they relate to Black people."[4] The historical irony of the black insurgents is that they created an intellectual and aesthetic legacy from which younger directors like Spike Lee could then draw and, through crossover success, create a broader market and greater accessibility for directors like Julie Dash who blazed a trail before him.

The "Spike Lee phenomenon," which as Sharon Willis argues is largely a creation of dominant white culture,[5] no doubt helped create market opportunities for directors like Julie Dash, but, unlike Lee, Dash is representative of an important group of Afro-American independents who resisted, or downright rejected, the crossover strategies Lee adopted.[6] As *Daughters of the Dust* demonstrates, Dash chose instead to create an aesthetic consistent with the principles of the black insurgents, an aesthetic committed to interrogating conventions of dominant cinema and to altering significations as they relate to black people. *Daughters of the Dust* tells the story of an extended family of Afro-Americans, living at the turn of the century on the Sea Islands off the Carolina and Georgia coasts. The story begins with a family reunion called on the occasion of the family migrating from the islands to the mainland and its promise of economic, social, and material security. Such a migration, however, threatens the cultural integrity that the family has maintained, in part because of their geographic remoteness.

In telling the story of a family of Afro-Americans, *Daughters of the Dust* becomes the occasion for supplanting the stylistic norms of the classical cinema, constructing instead representational strategies that provide a sense of Afrocentric style while at the same time conducting the interrogation of classical film as the basis for creating an emancipatory cinema. This aesthetic agenda is engendered within the opening images of the film. The first image of the film is a medium shot of a pair of open hands, holding onto soil as, in slow motion, the wind blows the grains into small clouds of dust. This image dissolves into a long shot of a woman, strongly backlit, clothed in a dress, washing in a body of water, with the left and right edges and bottom of the frame bordered by trees. As she washes, a voice-over begins, stating:

I am the first and the last.
I am the honored one and the scorned one.

This image then dissolves into another image of a bedroom, draped with sheer white lace, as the voice-over continues:

I am the whore and the holy one.
I am the wife and the virgin.
I am the barren one, and many are my daughters.

The image of the bedroom then dissolves into the image of a boat slowly being navigated through a channel, trees surrounding each side. The voice-over continues:

> I am the silence that you cannot understand.
> I am the utterance of my name.

Two stylistic features stand out from this opening: first, the repetition of binary oppositions in the verses of the voice-over, and second, the ambiguous relationship between the voice-over and the image track.

The significance of the binary oppositions within the verses is the manner in which they interrogate conventions of the classical Hollywood cinema, and function within a process of altering the manner in which Afro-Americans come to be signified. In foregrounding the structure of the binary opposition, the verses reference the dominant mode of narrative organization within the classical Hollywood cinema. Yet if the binary oppositions of the verses seem to uphold the norms of Hollywood cinema, they subvert another important element to the classical style: character consistency. As Bordwell, Staiger, and Thompson argue: "Screenplay manuals demand that a character's traits be clearly identified and consistent with one another." They further argue that the Hollywood cinema conforms to "sharply delineated and unambiguous traits."[7] The verses in the opening to *Daughters of the Dust*, however, work against such consistency by situating the binary oppositions within one character, and further, by making such placement function as a contradiction. Whoever the voice-over is referring to, its organization of traits as seemingly contradictory cause the spectator to question the character, not form conclusions about her. How, for example, can the character be both wife and virgin? What does it mean to be the silence that you cannot understand?

In this respect, the opening establishes what will become the most dominant stylistic trope for the film's creation of alternatives to signifying Afro-Americans, resisting the final assigning of meaning. The enigma created by the contradictions of the verses can only be understood with the unfolding of the time and history of a character. This stands as a subversion of the classical mode, in which characters are quickly defined as a set of traits based on actions, gestures, or costume. Further, this subversion will directly challenge the function of this convention as it relates to the process of racism, by engendering resistance to the finalization of meaning.

As opposed to such a breezy, uncomplicated establishment of static traits, *Daughters of the Dust* structures both its narrative and its characters in such a manner that the spectator must frequently wait for information that comes later in the plot in order to assign meaning to specific story elements. This dependence on the relationship between past, present, and future inscribes the underlying ideology of the film's story into the structure of the narrative. The film emphasizes neither racial purity nor cultural stasis, but rather, familial and cultural integrity—an integrity that can only be maintained by remembering the past and integrating it into the future.

The narrative's unwillingness to assign meaning in a finalized way is also articulated in the opening by the manner in which the verses do not orient the spectator to the relationship between images. The verses that accompany the images do not serve as a literal description of the images, and thus do not clarify what narrative relevance, if any, the images hold. Lacking both narrative relevance and spatial/temporal relationships, the sequence of the images fails to make clear the relationship that connects its components. Instead, the opening sequence privileges a more figurative mode of representation that functions metaphorically. In this respect, the opening establishes a mode of signification that is detached from the illusion of finality that literal or denotative signification frequently attempts to create.

As the film progresses, problematizing the relationship between word and image becomes a principal means by which the film interrogates the conventions of dominant cinema. Two more subversions of word-image relationships early in the film demonstrate this point. The first of these comes with the introduction of Yellow Mary to the photographer Snead. After Viola introduces her cousin Mary to Snead, the photographer shifts his glance to the light-skinned woman accompanying Mary. As his gaze rests upon the beautiful woman in yellow hat and dress, Mary comments: "Yellow." The statement startles Snead into shifting his gaze, as if he has been caught in the act of voyeurism. Mary continues, however, by saying, "They call me Yellow Mary."

The sequence is a series of unmet expectations, both diegetically and conventionally. After being introduced to Viola's cousin Mary, Snead expects to be introduced to Mary's companion. It is an expectation that will not be met. The sequence of shots follows that expectation seamlessly by combining Snead's gaze of the beautiful woman to the shot/reverse-shot convention. The camera's framing of her follows Snead's expectation that she is going to be introduced next. This motivation helps mask the erotic gaze that is then directed at the woman. Mary's comment functions to disrupt that concealment as well as denying the narrative expectation. By insisting on her nickname, Mary breaks the trajectory of expectations around the introductions, and keeps the introduction of her companion from being fulfilled.

This breaking of expectations functions to resist the final assigning of meaning. Given Mary's nickname, Snead now looks for an explanation for it. Viola's explanation—our fathers were brothers—does not provide one. The meaning of Yellow Mary is thus temporarily suspended. The same can be said with respect to Yellow Mary's companion. The plot refrains from introducing the woman who accompanies Yellow Mary, and thus resists a designation being assigned to her: it is not made clear whether she is friend, lover, or relative of some kind. Though Yellow Mary does refer to her as Trula, the reference is not for the ears of the others who are nearby when she makes it. Trula thus remains as unsymbolized to the others.

In resisting a designation for Trula, the plot foregrounds what is at stake in the final assigning of meaning. Without a designation—a signifier to be attached to her—Trula cannot be assigned a place, especially a place of contempt that the Peazant women are all too ready to apply to her by virtue of her association with Yellow Mary. Within the process of racism, the finalization of the signifier functions to assign Afro-Americans (and other people of color) a place outside of privilege and to deny people of color the means to resist such placing. Trula thus functions as an image of resistance to that process. She and Yellow Mary refuse to participate in the process that will allow the others to assign Trula to a place of contempt, a place below the one to which they have assigned Mary.

The placing function of the signifier, and its relationship to the final assigning of meaning, is very much a target for subversion in the film's signifying practice. This can be seen in the plot's consistent subversion of word-image relationships, as in the film's opening, and the shifting application of "Yellow" in Snead's introductions. Another significant site for this kind of subversion occurs with the introduction of the character of the Unborn Child, one of the voices that narrates the story. After the uneasy meeting of Yellow Mary and Viola, the plot changes to the island itself, introduced by two unnamed characters pounding yams in the traditional way. Soon a voice-over narrates a sequence of images:

My story begins on the eve of my family's migration north.
My story begins before I was born.
My great-great-grandmudda Nana Peazant saw her family coming
     apart,
Her flowers to bloom in the distant frontier.

And then, there was my ma and daddy's problem . . .
Nana prayed and the old souls guided me into the new world.
I came in time for the big celebration,
To be among my cousins, my aunties, and uncles.
I can still see their faces, smell the oil in the wicker lamps.
I can hear the voice of Auntie Haagar calling out for her daughters,
    Iona and Myown,
And teasing the newlyweds.

The verselike structure of the voice-over narration serves as a cue that it is to be read figuratively, yet unlike earlier verse, the relationship of word-image here grounds the voice-over with a degree of literalness. The verse about "ma and daddy's problem," for instance, occurs over the image of a couple lying in bed awake, the male having turned his back to the female. Unlike the voice-image relationship in the film's opening, in this case elements within the image can be seen to correspond to the words of the voice-over. The verses about being among cousins and teasing newlyweds also share similarities to the images that are shown. As a result of this correspondence between word and image, the voice-over takes on a degree of literalness: explaining, as it were, the images that are unfolding.

The literal operations of the verses, however, also create contradictions to the voice-over, which, like the contradictions of the earlier voice-over, function to resist the finalization of signification. The contradiction occurs as a result of the literal mode not being able to provide a definitive basis of interpretation for the verses. The literal mode here is guided by the plot's need to introduce characters and settings, and by the trajectory that the verses undertake. The verses establish a prologue, the family dynamics before the birth, and what seems to be a causal chain: Nana prays, old souls guide, child is born. This latter event is suggested by the phrases "the old souls guided me into the new world," and "I came in time for the big celebration." As a result of her coming into the world, the child sees all the sights of the family gathering. In this respect, the verses, and their corresponding images, function to fulfill the expositional—or informational—needs of the plot: it establishes a new character.

The contradiction lies, however, in the voice-over's assertion that it remembers the sights, smells, and sounds of the events being depicted, a memory that defies the cognitive abilities of a newborn. In this respect, the contradiction is a conflict between literal signifying modes, with their tendency to finalize signification, and the figurative or poetic modes, which allow for greater flux and dynamics within signification. In addition, the contradiction structures a conflict between modern thought, grounded as it is in literal signification, and traditional tribal modes of understanding, which are rooted in a spiritual orientation to reality and lend themselves more to metaphorical signification. The verses make sense only through a figurative/tribal/spiritual mode: the child as baby did not arrive, but rather, the child's spirit came to dwell among its relatives and witness the events.

Here too, the film structures retroactive interpretation into the plot. Throughout the narrative, the image of the child as spirit, dressed in white with a blue bow in her hair, repeatedly enters into diegetic space, at one point literally manifesting herself in front of the lens of Snead the photographer (whose character is a modernized assimilationist, and thus, least likely to "see" a spirit). With this narrative information, the spectator can retroactively discern the meaning of the unborn child's first voice-over—that rather than signifying her birth, the child's spirit preceded her corporeal existence among the family. In addition, specific images within the sequence the child narrates are made clear not by the narration itself but by plot events that occur much later, as for example the glass of water on top of a piece of paper (which Eula later explains is a means for her to reach her mother's spirit). As such, the narrative engenders, as it did with the first set of verses, the significance of remembering.

The character of the unborn child thus holds a complex function within the plot. She is of the future, but functions within the plot as an important link between the present, which finds the family headed for migration and assimilation, and the past, at which time the family functioned as an important site of survival and resistance to slavery. This kind of temporal dynamic further functions to disallow efficient, literal, and final meaning to be assigned to the character. In this respect, the unborn child functions within an overall film style that resists finalizing meaning.

The film's resistance to finalizing meaning is not articulated solely through style, but through plot as well. Bambara argues, for example, that "the narrative is not 'classical' in the Western-specific sense. It is classic in the African sense. There are digressions and meanderings—as we may be familiar with from African . . . and other cinemas that employ features of the oral tradition."[8] The digressions and meanderings Bambara identifies are integral to the film's abandonment of the classical style's ideological obsession with the finalization of meaning. Rather than striving to achieve the tight linear trajectory of character-centered, goal-oriented narrative, *Daughters of the Dust* is concerned with the relationships between characters and how each contributes to the composition and continuity of the family legacy.

In this respect, *Daughters of the Dust* is structured far less around action than around interaction. As in the classical cinema, individual characters come to represent broader sociological types: the matriarch (Nana), the domestic/prostitute (Yellow Mary), the "Christianized" assimilationist (Viola), the victim of white rape (Eula), the outsider and contemporary assimilationist (Snead), and so on. In contrast to the characters in classical cinema, however, the characters in *Daughters of the Dust* are neither static nor finalized in the meanings assigned to them. Through their interactions with other characters, they not only evolve, but reveal how their own individualism and place within the family enable them to transcend their sociological typing.

The film's abandonment of a plot organized around a single character and the actions this character undertakes to achieve a goal does not, however, eliminate the strong presence of goal orientation in the narrative. *Daughters of the Dust*, however, reverses the structure of goal orientation. In classical cinema, the goal of the main character may be stated early in the narrative, but the goal itself is situated toward the end of plot, where it is achieved through a series of actions that shape the finalization of both the narrative goal, and the film's overall meaning. In *Daughters of the Dust*, however, the goal of crossing over to the mainland not only transcends individual character, but is the whole reason for the narrative to begin. As an action, it is a foregone conclusion, it is already going to occur. Its status as foregone conclusion is the very reason for the reunion. Thus, characters will not work towards this end—that work has already been done—but rather, will struggle with what the goal will do to the family. In this respect, there is no narrative drive to achieve the action, but rather, the meandering investigation of whether the family will be able to survive it. In its probing, figurative, and circuitous examination of the family and its upcoming crossing, the film displaces narrative drive and resists finalizing the meaning of the event, rejecting a fixed and singular definition of it.

In addition to the structure of the plot, specific plot events also function to resist finalizing meaning. One of the earliest plot events that reinforces this position occurs in the confrontation between Yellow Mary and Viola. In her introduction of Snead, Viola begins to give her interpretation to the meaning of the family's coming migration, stating: "I see this day as the first steps towards progress; an engraved invitation to the culture, education, and wealth of the mainland. Yellow Mary, wouldn't you agree?" Instead of offering a response, however, Yellow Mary only looks at her companion, and the two burst out laughing. Viola's reaction makes clear her feelings that she has been rudely rebuffed.

Several elements of the plot function to invalidate Viola's position as missionary-Christian assimilationist, not the least of which is the temporal relationship between the film's story, which is set at the turn of the century, and its telling, which occurs almost 100 years later, in 1991. The future that Viola envisions is already long past for the spectator who listens to her interpretation. From their position in history, spectators know how painfully naive Viola is in terms of the "engraved" invitation. The racist society that the Peazant family is about to face is going to give neither culture nor education nor wealth to Afro-Americans. Rather, the Peazant family is headed to a racist, segregationist society that still outlaws interracial marriage, refuses to provide adequate education, allows lynching to go on unabated, and makes it nearly impossible for people of color to obtain justice.

As the plot continues, it further undermines not only Viola's interpretation but nearly all pronouncements that are made with certainty and finality. Indeed, soon after Viola's naive assessment of the migration, Snead self-assuredly corrects Viola's history of the islands, asserting that "our" government had outlawed the trafficking of slaves fifty years before the Civil War. The plot's visual emphasis on the island's isolation and intimidating landscape, however, work to validate Viola's correction of Snead's perspective: in the remote and inaccessible Sea Islands, slavers had the means and abilities to conduct their trade, especially in the absence of a strong and committed federal government rigorously enforcing the law. The shifting within the plot of the credibility of character's positions is evident here. While Viola's rigid appropriation of Christianity will be consistently critiqued by the plot's evaluative system, here the plot allows her to critique Snead's naive judgment about the relationship between law and actions. As the narrative trajectory continues, the plot will consistently undermine the finality that signifying practices impose.

In contradistinction to the sites of signifying practices of the contemporary world—Christianity, history, contemporary society, the law—the film validates the signifying practice of the Gullah culture, which resists finalization. As Bambara argues: "*Daughters of the Dust* advances the idea that African culture can subvert the imposed one."[9] The film's subversive potential, however, lies precisely in its rejection of the linear opposition and finalization upon which Eurocentric language and culture rest, derived as they are from rationalism and empiricism. The signifying system that Nana Peazant embodies inclines far more toward the metaphorical, spiritual, and circular, stressing continuity—especially the continuity of past, present, and future—over opposition.

In this respect, the film's most pointed critique is leveled at those characters who adopt the values of contemporary culture—values imbued with racism and privilege—over their own cultural heritage, which constitutes a means for survival and resistance to a social system of privilege, violence, and oppression. This is most clearly articulated through the Peazant women's reaction to Yellow Mary's entrance. While two of the younger daughters—Iona and Eula—greet their relative with wonder and affection, Haagar, Viola, and others offer only contempt and scorn for her, describing her as a shameless hussy, and commenting that a "buzzard don't circle the air just for fun, that gal done come back here for something." The good will that has come to characterize family relations to this point is notably lacking, and the tension between the Peazant women, with their "upright" views, and Yellow Mary is palpable.

While perhaps not as pronounced as in classical Hollywood cinema, the film's critique of the Peazant women at this juncture is nonetheless articulated through several elements of plot, including the above described inconsistency of character (family relations are suspended with respect to Yellow Mary) and the comparative behaviors the plot draws. Immediately following the standoff with Yellow Mary, the Peazant women are shown preparing for the picnic. In addition to showing the elaborate preparations that go into the meal, the sequence is striking for the tenderness it shows among the characters, even as they criticize and malign each other. Within the rituals of their cultural heritage, as the scene makes clear, the preparation of food is of vital importance. Enveloped within that ritual, the characters take on behaviors that are far more authentic to them than the hierarchical, moral-judgmental mode they adopt with respect to Yellow Mary—a mode adopted from the culture of domination and privilege of the mainland.

Another comparison that critiques the Peazant women's appropriation of the values and signifying practices of dominant culture is Nana Peazant's greeting of Yellow Mary. Rather than stand over her in confrontation, Nana greets Yellow Mary while sitting and in a loving embrace, stroking her hair. Nana's position with respect to Yellow Mary is based on familial bonds that are grounded in the knowledge that the family and their cultural heritage constitute the principal means of survival and resistance against the trauma and violence of slavery and racism. Nana, Eula, and Yellow Mary thus come to constitute an important site for the plot's articulation of this position. For these characters, the family is an important site of shared suffering whose collective strength can overcome individual vulnerability and victimization, precisely because of its privileging of unconditional love over the norms and values of contemporary society. The family is thus an important site of resistance because it functions as an alternative meaning system. It engenders flexibility and transformation rather than fixity and finalization in signification precisely because its relations are in a constant state of change: Eli used to be a little goober-head, but he is now a young leader, and will one day have to function as knowledgeable elder.

The family as alternative meaning system is precisely what is abandoned by Viola, Haagar, and the others in their attempt to ostracize Yellow Mary. The contradictions at stake in their appropriation of the values of dominant white culture and its potential for self-destructiveness is evidenced in Viola's observation of Yellow Mary as "all that yalla wasted." The statement simultaneously expresses contempt and admiration for whiteness that is directed at Mary as a result of her status as mulatto. Mary stands as a reminder of the institutionalized rape of black women by white men, provided for first by slavery, then by a judicial system that gave black women no standing. Yellow Mary's position is further complicated for the Peazant women by her status as a domestic and prostitute. Though the latter becomes the convenient excuse for condemning Yellow Mary on the basis of morality, it is distaste for each profession's servicing of whites—the race and culture that is despised for its violence and domination of blacks but nonetheless holds out a promise of enrichment—that creates such hostility toward Mary.

Both Nana and Eula, however, reject this position towards Yellow Mary, insisting on the maintenance of family unity as the basis of individual empowerment. Eula points up the family's hypocrisy—they take Yellow Mary's money to help a family member in trouble with the law, but reject her personally. In addition, Eula also passionately entreats the family to accept Yellow Mary, delineating for them the family dynamic whereby individual members depersonalize and subsequently reject Yellow Mary as a way of mastering the traumatic legacy of slavery and racism. "We carry too many scars from the past," Eula informs them, and critiques this by warning that, "We wear our scars like armor, for protec-

The family as healing community. Yellow Mary, Nana, and Eula share their pain and their love for each other, rejecting the white bourgeois values of stoicism. Courtesy of Kino Films International.

tion." Eula makes clear that such a dynamic plays into myths of individualism and goes against the strength that the family as site of shared suffering and unconditional love can offer. Her argument demonstrates that rejecting Yellow Mary only functions to destroy their own humanity, as well as the family collective.

In her entreaty, Eula thus warns the family against adopting the signifier and its finalization—Yellow Mary as "ruint"—as decidedly dehumanizing and at cross-purposes to the cultural integrity of the family and its survival.

The film's resistance to the finalization of meaning is also articulated by the comparison of the ideology of assimilation to the ideology of *nommo*, what Bambara describes as "that harmonizing energy that connects body/mind/spirit/self/community with the universe."[10] The ideology of assimilation is articulated in the text by and through the characters of Haagar and Viola, while the character who most represents the ideology of *nommo* is Nana Peazant. Each of these characters insists on the validity of their beliefs throughout the narrative, but the plot evaluates each through an opposition between rigidity and flexibility. Hagaar and Viola are rigid in their assimilationism, the former having neither sensibility nor affection for the past, the latter expunging it through her adoption of missionary Christianity. Their inflexibility is articulated at several points in the narrative, but never more clearly than towards the end, where Nana asks each individual to engage in a ritual to preserve family unity. Viola, who sees the ritual of kissing a Bible that Nana has bound with mojo as blasphemous and heretical, breaks down before she can bring herself to act in love and solidarity with the family. Hagaar, however, rigidly refuses to do what she is asked, seeing the action as betraying the necessity of looking to the future. She is thus shown as being committed to assimilationism at the expense of family unity.

By comparison to the rigidity with which Hagaar and Viola adopt assimilationism, Nana Peazant and *nommo* function with enormous fluidity and adaptability. To begin with, Nana's position is not in opposition to the crossing, as her conversation with Eli demonstrates. Nana is trying less to hold the family to the island as a geographical site than to hold together their unity and cultural integrity as a spiritual site. As she says to Eli, "I'm trying to teach you how to track your own spirit. I'm trying to give you something to take north besides big dreams." In this respect, Nana tries to provide the family with the means by which to survive and resist a society and cultural mode that seek nothing less than their dissolution.

The iconography of Nana's *nommo* also articulates the fluidity and adaptability that are at the core of its unifying function. Nana's spiritual practice includes fashioning bottle trees, writing notes to the dead, making amulets, and engaging in other practices that incorporate objects of the contemporary world. Rooted though it is in ancient tribal religions, this spirituality neither rejects nor is confounded by the contemporary world, but weaves it into its ongoing process of harmony, unity, and continuity between the past and present, the dead and the living, the individual and the community. As a result, Nana does not see the modern world, or the crossing itself, as the death of the family; rather, she sees the modern world and its changes as important sites in which *nommo* must be maintained.

Nana is not the only character who articulates this position, however. When Snead, the photographer, comes upon the male elders, he states, "I see your family still sticks to the old ways." A Peazant male responds,

"Yeah, yeah, we stick to 'em. But times are changing. And you know Mr. Snead, you have to change with the times." The irony of the statement is indicative of the balance between the old ways and contemporary culture. The last thing that Snead, the assimilationist, needs to be told is that one must change with the times. The statement is thus not meant to favor assimilationism, which expunges the past, but rather, to favor adaptability, which engages the contemporary world with a commitment to the past. As with Nana Peazant, this adaptability and commitment to the past are rooted in maintaining harmony and unity, and function to resist finalization by insisting upon the fluidity of all things rather than static categorization.

This fluidity as a means of fostering multiple meanings is figured in the film through the tale of the Ibo, a story within the story. As Eula tells it, the Ibo were Africans brought over in bondage to the Sea Islands for a life of slavery. When the Ibo stepped onto the land and saw the life that their "masters" had planned for them, they turned around and walked all the way back to Africa.

Within the film, the status of the supernatural story changes from character to character. For some characters, the fantastic tale is "true" and thus serves as a model of resistance and defiance to bondage and slavery. For these characters, there is a duality to this tale. In one respect, they understand the tale as describing the spirit of the Ibo people—the tale speaks of the manner in which bondage failed to take their spirit and their souls. In another respect, however, they insist on the literalness of the story as a means of expressing the totality of the Ibo's resistance. Fantastic and improbable, the story gains significance not from its relationship to reality but from its ability to provide an image of total resistance to slavery and domination.

For other characters, such as Bilal, the tale of the Ibo is not true. Bilal is defined by the other characters as a "saltwater negro" who "come over on the very last slave ship."

Bilal tells Snead how he came over on the slave ship with the Ibo. He emphasizes a literal version of the tale by stating, "but Mister, I was there." He then tells Snead, "Those Ibo men, women, and children, a hundred or more, shackled in iron, when they go down in that water, they ain't never come up. And nobody can walk on water."

As with most elements of the story, however, the function of the Ibo tale lies not in its truth value, but in its contribution to the characters' lives. This is made clear by the manner in which each telling of the story occurs in the presence of Eli, distraught over the rape of his wife and his fear that the child she now carries is not his. When Eula tells the fantastic version of the tale for Eli, its function is for healing—to help Eli overcome domination ideology and maintain family wholeness despite the trauma. The success of the healing is demonstrated by Eli's ability to receive a vision of the unborn child wandering into the past, a vision that the child describes as the "eternal" and that reminds Eli that he—and the whole family—are "children of those who chose to survive."

Eli hears Bilal's version of the tale after he has experienced his vision. Bilal's insistence on the literal, then, is not so much a contradiction as a confirmation of the brutal social reality that is the basis of the family, its lineage, and its endurance. Rather than validate one version over another, which would engender the ideology of domination, the plot instead articulates the function of the telling: to give meaning to the tragedy of domination in order to both survive and transcend it—both of which are important.

The plot emphasizes the function of the telling by demonstrating the transformative effects of *nommo* on both Eli, who achieves unity and harmony with his wife, and Snead, the ultimate assimilationist who goes from being thoroughly ensconced in the modern world to being in harmony with the cultural richness and vitality of the past. The more contact Snead has with the Gullah traditions and stories, the more animated he becomes—to the point where it pushes him to envelop Viola in an embrace and kiss her passionately, a transcendent action that helps free Viola from the stagnant primness of her missionary Christianity.

In addition to its effects on Eli and Snead, the transformative effects of *nommo* are experienced by Yellow Mary, who in the end chooses to stay on the island rather than go north to Nova Scotia. Hardened and not a little cynical from her experience of being a "ruint" woman, Yellow Mary is healed through Eula's affirmation and Nana's love and commitment to family unity. Yellow Mary comes to recognize her need to have a place where people know who she is, and accept her for who she is. As she states, "I need to know that there's a place I can come back to. Where I can say my name and be proud of who I am." What Yellow Mary comes to see is that the comforts of the material world are vastly inferior substitutes for the love and acceptance she has with her extended family. Yellow Mary thus forgoes the materialism that the crossing offers in order to stay behind, which the unborn child describes as a means of "growing older, wiser, stronger"—a pointedly nonmaterialist endorsement. The privileging of this position over the materialism of assimilation is further articulated through the unborn child's pride and emphasis on being born on the island, and by the manner in which the plot closes the narrative not with the crossing, but with those that stayed behind.

As with many stories within a story, the tale of the Ibo functions as a model for the larger story that frames it. Just as the Ibo tale functions to resist finalization, so too does the story of *Daughters of the Dust*. The story's long-delayed conclusion of the family crossing over to the mainland is constructed as a site of multiple meanings rather than as a final action validating the narrative's predetermined ideological position. Several elements of plot function to create this multiplicity of meanings. One is the meandering narrative trajectory itself. Despite its having taken several digressions and diversions, the narrative does arrive at the point of the family's departure. Having invested the structure of the plot with a focus on character interrelationships, however, the narrative continues that focus with the departure. The departure is not coded as one singular action, but rather, as a focal point for several character interactions. This is particularly emphasized by the manner in which the plot dynamics result in some family members staying on the island while others leave. Within the plot trajectory, then, what unites the family members is not the action of crossing over, but rather, the possibility of maintaining unity and harmony if they will embrace *nommo*.

Another element of plot that functions to diversify the meaning of the ending is the temporal relationship between story and telling. The knowledge of the characters, set as they are in the past, is not equal to the knowledge of the spectators, who know—to some extent—what the future holds for both those migrating north and those staying behind. Though each group is full of hope and possibilities for the future, the spectator has potential to know that what the future holds for both groups is continued subjection to the effects of racism and domination ideology. The group heading north will not receive the material comfort promised to them in picture catalogs, but instead will be exposed to racism, violence, and exploitation of their labor. Likewise, the future of the group that stays behind will not only be shaped by the continuing struggle against racism, but will see displacement and encroachment of their lands when American leisure culture takes interest in the seashore for vacation spots. The isolation that made possible the continuation of the Gullah culture will later contribute to its demise, as developers create luxury hotels, golf courses, and gated communities for moneyed whites who desire exclusive locations.[11] For those who remain behind at Ibo Landing, the future holds equal threats to maintaining cultural integrity.

Yet although these meanings are engendered in the plot, *Daughters of the Dust* resists finalizing that meaning as the sole or ultimate message of the film. *Daughters of the Dust* is not a tragedy of what the crossing represents—the demise of cultural integrity—but rather, an object lesson in the Gullah culture's vitality, richness, and potential for recovery and continued resistance. Like the Ibo tale of which it tells, the narrative gives evidence of the reality of tragedy, but insists on the power of *nommo*—of Afro-American cultural integrity—to contest it.

Notes

1. Toni Cade Bambara, "Reading the Signs, Empowering the Eye: *Daughters of the Dust* and the Black Independent Cinema Movement," in Manthia Diawara, ed., *Black Cinema* (New York: Routledge Press, 1993), 119.

4. Ibid.

5. Sharon Willis, *High Contrast: Race and Gender in Contemporary Hollywood Film* (Durham and London: Duke University Press, 1997), 160.

6. Bambara, "Reading the Signs," 137.

7. David Bordwell, Janet Staiger, and Kirsten Thompson, *The Classical Hollywood Cinema: Film Style and Mode of Production to 1960* (New York: Columbia University Press, 1985), 13–14.

8. Bambara, "Reading the Signs," 123.

9. Ibid.

10. Ibid., 131.

11. See, for example, Marquetta Goodwine, "YEDDY WE: Statement to the UN Commission on Human Rights from the Gullah/Geechee Community of the United States," Geneva, Switzerland, April 1, 1999, where she states, "Wealthy developers have built 'gated communities' throughout the Sea Islands and left cultural destruction in their wake. Our graveyards and burial grounds have been desecrated. Grave markers have been removed and areas leveled. Club houses, golf courses, and other recreational facilities for rich affluent people have been placed on top of graves. This has gone on in spite of us bringing these issues out in courts which are supposed to uphold the laws that they have on their books that clearly state that this is an illegal practice.

We are not allowed to visit some of our burial grounds and graveyards or other sacred lands due to gated communities being located there. We are not allowed to enter these resort and retirement areas unless a person that lives within the gates leaves our names at the entrance to allow us 'permission' to enter."

10
The Great White Man of Lambarene and the Limits of Representation

A book that begins with colonialism, racism, and representation ends there too. This book began by taking up Stam and Spence's call for new methods to analyze film texts and their participation in the process of racism. It then started its investigation with *The Birth of A Nation*, a film that begins its story with "the bringing of the African to America," a highly romanticized way to characterize the slave trade. The European slave trade began what is now known as the African diaspora, the forced dispersal of Africans throughout the world. As *Daughters of the Dust* attempts to demonstrate, the maintenance of cultural integrity despite relocation and oppression is one of the primary challenges of the diaspora.

In addition to the slave trade, however, Europe devastated African cultures and social systems through its exploitation of the continent and oppression of its peoples conducted under the ideological institution of colonialism. The complex legacy of colonialism as a collision between two different social systems forms the subject of Bassek ba Kobbio's film, *Le Grand Blanc de Lamberene* (hereafter *The Great White Man*). Made in 1994, the film undertakes both the story of Albert Schweitzer, Nobel prize–winner and (in)famous humanitarian, and the African continent he served and tried to protect. Beginning with Schweitzer's work at his hospital in Lambarene during World War II, the film then follows what happens to both Schweitzer and the village as the end of the war brings about the end of colonialism and its ideologies. As Schweitzer continues his work, the continent around him undergoes enormous social changes and upheavals, as modernism supplants tribal culture, and Africa struggles towards self-determination. Through the enigmatic figure of Schweitzer, *The Great White Man* examines the complex relationship between colonialism, racism, and representation.

The film's concern with the last of these elements results not so much from the legacy of European colonialism as from another important social phenomenon within the African continent: American cultural and economic imperialism. Specifically, the film's style resists the passive adoption of classical Hollywood narrative. Similar to the American films *Daughters of the Dust* and *Do the Right Thing*, *The Great White Man of Lambarene*, organizes its style as a confrontation with the norms and conventions of the Hollywood style and the ideological frameworks they engender and articulate. In this respect, *The Great White Man* is representative of currents within African filmmaking that seek to interrogate African culture and society outside the limitations and ideological positions that the Hollywood style imposes. The style of *The Great White Man* is engaged in a process of dismantling and rejecting several of the conventions of the biography genre in order to resist the finalization of meaning. As with *Daughters of the Dust*, resistance to the finalization of meaning functions to articulate the role that representation can exercise in the process of racism and oppression.

A fundamental site for such resistance is structured through the film's dismantling of character consistency—an important convention of the Hollywood cinema. As discussed previously, Bordwell, Staiger, and Thompson argue that characters in the classical Hollywood cinema must be defined as a bundle of qualities or traits that are clearly identified and consistent with each other. They further assert that consistency of character is particularly important to classical cinema if the character must act as the prime causal agent of the narrative. Two important narrative operations go on within *The Great White Man* to dismantle this convention. First, the character most constructed to act as the prime causal agent, Schweitzer, is in fact the least consistent. The self-assured and driven Schweitzer that the film introduces moves erratically from one set of ideologically determined responses to another with such frequency that his reactions to narrative actions and events are unpredictable. Further, as the narrative trajectory unfolds, the plot undermines Schweitzer's position as prime causal agent, revealing instead the profound, decentralized, and unlocalized social forces that impact the narrative world: the demise of colonialism, African self-determination, modernization.

The film's beginning establishes the framework for such a dismantling by constructing Schweitzer as the central character with strong personality traits. He is driven (not only is he a humanitarian physician, but also a musician, theologian, and lecturer), detached, and dismissive—not only with respect to the African people he serves, but in all his interpersonal relationships. The film's opening establishes all of these traits. The first images of the film show an African man having his teeth pulled, a procedure the camera shows in tight shots that emphasize its excruciating effects. After the tooth is pulled and put into a metal basin with other teeth, a bucket of water is thrown on the patient, who is clearly in agony. At that moment, a young boy runs into the room, calling for the doctor and handing him his white pith helmet. The two make a quick exit, as French horns nondiegetically begin to play with a sense of urgency. The young boy and white doctor are next seen from a window as they run to the shoreline. The patient is left alone, both diegetically—there is no nurse or hospital staff to assist or care for him—and by the plot itself, which incorporates several elements—soundtrack, action, point-of-view editing, and a title sequence—to lure spectator attention away from the patient and towards the doctor.

This narrative ploy itself articulates the detachment of the doctor from the effect of his work on the patients. Through the above-mentioned plot devices, the narrative seeks to align the spectator with the doctor by giving assurances that there are far more important things going on that must be attended to. The plot does not wait long to relate to its audience what those things are. The young boy and the doctor wait by the shoreline in anticipation of arriving canoes. As the boy sadly observes, however, the canoes bring no medicine. The camera then slowly tilts and pans to reveal the reaction of the white mustached doctor who gazes, almost expressionless, at the procession of canoes on the expanse of river. He refrains from acknowledging either the boy's observation or his shared disappointment. Instead, the plot ends the scene by cutting to a wider establishing shot that shows the doctor and the boy from behind, looking out across the water, as a subtitle fades in on the left of the screen, informing spectators that the setting is Lambarene in 1944.

In her discussion of *Daughters of the Dust*, Toni Cade Bambara highlights the title that establishes the narrative setting as an important plot element. Bambara argues that in *Daughters of the Dust* the title lingers on the screen as a means of conveying the historical significance of time and place as an important interpretive element to the plot.[1] The title establishing the setting of *The Great White Man* likewise emphasizes the historical significance of the film's setting as an interpretive element, yet it does so through a quite different means. Rather than being centered, the title is placed in the lower left of the screen, and rather than lingering, it fades up and fades back out in under five seconds (the title in *Daughters of the Dust*, in contrast, lasts over ten seconds).

Composition and duration thus work to understate the title, but the narrative placement of the "statement" that the title articulates functions to invest it with dramatic force and significance. The title comes after the disappointing pronouncement that there is no medicine (for example, anesthesia for pulling teeth), and, by its date, the title informs the audience why there is no medicine: not so much because the setting is remote and primitive Africa, but because it is the height of World War II. Later, the plot, through the character of Helene, will articulate in more detail how the war has cut off supplies to the hospital, a shortage that is conveyed in several other places within the narrative. The setting title, however, serves a function beyond explaining the lack of medicine; in addition, it marks the significance of the historical period within which the film is set. The understated title establishes that the narrative is not going to be the biography—the complete life history—of Schweitzer, but rather, that it will privilege a select period in that history. As later narrative events will demonstrate, the period is privileged precisely because of its significance to colonialism. With the end of the war, the period of European colonialism will slowly and painfully come to a close. What that *means,* in terms of Africa—its future possibilities, pitfalls, and potential—becomes a key focus of the film.

Through the contradictory figure of Schweitzer, however, the film makes clear that ideological certainty with respect to the meaning of postcolonial Africa is only an effect of representation and not an indicator of truth. The narrative trajectory represents Schweitzer within and through a variety of competing and conflicting attitudes and discourses, some of which he embodies, others of which are attached to him via the observations of other characters—as with the observations made by Helene, Koumba, and Bissa.

One of the traits that the plot establishes and then contradicts, is the doctor's dismissive and condescending attitude towards Africans. This is pointedly established when he rebuffs the young Koumba's aspiration for growing up to be a doctor like Schweitzer himself. The film underscores the callousness of Schweitzer's dismissiveness by having the doctor immediately turn and affectionately play with a young chimpanzee, expressing

The character of Altmeyer adds to the complexity of Schweitzer by changing from admirer to critic, Courtesy of California Newsreel.

more warmth and devotion to the animal than to the boy at his side (a boy whom, the plot will later establish, the doctor brought into the world). As if that were not emphasis enough, the plot has the doctor pause, call to Koumba, gesture for the boy to come forward, and then hand him a piece of candy, a token expression that is clearly ignorant of the crushing impact the doctor's dismissal of Koumba's ambitions has had on the boy.

As the narrative progresses, however, each of these character traits, and others that the plot establishes—moral rectitude, affection for European sensibility and culture, exclusive belief in Western medicine, and Franciscan piety—will be contradicted. The dismissiveness and condescending attitude is gone when Schweitzer speaks to a witch doctor, attends to a dying chief, or an injured old man. What is significant in terms of the film's evaluative system and its dismantling of classical Hollywood narrative is that contradictory character actions and traits are conveyed neither as correctives nor as transformations of character. Rather, Schweitzer is shown as a figure struggling with and sometimes overcome by contradictions. Schweitzer's actions and attitudes seem to impulsively leap from him, whether as an explosion of righteous anger, or as a flood of compassion. What is significant for the plot is the manner in which contradictory responses and attitudes are not shown to be integrated and controlled through the agency of character identity, but rather disconnected and unbridled impulses that at any time determine Schweitzer's character.

That impulsive constitution is articulated early in the film when Chief Mata and his retinue enter the hospital grounds. A herald loudly announces the chief's arrival and demands the presence of the Great White Man. The booming voice of the herald disrupts the courtyard of the hospital, and the tone of the demanding request makes Schweitzer bristle. As a revered figure, Schweitzer is accustomed to being treated with the utmost respect and deference; he is thus angered by the herald, and shouts back his own demand to know the source of the disruption. Upon finding out the source, however, Schweitzer immediately abandons his authoritative position and patiently listens to the herald announce the great chief.

The narrative emphasizes through repetition that Schweitzer's initial impulse is to assume a position of authority and expect deference. Later in the plot, when the chief vociferously demands the deference accorded to his position by being given extra doses of medicine, Schweitzer's first response is to assert his own position and authority. That Chief Mata's request makes no medical sense gives reason for Schweitzer to maintain this assertion of authority. Here too, however, Schweitzer abandons his own position in order to defer to the values of native culture that give Mata an elevated status.

This repetition of Schweitzer adopting and then abandoning his position of authority and status functions to emphasize the conflicting traits within his character. The first trait is Schweitzer's obvious attachment to the authority and deference he commands, a status he believes he has earned through his hard work and sacrifice. The narrative also makes clear, however, that Schweitzer is fully cognizant that he lives and works within a cultural and symbolic framework different from his own, and demonstrates a commitment to respecting this other culture's values. The narrative trajectory, however, structures Schweitzer's commitment to alternative cultural values as unpredictable and unreliable. At certain junctures he maintains the commitment even when it requires foregoing his own revered status, as his interactions with Mata demonstrate, but at other points he abandons that respectful stance, as when he derides the woman with venereal disease.

Another site of Schweitzer's inconsistency of character is his arrogant belief in the superiority of Western medicine. Early in the film he condescendingly rejects Lambi's suggestion that they turn to the native *iboga* cure when they run out of medicine. Later, he not only turns to this cure in desperation as a placebo, but begins to research its possible efficacy. Unlike traditional biographic narrative, however, Schweitzer's interest in the efficacy of *iboga* is not an event that signals a transformation of character. Schweitzer does not come to reconcile Western medicine with the herbalism from which it evolved, nor is he led to a new respect for the wisdom of traditional African culture. Rather, his interest in researching the efficacy of *iboga* is only fleetingly justified as his desire for more control in operating a clinic, but then is abandoned in the course of the narrative, another fleeting and impulsive desire of the doctor.

Schweitzer's inconsistent adoption of traits is emphasized in the aforementioned scene of his treatment of the African woman with venereal disease. The respect for African values afforded to Chief Mata is clearly abandoned in this scene. Instead, as Lambi informs him, he showed respect neither for the woman nor for her husband's polygamy. Indeed, in his arrogant assertion of European prudery, Schweitzer ignorantly and arrogantly tells the woman to disobey her husband. Significantly, the scene emphasizes both the callousness of his tirade and its impulsiveness, by showing him immediately moved to compassion at the sight of an injured elderly man who is next for treatment. The performative element of the plot and its choreography is crucial here. The manner in which the character of Schweitzer is shown responding to each of these characters downplays the agency of identity as site of control. Schweitzer's responses are instead shown to irrupt uncontrollably out of him. He is no sooner shown to be berating the woman and lamenting his position as Great White Man, when the camera shows his gaze being directed to the old man's deeply scarred leg, and being immediately reduced to pity. What is particularly significant to the rhetoric of the plot is not just the pronounced contrast between the two responses and the lack of agency in their articulation, but the manner in which the narrative resists resolving the difference. There is no clear hierarchy of traits that can resolve the differences, no explanations for the inconsistent manner in which traits are adopted.

Character inconsistency is further articulated in Schweitzer's mistreatment of Lambi, the faithful and steadfast native male nurse. Here too the commitment to African values and culture is abandoned in favor of an emotive outburst. Prior to the scene, the plot demonstrates a range of attitudes towards Lambi: Schweitzer addresses him as Westerner to African, doctor to nurse, and significantly, man to man (about Bissa). This range of positions within the relationship serves as narrative motivation for Lambi to not only take corrective measures for the doctor's cultural mistakes, but to confront the doctor about his mistakes—as he does at the doctor's mistreatment of the woman with venereal disease. Here, however, Lambi makes clear to Schweitzer that the doctor has failed to negotiate the nuance and implications of Mata's imminent death, but Schweitzer angrily and arrogantly assumes his position as the Great White Man, and strikes Lambi for informing the chief of what Schweitzer has kept hidden from him. The violence, while motivated by Schweitzer's anger, arrogance, and driven personality, nonetheless serves within the plot as the height of Schweitzer's character flaws: it is directed at a loyal and steadfast assistant and is followed by the most arrogant assertion of Schweitzer's status in the entire film. Furthermore, its emotional tenor is emphasized by the traumatic effects the action has on Lambi's son, Koumba, who witnesses his father's humiliation. The scene's closure with the young Koumba weeping as he cradles his father in his arms makes clear that the film's evaluative norms are critical of Schweitzer's action.

The scene is significant for several reasons. To begin with, it structures an inconsistency to Schweitzer's behavior, drawing a parallel between an earlier point in the plot where Lambi corrects Schweitzer's cultural insensitivity without such repercussions. The result of the comparison is that Schweitzer is rendered as not in control of the competing and contradictory forces that operate within him, the compassionate humanitarian is immediately transformed into violent overseer when his work is compromised by another. The degree to which these competing forces function as character inconsistency is demonstrated by the lack of connection between Schweitzer's mistreatment of Lambi and his compassionate, driven humanitarianism. The potential for the action to serve as a culminating event is articulated within the plot by its effect on Koumba: it motivates him into permanent opposition to the doctor. The child will leave Lambarene and not return until he is educated as an adult and ready to supplant Schweitzer. The event has no such effect on Schweitzer, however. He does not come to see his violent mistreatment as antithetical to the Christianity he preaches, or the humanitarianism that drives him. Indeed, what the plot emphasizes instead is that Schweitzer never seems to think twice about his outburst, and replicates the behavior on a smaller scale during the photo shoot at the riverbank, first striking Africans to get them out of the way, then embracing them for the purpose of a photograph.

In addition to functioning as a heightened articulation of character inconsistency, the scene also operates to illustrate the complexities involved when the ideologies of two different social systems come in contact and conflict with one another. This complexity is demonstrated by the manner in which neither Lambi nor Schweitzer comes to occupy the place of truth. Schweitzer's withholding of information *is* having a placebo effect on Mata, but it will not cure him, as Schweitzer himself admits to Helene and Lambi. As Lambi's position makes clear, however, Schweitzer is not considering the cultural impact of Mata's death; that the tribe must be made ready for such a devastating event to their social system. In this respect, Schweitzer is wrong. The plot, however, does not validate Lambi's position as being any more right. Lambi's confession to the chief hastens Mata's death; without the placebo effect, he has nothing to counteract his terminal illness, and quickly deteriorates. Lambi's action thus forecloses the possibility for preparation that motivated him to begin with. In this respect, Lambi's position is undermined by his inability to handle the consequences of his actions.

The complexity of the situation is articulated by the manner in which the events do not ultimately invalidate each character's position. Lambi's position—his claim that the doctor does not understand the social consequences of his treatment—remains valid even if Lambi cannot provide the proper corrective. On the other hand, Schweitzer's decision to treat the terminal patient through the placebo effect in order to diminish suffering and prolong life is likewise valid, as demonstrated by Mata's vitality during his treatment. The plot thus denies either Schweitzer or Lambi, and their respective positions, sole claim to the place of truth. Rather, their positions are strictly bound to the ideologies from which they emerge. Lambi's assertion of tribal customs and propriety cannot take into account how Schweitzer's treatment is working, and conversely, Schweitzer's placebo effect cannot function within tribal customs and propriety: it cannot work if Mata is to prepare for his death.

The ideological limitations placed on their positions—on their ideas and subsequent actions—is a central concern of the film's rhetoric, which insists on the inability of truth to exist within representation. Rather than simple revisionism, which replaces one finalized ideological interpretation (Schweitzer as a hero) with another (Schweitzer as colonial racist), *The Great White Man* organizes several competing and antagonistic discourses in order to construct Schweitzer—and the contact between Africa and Europe—as an enigma. The function of this enigmatic construction is to caution against ideological certitude and point instead to what lies beyond representation: Schweitzer as a reality beyond what he believes and how he acts, beyond what the accurate assessments people level at him and the impact he has. Further, the film extends this enigmatic complexity to the continent itself: the Africa beyond the political machinations of extricating itself from colonialism, beyond the modern states it now erects, beyond the tribal societies it has left behind. As further discussion will demonstrate, the narrative disallows any discourse or image the privileged status of conveying truth. Rather, the plot insists on truth as existing only beyond representation and meaning systems.

One of the means by which the plot conveys this position is by undermining the meaning of the sign. Schweitzer's gift of candy to Koumba demonstrates this point. As discussed previously, the gesture is situated within the plot as a means of articulating Schweitzer's detachment and arrogance. Later in the plot, however, when Schweitzer hands a piece of candy to Koumba's ill child, the gesture is read as a sign of Schweitzer's cleverness, compassion, and effectiveness. Koumba stands by impotently as his child suffers from meningitis, science having exhausted itself without result in treating the child. Schweitzer, however, responds to the child's pain by handing him a piece of candy—a gift that temporarily distracts the child from his suffering. The same gesture—handing candy to a child—is thus structured by the plot as not having the same meaning. Rather, as an outward sign about Schweitzer's character, the gesture cannot be read consistently. As a result, the plot undermines the ability of the sign to convey truth, pointing instead to a reality beyond representation: a Schweitzer that cannot be reduced to his actions and gestures.

The primary means by which the plot articulates this position is through the interrelationship between different characters and the discourses they represent. Although several characters—Mikendi, Bissa, and Koumba, as well as Schweitzer—come to articulate valid statements, each of their discourses fails as truth precisely because they cannot represent the totality of the situation, despite claiming that goal. One of the earlier indications of this failure, and thus of the film's reticence towards ideological certitude, is demonstrated through the character of Mikendi. After his return from the war, Mikendi speaks to his village as they are gathered around the fire, warning them of white culture by describing the racism he experienced while fighting with the Allied Armies. When he finishes, his father, the village chief, remarks that "wisdom itself flows from your mouth." Such a statement, which clearly functions as a confirmation, is nonetheless immediately followed by the chief's pronouncement that, "There are days like this when I am sure your good mother screwed with a hare."

The chief's discourse is thus cause for confusion, as the two statements appear to be antithetical to each other. Mikendi's statements are made immediately after the proprietor of the trading post attempts to cheat an African soldier for participating in the victory party. The prior scene thus functions to establish the veracity of Mikendi's statement that the whites are cheats. Further support is then leant to this statement by the chief's first remark, which compliments the son in a manner that validates Mikendi's discourse.[2] The immediate criticism of Mikendi after the compliment then creates a contradiction.

Within the plot's rhetorical position against discourse claiming to represent a totality, however, the contradiction can be resolved. Mikendi's discourse, so clearly delivered to a public audience, and so emphatically conclusive about the white race, attempts to represent the totality of the relationship and future relationship between black Africa and the white race. The chief's criticism is thus directed at that totalizing function. As the prior scene of the victory party demonstrates, Mikendi's position based on his experience in the war is valid; whites do consistently seek to subject blacks to inferior positions and status. Despite this validation, however, his experience is insufficient to sum up the totality of the white-black relationship. The chief's criticism is motivated by his experience of Schweitzer, and the positive contributions that white culture can make to Africa. He thus rejects Mikendi's model as too one-sided and overly simplistic for determining the course that black Africa must take in the postwar world.

The complexity of the film's organization of antagonistic discourses is evidenced at this juncture. Mikendi's criticism of whites is an accurate assessment—and prediction—of how the white nations exploit Africa and its peoples. The future will hold even more economic and political exploitation, as Africa is subjected to the role of pawn in the Cold War, and used as an inferior trading partner for multinational corporations. It is important, however, for the film's rhetorical position—its criticism of discourse as bound to its ideological limitations—that the validity of Mikendi's statements coexists with the validity of the chief's; neither is privileged over the other and confirmed as the truth—in all its totality—about Africa.

In addition to demonstrating the limitations of Mikendi's discourse as signification, the plot also conveys the ideological limitations of Mikendi's discourse by pointing up its contradictions. Mikendi's position is to reject whites, but is nonetheless assimilationist. He disposes of the tribal social system and seeks instead to adopt white culture, though without whites. Mikendi thus espouses a somewhat contradictory position of dispensing with traditional tribal culture for the adoption of white culture as a means of ensuring African self-determination.

The contradictions and limitations of Mikendi's position are further emphasized through his interactions with Bissa, a woman of Mikendi's tribe assigned by the chief to be Schweitzer's concubine. When Bissa learns of Mikendi's political maneuvering to claim the hospital, she confronts him immediately. In that confrontation, Bissa articulates the collective logic of tribal ideology that Mikendi is now sweeping aside in his quest for African self-determination. Mikendi attempts to silence her by accusing her of being a traitor to her people by sleeping with Schweitzer. Mikendi's accusation, however, carries no weight because, as Bissa makes clear, her responsibility to Schweitzer is a matter of doing the will of the people expressed through the chief. As she states, "I didn't ask to look after the *n'djembe*."

The iconography of the setting is an indicator of the film's evaluative position in the confrontation. As Bissa squares off against Mikendi, two photographs in the background—one of Marx and one of Lenin—divide the characters. Bissa repudiates Mikendi's accusation first by defending her role as the expression of the tribe, and then by admitting Schweitzer's rejection of a sexual relationship. Further, Bissa not only defends the doctor's commitment to the community—he has stayed while others have left—but also reasserts the village's commitment to the doctor, a commitment that Mikendi is now betraying. Bissa's position can thus be characterized as fidelity to the cultural traditions of the village. Mikendi, however, occupies a far more compromised position. He is consumed with adopting the power politics of white culture—signified by Marx and Lenin—at the expense of respecting the cultural integrity of the village. Indeed, his position against the "mixing of the races" reflects more the paranoia of colonial ideology than a commitment to tribal culture.

What is significant for the film's rhetorical position, however, is that the limitations and contradictions of Mikendi's position do not function as validation of Bissa, nor do they completely invalidate Mikendi. His observation that the time of the chiefs is over, and that politics and education will rule Africa is accurate. Further, his drive for self-determination during the waning of colonialism in Africa is an important preemptive strategy for containing the neocolonialism that is coming to Africa through multinational corporate exploitation of the continent. The plot thus constructs Mikendi's position as valid, but limited and contradictory. Further, it structures every other character and their position in the same way, refusing to privilege any discourse as occupying the place of truth.

As a result, while Bissa points up the contradictions Mikendi engenders, her own position is shown to be limited as well. While the plot positively evaluates her loyalty to tribal custom and tradition, it withholds from the position the means by which to build a social system in the postcolonial world. The powerful and volatile effects of colonialism on the continent foreclose the opportunity to simply return to tribal society. As such, the plot makes clear that, although it is valid, Bissa's position is also limited. The plot's refusal to allow any discourse to hold the place of truth is then further emphasized by synthesizing the antagonistic positions between Mikendi and Bissa. In the construction of the character of Koumba, the plot resolves the opposing positions of Mikendi, who abandons cultural integrity for contemporary power struggle, and Bissa, who maintains fidelity to cultural traditions. Koumba reintegrates the collective traditions of village culture into the postwar postcolonial struggle for self-determination through his commitment to the Pan-African movement. Here too, however, the plot will both validate and undermine the position of the character. The recurring photograph of Koumba as a young man confidently smoking a cigarette, his own completely Europeanized house, and his decision to study the law as well as medicine all function to convey the degree to which Koumba has situated himself decidedly within the modernist sensibility from which Schweitzer tries to protect Africa.

The film also makes clear, however, that Koumba is not a complete assimilationist. He does not abandon his respect for cultural tradition as Mikendi has. When prompted by his wife, he accompanies Schweitzer as the doctor exits their home—as codes of hospitality and respect would dictate. Furthermore, he honors the doctor's request to organize his funeral, maintaining, as does Bissa, the village's commitment to Schweitzer as a revered figure.

While Koumba represents one attempt at resolving cultural tradition with the modernist realities imposed on Africa, the film refrains from designating his character as an ideal model for such a resolution. Instead, as with every other character, the film evaluates Koumba ambivalently: the discourses located at the site of his character have validity, but cannot express the totality or the complexity of the situation. The plot's ambivalence towards Koumba is articulated by the manner in which he cannot live up to the symbolic mantle created for him, first by Mikendi, then by others. At several points in the film, characters invoke the return of Koumba with such hope and anticipation as to afford him savior status. Story events, however, do not grant him the ability to achieve that status. Indeed, rather than save the village from the complexities that confront it, Koumba is not even able to save his son from illness.

The plot's refusal to construct Koumba as a privileged site within the narrative confirms its rhetorical refusal to grant discourse, bound as it is to representation, the ability to occupy the place of truth about reality. Precisely what Koumba cannot live up to is a symbolic mantle that is created for him by others. It is not for lack of integrity that Koumba cannot live up to others' expectations; rather, his failure lies not in him but in the inability of any symbolic mantle to be real. The complexities facing the village, and by extension, Africa, are the result of different social systems—each bound by their own ideological limitations—coming into contact with each other. Within the sites of that contact, no position can successfully and completely resolve the conflict that is generated. To do so would be to assert that some social system, and the meanings that it creates, hold a privileged relationship to reality.

The Western world, backed by what Schweitzer calls its "fascination with science," has come to believe that it does possess such a relationship with reality—that through science, every aspect of reality can be known and conquered. The rhetorical position of the film, however, argues just the opposite. The scene in which the witch doctor points out the limitations of Western medicine articulates this position, one that Schweitzer will himself adopt in his confrontation with Altmeyer.

The film's critical stance towards the truth claims of representation is not limited to character interaction; plot events and the film's iconography also critique the process of representation and delineate the ideological limitations of meaning systems. The most pronounced of such scenes is the scene of Ingrid Lombard's arrival. A visiting journalist, Lombard arrives to write a story about Schweitzer, whose humanitarian renown is becoming so large as to make a Nobel Prize imminent. When Lombard first arrives, however, Schweitzer prohibits her from taking photographs, assuring her that there will be opportunity later. That opportunity, however, turns into the construction of an image, not the candid shot Ingrid attempted earlier. As Schweitzer's staff, followed by many natives, run down to the landing to unload hospital supplies from the boats, Schweitzer and Lombard follow, giving him the opportunity to strike poses invoking his "Great White Man" image. The scene is then transformed for Lombard's camera from unloading boats, to the doctor's arrival by boat. Schweitzer determinedly and arrogantly pursues the manufacture of this image, screaming and pushing at natives to conform with the requirements of the process. What Schweitzer fails to see, however, is that Ingrid is photographing his bullying as well as the image he wants to create and maintain. In addition to the humanitarian and paternal Schweitzer created through staging and posing, Ingrid also photographs his contemptible treatment of the people he serves.

In addition to demonstrating Schweitzer's cunning willingness to manufacture the image of the Great White Man, the scene details the artificiality of the process. It describes to the spectator the means by which elements are organized and framed in order to give evidence of a reality that does not necessarily exist. Significantly, the film chooses the photograph, an indexical sign, for its critique. Because the indexical sign bears a physical relationship to that which it represents, its meaning is typically invested with truth value. Precisely what the plot demonstrates, however, is that the meaning of the indexical sign is still arbitrary—the preexisting reality that the photograph captures does not necessarily exist.

Here too the plot does not simply substitute one truth for another. As the confrontation with Ingrid at the dinner table demonstrates, Ingrid no more possesses the truth about Schweitzer than does he, or anyone else. Her ability to capture Schweitzer berating the natives, and her critical stance towards the separate and unequal living conditions of his facility, is no more truthful than any other interpretation of Schweitzer—something she herself does not understand. As his participation in the manufacture of his Great White Man image indicates, representation is a matter of creating meaning for a desired purpose. The real Schweitzer is a complex reality beyond representation.

The inability of the signifier to produce reality is also a central issue in the film's treatment of independence. The period of African independence is introduced immediately after the departure of Helene, an exit marked by ceremonial good-byes in the tradition of the village. Its contrast to the scene that marks the beginning of independence is striking. The simple clothing and bare feet of the previous scene are gone, replaced by

European fashions. The river, which serves as the foundation of the village, is replaced by a fabricated plaza, decorated in the bright colors of the newly adopted flag. To punctuate the visual contrast, the ceremonial sounds of village life are replaced by European-style pop music played on electric instruments. The plot thus undermines the celebratory atmosphere by constructing the village's transformation into a modernized city as an abandonment of cultural heritage and traditions. This is further conveyed by the manner in which the scene ends with a villager playing a trumpet in the band—a trumpet that Schweitzer gave him in an attempt to silence his drum playing. The closing shot is then of Schweitzer walking away dejectedly, demoralized over the triumph of modernism over tribal culture—a process he naively thought could be contained.

In addition to undermining the celebration, the plot demonstrates the limitations of independence by focusing on how little it affects the material reality of the citizens of Lambarene. The food-distribution scene emphasizes this point. As one villager tells Bertha, the people thought they would see more food as a result of independence, but they do not. Just as with the African staff of the prior scene, independence does not affect the material lives of the people. In addition, however, the scene articulates the complex issues at stake in independence. The scene begins with the distribution of food according to the colonial customs of patrician philanthropy: each villager is expected to thank the Great White Man for the rations he or she receives. When the people realize that independence is not going to affect their material existence, they nonetheless insist on the dismantling of these customs, which afford them no respect or equality. The film validates this position by conveying the inappropriateness of Bertha's behavior; her response to the villagers' request to be treated with respect is contempt, a response that is antithetical to the humanitarianism that supposedly guides the Schweitzer enterprise.

The means by which the scene degenerates into anarchy, however, demonstrates how complexly colonialism imposes itself on a social system. The anarchy of the food distribution parallels the celebration of independence—neither changes the material existence of the villagers. Independence expunges colonialism from the political realm, but to no material effect. Likewise, the popular rebellion against patrician philanthropy can offer no material changes beyond the moment. The crowd may get more goods from the wagon, but it has no means to fill the wagon again. The conclusion, which the following scene will also work to convey, is that colonialism cannot be "removed" as if it were a lice infestation.

Mikendi's torching of the hospital will no more expunge colonialism than will the change of governments, and like the anarchy of the food wagon, will ultimately not provide anything to the people the actions are intended to serve.

Another important site for the film's unraveling of the complexity of colonialism is the trading post. As with the hospital, Mikendi's plans for self-determination call for the transfer of the trading post to the Africans. That transfer is effected, but like the change in governments and the takeover of the hospital, it does nothing to change the material condition of the lives of the villagers. The drunken proprietor's resigned reaction to the impending transfer of the trading post motivates his comments on the material effects that the ideology of colonialism and modernism cause.

The proprietor does nothing as Schweitzer rampages through the post's alcohol supply, not only because he knows his time as owner is nearly finished, but because he knows Schweitzer's rampage is in vain—it will do nothing to stop the village's now inevitable transition to modernism. As the proprietor observes, "Africa, the real Africa, is finished. Because of people like you." The proprietor's pronouncement is striking because it implicates Schweitzer in the very process against which he struggles—the transformation of African social systems into modernism. As a missionary, Schweitzer performs a role just as vital to the colonialist enterprise as mercenaries and traders. Part of that role, as the proprietor indicates, is the dissemination of ideas whose function and purpose is ultimately to dismantle the meaning system of African tribal culture—a meaning system upon which, as is the case with all cultures, their social systems depend.

The proprietor's observation, however, also deftly represses the equal culpability of the trading post in that process, a culpability to which the piles of timber nonetheless testify. The trading post as economic institution is the result of a meaning system that commodifies reality, instituting a symbolic system of individual ownership. If the "real Africa" is finished, it is because the ideology of colonialism has completed its task, and the collective logic of tribal culture has been vanquished by colonialism's imposition of private ownership. Schweitzer vainly struggles against modernism and insists on Africa's need for farmers in a manner that seems to ignore that the need for farmers was created by the shortages of resources that the confiscation and privatization of land under colonialism created. The transfer of the trading post to African ownership is thus largely limited to the symbolic realm; it will have little or no impact on a social system of private ownership that will inherently create the shortages upon which its system of exchange depends. Koumba's belief in collective participation, while attempting to integrate tribal culture into the new social system, is nonetheless unable to resist or alter the disruptive and continuing effects that ownership, property, and industrialization exercise on the cultural and material existence of the African people.

In articulating colonialism's economic and cultural impact, however, the film refrains from establishing tribal culture as a mythological Edenic opposite. Several scenes, for example, emphasize the profoundly hierarchical and patriarchal character of the tribal systems, establishing, for example, the elevated status of the chiefs among the people. The film also constructs the social code of polygamy as a function of the privileged status of male sexual desire, repeatedly demonstrating how the status of women can be reduced to objects of trade within the reification of male sexual desire. Bissa is given to Schweitzer early in the film, and Mata attempts to demonstrate his status as powerful chief by offering a woman to Lambi as a gesture of thanks. The scene where the chief rebukes the males of the tribe for not controlling their women further emphasizes both the patriarchal and hierarchical structures within the tribal social system.

The plot also prevents romanticization of tribal culture through the operation and iconography of Schweitzer's hospital. The ability for the hospital to compensate for the limitations to tribal healing is articulated through the introduction of its operation. The first procedure after the opening that Schweitzer is shown performing is a cesarean section birth. Within the rhetoric of the film, the procedure exercises an important signifying function. Within the film's rhetorical operations, human reproduction is a site of limitations for the meaning systems of each culture. The witch doctor points out to Schweitzer, for example, that Western medicine cannot cure infertility, whereas he can, a point that Schweitzer humbly concurs with. Tribal healing practices, however, were not as effective in dealing with the risk and peril of childbirth, and its resulting mortality. The cesarean section procedure was refined by Western medicine as a means of saving the life of both mother and child from the dangers and complications that can result from the birthing process. Theresa DeLauretis, for example, recounts Claude Levi-Strauss's documenting of how tribal societies developed shamanistic healing practices for difficult and protracted labor.[3] These practices, however, were not as effective in protecting women from the high mortality of childbirth. The plot's introduction of Schweitzer's work thus functions as a reference to the limitations of the meaning systems of tribal culture—a culture that the film clearly values, but refuses to overvalue.

The narrative refrains from romanticizing tribal culture precisely because the rhetorical position of the film is to deny any meaning system a privileged relationship to truth. The plot's consistent refusal to allow any meaning system to occupy the place of truth is a significant site for confronting both colonialism and racism. Similar to the rhetorical operations of *Daughters of the Dust,* the plot of *The Great White Man* constitutes its signifying practice in such a way as to resist the finalization of meaning and its role in the process of racism. As earlier discussions have indicated, racism itself depends upon the process of signification and the absolute truth value assigned within its operations. Colonialism depends on racism and the truth claims it attempts to fix and finalize, in order to justify and legitimize the subjugation and oppression of people that lie at its core. *The Great White Man* constitutes a direct assault on that process by denying any signifying process its truth claims.

In this respect, the film makes clear that tribal cultures—though with different effects—were just as limited by their own ideological frameworks as the modernist states that replaced them. As a result, the film portrays the dissolution of tribal culture as tragic not because it was an unspoiled Eden, but rather because it did not have to be inevitable. The social systems that supplanted tribal culture—colonialism and modernism—rest upon and function through illegitimate truth claims, which form part of their drive to dismantle other meaning systems. The film's ironic ending, however, emphasizes an alternative to the necessity of meaning systems vanquishing each other through false claims of privileged knowledge.

Following Schweitzer's burial, the film closes with a shot of the river, framed by the African countryside. A title appears in the lower left side of the frame, quoting Schweitzer from outside the narrative: "All we can do is allow others to discover us as we discover them." By closing with this statement, the plot continues in a process of dismantling the structure and operations of classical narrative. Here, the plot resists the resolution and closure of classical narrative, with its finalization of meaning, and instead maintains contradiction. The quote is striking precisely because Schweitzer neither speaks the line in the film, nor acts in a manner that would have motivated it—as Bissa so clearly articulates at two different junctures in the narrative. As a result, the quote seems enormously contradictory to the driven and self-assured missionary.

In addition to maintaining contradiction, the quote also works against the finalization of meaning that the plot has resisted throughout the narrative. Pronouncements at the end of a narrative function to establish a finality and stability to the meanings assigned to a signifier. In closing with a quote that functions so ironically, the narrative resists such a finalization, and instead foregrounds the problem of truth and representation as a means of closure. As with the other discourses in the film, the contradictory or ironic nature of the statement does not function to undermine the validity of the statement. Indeed, the trajectory of the narrative and its character interrelationships would seem to confirm its validity, even if Schweitzer himself did not live up to it. Furthermore, the quote functions to problematize the truth claims of its own representation. The basis of the contradiction lies in the dissonance between the character as constructed and the profoundly personal insight of the observation. The film, however, lacks any motivating elements to produce such an insight. As a result, it points to its own inability to represent the totality of Schweitzer.

In this respect, the statement does not so much function to close the narrative, but to reopen it through a different interpretive framework. Rather than capping the biography of Schweitzer, the ending maintains that the story of the Great White Man is a broader tragedy that ensued when two social systems, each bound by ideological limitations, came in conflict at the site of representation. The alternative, the ending suggests, is to resist the truth claims found at the finalization of meaning, and engage instead in a never-ending exploration, and struggle, to discover what lies beyond representation.

Notes

1. Toni Cade Bambara, "Reading the Signs, Empowering the Eye: *Daughters of the Dust* and the Black Independent Cinema Movement," in Manthia Diawara, ed., *Black Cinema* (New York: Routledge Press, 1993), 131.

2. In some African cultures, it is customary to begin addressing an individual by complimenting the person first. The chief's statement that wisdom flows from Mikendi's mouth can certainly be read within this context, but its rhetorical function is not limited to that end. The chief could have complimented Mikendi in any number of ways, but chose to validate the discourse of his son.

3. Theresa DeLauretis, *Alice Doesn't: Feminism, Semiotics, Cinema* (Bloomington, Ind.: University of Indiana Press, 1984), 122.

Epilogue: Racism, Representation, and the Role of Theory

In denying truth a position within representation, *The Great White Man of Lambarene* structures its narrative around one of the core structures to the operation of racism, the process of signification. *The Great White Man* attempts to draw the distinction between truth, as that which lies beyond representation, and meaning, the social constructs that human communities create through signification in order to organize and stabilize the realities that confront them. What *The Great White Man* seeks to demonstrate is that the latter process, the construction of meaning, is inherently political to the degree that it involves relations of power that determine how a society will be ordered in one particular way and not another. Mikendi's prophetic line that "the time of the chiefs is finished" articulates that the structure of African society is about to undergo a profound change, from tribalism to liberal democracy.

Furthermore, the film underscores how such a change cannot occur without fundamental shifts in the social-symbolic system, shifts which are glaringly obvious in the juxtaposition between Helene's departure, and the Independence celebration. In this respect, the film emulates the goals and practices of cultural studies, which largely focuses on the production of meaning as central site of power relations within a given society. Indeed, the circulation and affirmation of specific discourses is a primary means by which the power relations operate and maintain themselves—and is a primary site for contesting dominant relations.

What this study has tried to demonstrate is that the operations of race and racism not only conduct themselves through the circulation and affirmation of specific discourses and meanings, but also through a process of repression and denigration of countervailing discourses and signifying practices. Within each process, however, the status of the signifier and its meaning function is central. In the former process, however, the status of the signifier is made to be invisible, a strategy to reinforce the meanings of race by making them seem "natural" or "inevitable." It is precisely this process that Wahneema Lubiano attempts to expose in her essay on realism and representation when she rhetorically asks "What is race in the United States if not an attempt to make 'real' a set of social assumptions about biology?"[1] This making real of social constructs is a process that *Mississippi Burning*, for all its flaws, tried to make visible in the media interviews scene, when the middle-aged white woman asserts that there is real difference between whites and Negroes, arguing: "they're not like us, they smell, they don't take baths, they're nasty."

Arguing for race as a social construct, however, is something of a double-edged sword: its tendency is to dispense with both the negative stereotypes heaped upon a particular race *and* the positive cultural identities that races construct for themselves. To cast off as arbitrary the core features of how a race defines itself is not easy—nor is it likely to be immediately empowering. Indeed, it amounts to surrendering claims that there is any real essence or essential features that determine the composition of a specific race, racial category, or group. Stuart Hall recognizes the vulnerability such a position incurs when he asks, "Where would we be, as bell hooks once remarked, without a touch of essentialism?"[2] Nonetheless, Hall argues that:

> The essentializing moment is weak because it naturalizes and dehistoricizes difference, mistaking what is historical and cultural for what is natural, biological, and genetic. The moment the signifier 'black' is torn from its historical, cultural, and political embedding and lodged in a biologically constituted racial category, we valorize, by inversion, the very ground of the racism we are trying to deconstruct. In addition, as always happens when we naturalize historical categories (think about gender and sexuality), we fix that signifier outside history, outside change, outside political intervention.[3]

Hall's argument underscores both the dialectical relationship and the political dimension to racial identity. A social construct, race is a network of signifiers and meaning assigned to and by particular groups to create and respond to the real effects of social organization and its operations.

The reluctance of racial groups to concede as arbitrary the traits it assigns to itself is understandable. Formed by the imposition of the signifier, racial groups are nonetheless able to carve out of that imposition the space for collective solidarity and support—even if the original intent of the racial construction is oppression and disenfranchisement. To relativize the signifier that constructs the group thus puts at risk the network of solidarity and support that can grow out of it. Further, such a position increases the vulnerability for further assignation of traits by the dominant power structure and its insistence on the reality of the signifier. Here too, however, Hall's argument is instructive, for just as dominant signifying practices structured around race function to confuse the historical and the cultural with the natural and the biological, so too is the essentialist position Hall argues against, but sees some value to, confusing "authentic" with "real." The manner in which Afro-American culture has sought to define itself through history is an authentic response to the very real effects of conditions and restraints imposed by dominant white culture. To recognize the symbolic nature of Afro-American identity and culture is thus not to deny its authenticity, but rather is a means by which to rediscover specific symbolic responses and strategies resistant to the very real effects of domination and oppression.

The dominant signifying strategies of the mass media, especially of film and television, by and large function to foreclose such a discovery, insisting instead on the permanence, naturalness, and consistency of race—laying the foundation for the discourses and strategies of naturalization, legitimization, and justification described previously. This study has tried to demonstrate that the symbolic process in general, and the signification of race specifically is never complete, nor completely successful—that the process is not only susceptible to analysis and exposure, but that competing or contradictory discourses will always resist, escape, and even contest the ideological function of the text. As was argued earlier, the point of interpretation then becomes to elucidate how those resistant meanings image more equitable societies, articulate alternatives, and map out methods of transformation.

In this respect, critical analysis contains enormous political potential—as a means for establishing critical consciousness, and as a site for engaging the possibilities of social transformation. Whether the potential is realized will depend on the degree to which such critical analysis can be put into practice—not just shouting it from the rooftops, but taking it to the streets. bell hooks, for example, has discussed the manner in which the acceptance and popularity of cultural studies has created more opportunities for radical practice, but at the same time created a situation where "many critical thinkers . . . prefer to score points by remaining in the academic world and representing radical chic there. This is especially the case when academics feel they are less cool if they attempt to link cultural studies' intellectual practice with radical politicization."[4] Despite the kind of containment that academia exercises against critical/cultural theory as practice, hooks nonetheless concludes that, "when we desire to decolonize minds and imaginations, cultural studies' focus on popular culture can be and is a powerful site for intervention, challenge, and change."[5]

In its analysis of select films and their signifying operations, this study has attempted to introduce the reader to some of the intellectual tools that provide a means to engage in such a process of intervention, challenge, and change. Not coincidentally, the terms describe a developmental process of contesting dominant power relations. Critical analysis as an intellectual tool challenges the invisibility within which dominant signifying practices frequently cloak themselves. This kind of invisibility is not solely a matter of the norms and conventions of film style, but is also operative as broader cultural practice.

The experience of two films examined here illustrates this point. In 1989, Spike Lee's tour-de-force *Do The Right Thing* created a media sensation (see Chapter 8). When the Academy Awards were presented, however, *Do the Right*

Thing was ignored, and the less contentious, more nostalgic *Driving Miss Daisy* won the award for Best Picture. The Academy, which is predominantly white, selected *Daisy* and ignored *Do the Right Thing* on the grounds of "taste," "aesthetics," "artistic merit," and other such criteria that it believes to be more or less objective. As with any other categorical distinctions, however, the criteria are both arbitrary and self-serving. They function to deny that the complicating factor of race had anything to do with selection, thus allowing the process to render invisible the manner in which the Academy's validation of films that justify and naturalize privilege serves the status quo of racial inequity.

That privilege and exclusion were operative in the ideological functioning of the Academy Awards might easily be refuted were it not part of a more general pattern. When *Daughters of the Dust* arrived at the Sundance Film Festival in 1991, it generated much critical acclaim. Gene Seymour of *New York Newsday*, for example, wrote that the film is "Daringly new . . . exuberantly African-American . . . spellbinding and altogether extraordinary! The kind of movie that can make you believe once again in the power of film to transform the way the outside world looks to you." The *Village Voice* described it as "A film of visionary power! *Daughters of the Dust* is an unparalleled, unprecedented achievement."[6] For all its acclaim, however, *Daughters of the Dust* did not win an award for its director, Julie Dash (the Filmmakers Trophy went to Yvonne Rainer), or for itself as a drama (the Grand Jury Prize for Drama went to *Poison* by Todd Haynes). Somehow, the drama produced by an intimate portrait of an Afro-American culture at the turn of the century, enhanced by its replacement of Hollywood style with an Afrocentric one, failed to connect with a jury by and large comprised of privilege. Rather, the film was awarded a prize for cinematography, almost as if to say "We didn't really understand it, but it sure looked nice!"

Years later, when the American Film Institute (AFI) announced its list of the hundred greatest films in the cinema's hundred-year history, neither *Daughters of the Dust* nor *Do the Right Thing* was among them. Indeed, no film made by a black director was on the list. *The Birth of a Nation*, however, was listed at number forty-four. The same process of exclusion is evidenced elsewhere in the list. Only a handful of films, among them, *Guess Who's Coming to Dinner*, *Unforgiven*, and *To Kill a Mockingbird* have Afro-Americans as principal characters (and one could argue that the Afro-American characters are not really that "principal" in either *Unforgiven* or *Mockingbird*).

The AFI official list of great movies is thus part of a pattern of cultural practices in which race is made invisible—to the benefit of privilege, and at the expense of racial minorities. The invisibility of this exclusion is furthered by the legitimizing practices that cultural institutions readily employ. The AFI, for example, legitimated its exclusion through the figure of its Blue Ribbon panel. The list was generated through the selection of films by 1,500 participants, composed of film directors, critics, scholars, and such cultural luminaries as Yogi

Berra. The process of selection (and exclusion) was thus made to seem as if it were conducted through the invisible hand of artistic criteria that an expert panel applied; that this panel was also largely white was made to seem irrelevant.

Cultural studies, however, provides a means for intervening and challenging such legitimizing practices and the processes of exclusion that they seek to obscure. Theoretical paradigms such as semiotics and psychoanalysis demonstrate that no criteria are objective, but rather are subject to the arbitrariness of the signifier and the symbolic dynamics of validation and recognition. Such theoretical tools allow individuals and the coalitions they form to intervene in the fluid transmission of the signifying practices of dominant culture and its institutions with the disruptive force of critical analysis.

Furthermore, such critical intervention provides the means to then effectively challenge the truths upon which signifying practices assert themselves, the assumptions within which they ground themselves—not by asserting an alternative truth but by insisting on the arbitrary foundation of all discourse. Who is on what list or wins what award is not the most pressing social concern; rather, it is the broader processes of which list-making and award-winning are representative—the patterns of exclusion based on race, and the denial of the operations of racism—which are pressing social concerns. This study has sought to demonstrate primarily that racism is but one mode of signifying relations (with very real effects), the purpose of which is to maintain a social system of inequity—a social system that is both very complex and very effective at perpetuating itself.

Yet for all its effectiveness at maintaining itself, our social system of inequity is vulnerable at the point of every discourse of legitimization, naturalization, and justification it appropriates and employs. Grounded as it is in the arbitrary nature of the signifier, it ultimately stands not at the apex of evolution, or upon the foundation of truth, but rather, on feet of clay. In this respect, critical analysis and cultural studies are not just pedantic tools by which academics work, but rather the means by which people can empower themselves to participate in the construction of a just, more equitable society. Such a world is imaginable—it can be glimpsed through the shroud of strategies of containment that dominant discourses exercise. Furthermore, such a world is feasible—especially given the technological and scientific capabilities now at its disposal. In this respect, it is no coincidence that abstract theory is so highly marginalized in mainstream culture: its potential when carried in the hands of many is enormous, and the disruption of power is no small affair.

The power engendered in the current social system of inequity is also no small affair, and the ability of the system to maintain itself should not be underestimated: it is entrenched, decentralized, highly adaptable, and supplied with a nearly inexhaustible array of containment strategies—all the more reason to be armed with theory to confront it effectively. In this respect, analyzing the operations of racism can be extremely instructive. As the twenty-first century begins, there is no doubt that social institution of racism has fundamentally changed since the 1950s; yet this does not mean it has been eliminated nearly as much as it indicates that its operations have been modified. The infamous war on drugs, which has selectively focused on Afro-American men and turned them into a commodity for a burgeoning privatized prison industry, is just one example of how privilege and inequity, functioning to the accuser's benefit and at the victim's expense, continues to flourish. As the institution of racism continues to modify itself, so too will the categories and signifiers of privilege be reconfigured, as will the discourses of justification, legitimization, and naturalization—perpetuating not only the institution of racism, but the social system of inequity and domination that endows it.

As the work of bell hooks, Stuart Hall, and Cornel West demonstrates, the critical consciousness and commitment engaged in the struggle against racism must take as its object the broader system of inequity and domination if social transformation is to occur. As bell hooks argues:

> We must . . . be able to examine critically ways in which the desire to be accepted into privileged-class groups within mainstream society undermines and destroys commitment to a politics of cultural transformation that consistently critiques domination. Such a critique would necessarily include the challenge to end class elitism and call for a replacing of the ethic of individualism with a vision of communalism."[7]

In arguing for such a fundamental replacement, hooks returns the politics of cultural studies to individual consciousness and desire.

Theory alone will not achieve social transformation as so many abstract discourses, but must become rooted within and shape individual desire—must counterpose the liberating freedom of the egalitarian community with the pleasure of individual gratification. In the end it must resubstantiate and reinvigorate the utopian impulse as both imperative and goal. The alternatives that the politics of individual consumption offers—alienation, domination, and materialism—pale by comparison.

Notes

1. Wahneema Lubiano, "But Compared to What?: Reading Realism, Representation, and Essentialism in *School Daze, Do the Right Thing,* and the Spike Lee Discourse," in Valerie Smith, ed., *Representing Blackness: Issues in Film and Video* (New Brunswick, N.J.: Rutgers University Press, 1997), 98.

2. Stuart Hall, "This 'Black' in Black Popular Culture," in Valerie Smith, ed., *Representing Blackness: Issues in Film and Video* (New Brunswick, N.J.: Rutgers University Press, 1997), 130.

3. Ibid.

4. bell hooks, *Outlaw Culture: Resisting Representations* (New York and London: Routledge, 1994), 4.

5. Ibid.

6. Excerpted from the 1999 Nontheatrical Catalog of Kino International.

7. hooks, *Outlaw Culture,* 148.

Bibliography

Ards, Angela. "When Cops are Killers." *The Nation,* March 8, 1999.

Baker, Houston A., Jr. "Spike Lee and the Commerce of Culture." In *Black American Cinema,* edited by Manthia Diawara. New York: Routledge Press, 1993.

Baraka, Amiri, "Spike Lee at the Movies." In *Black American Cinema,* edited by Manthia Diawara. New York: Routledge Press, 1993.

Bambara, Toni Cade. "Reading the Signs, Empowering the Eye: *Daughters of the Dust* and the Black Independent Cinema Movement." In *Black American Cinema,* edited by Manthia Diawara. New York: Routledge Press, 1993.

Bernardi, Daniel, ed., *The Birth of Whiteness: Race and the Emergence of U.S. Cinema.* New Brunswick, N.J. : Rutgers University Press, 1996.

Bogle, Donald. *Toms, Coons, Mammies, Mulattoes and Bucks: An Interpretive History of Blacks in American Films.* New York: Bantam Books, 1973.

Bordwell, David, Janet Staiger, and Kristen Thompson. *The Classical Hollywood Cinema: Film Style and Mode of Production to 1960.* New York: Columbia University Press, 1985.

Commolli, Jean-Luc, and Jean Narboni. "Cinema, Ideology, Criticism." In *Movies and Methods,* edited by Bill Nichols. Vol. 1. Berkeley: University of California Press, 1976.

Davis, Jennifer. "Squeezing Apartheid." *Bulletin of the Atomic Scientists* 49(9): 16–20 (November 1993).

Davis, Peter. Review of *The Gods Must Be Crazy. Cineaste* 14(1): 51–53 (1985).

DeLauretis, Theresa. *Alice Doesn't: Feminism, Semiotics, Cinema.* Bloomington, Ind.: University of Indiana Press, 1984.

Diawara, Manthia, ed., *Black Cinema.* New York: Routledge, 1993.

Doherty, Thomas. Review of *Mississippi Burning. Cineaste* 17(2): 48–50 (1989).

Goodwine, Marquetta. "YEDDY WE: Statement to the UN Commission on Human Rights from the Gullah/Geechee Community of the United States." Geneva, Switzerland (April 1, 1999).

Gray, Herman. "Television, Black Americans, and the American Dream." In *Critical Perspectives on Media and Society,* edited by Robert K. Avery and David Eason. New York: Guilford Press, 1991.

_____. *Watching Race: Television and the Struggle for Blackness.* Minneapolis, Minn.: University of Minnesota Press, 1995.

Guerrero, Ed. *Framing Blackness*. Philadelphia, Pa.: Temple University Press, 1993.

Hall, Stuart. "This 'Black' in Black Popular Culture." In *Representing Blackness*, edited by Valerie Smith. New Brunswick, N.J.: Rutgers University Press, 1997.

hooks, bell. "The Oppositional Gaze." In *Black American Cinema*, edited by Manthia Diawara, 288–302. New York: Routledge Press, 1993.

_____. *Outlaw Culture: Resisting Representations*. New York and London: Routledge, 1994.

_____. *Yearning: Race, Gender, and Cultural Politics*. Boston: South End Press, 1990.

Jaehne, Karen. "The Press and Politics at Cannes '88." *Cineaste* 16(4): 8–10 (1988).

Lacan, Jacques. *The Seminars of Jacques Lacan, Book I, Freud's Papers on Technique*, edited by Jacques Alain Miller, translated by John Forrester. New York: W. W. Norton & Company, 1991.

Lubiano, Wahneema. "But Compared to What?: Reading Realism, Representation, and Essentialism in *School Daze, Do the Right Thing*, and the Spike Lee Discourse." In *Representing Blackness: Issues in Film and Video*, edited by Valerie Smith. New Brunswick, N.J.: Rutgers University Press, 1997.

MacCabe, Colin. "Theory and Film: Principles of Realism and Pleasure." In *Narrative, Apparatus, Ideology: A Film Theory Reader*, edited by Philip Rosen. New York: Columbia University Press, 1986.

Memmi, Albert. *Dominated Man*. Boston: Beacon Press, 1968.

Norris, Christopher. *Deconstruction: Theory & Practice*. London and New York: Methuen & Co., 1982.

Schatz, Thomas. *Hollywood Genres: Formulas, Filmmaking, and the Studio System*. Philadelphia, Pa.: Temple University Press, 1981.

Sippl, Diana. Review of *A World Apart. Cineaste* 17(1): 33–35 (1989).

Small, Stephen. *Racialised Barriers: The Black Experience in the United States and England in the 1980's*. London and New York: Routledge Press, 1994.

Smith, Robert. *Racism in the Post Civil Rights Era: Now You See It, Now You Don't*. Albany, N.Y.: SUNY Press, 1995.

Smith, Valerie, ed. *Representing Blackness: Issues in Film and Video*. New Brunswick, N.J.: Rutgers University Press, 1997.

Spears, Arthur K. *Race and Ideology: Language, Symbolism, and Popular Culture*. Detroit, Mich.: Wayne State University Press, 1999.

Stam, Robert, and Louise Spence. "Colonialism, Racism, and Representation: An Introduction." In *Movies and Methods: An Anthology*, edited by Bill Nichols. Vol. 2. Berkeley: University of California Press, 1985.

Taylor, Clyde. "The Re-Birth of the Aesthetic in Cinema." In *The Birth of Whiteness: Race and the Emergence of U.S. Cinema*, edited by Daniel Bernard. New Brunswick, N.J. : Rutgers University Press, 1996.

Vann, Helene, and Jane Caputi. Review of *Driving Miss Daisy*. *Journal of Popular Film & Television* 18(2): 80–83 (Summer 1990).

West, Cornel. *Race Matters*. Boston: Beacon Press, 1993.

Willis, Sharon. *High Contrast: Race and Gender in Contemporary Hollywood Film*. Durham and London: Duke University Press, 1997.

Young, Lola. *Fear of the Dark: "Race," Gender, and Sexuality in the Cinema*. London and New York: Routledge, 1996.

Zook, Kristal Brent. *Color by Fox: The Fox Network and the Revolution in Black Television*. New York and Oxford: Oxford University Press, 1999.

Index